BECOMING THE TWIN CITIES

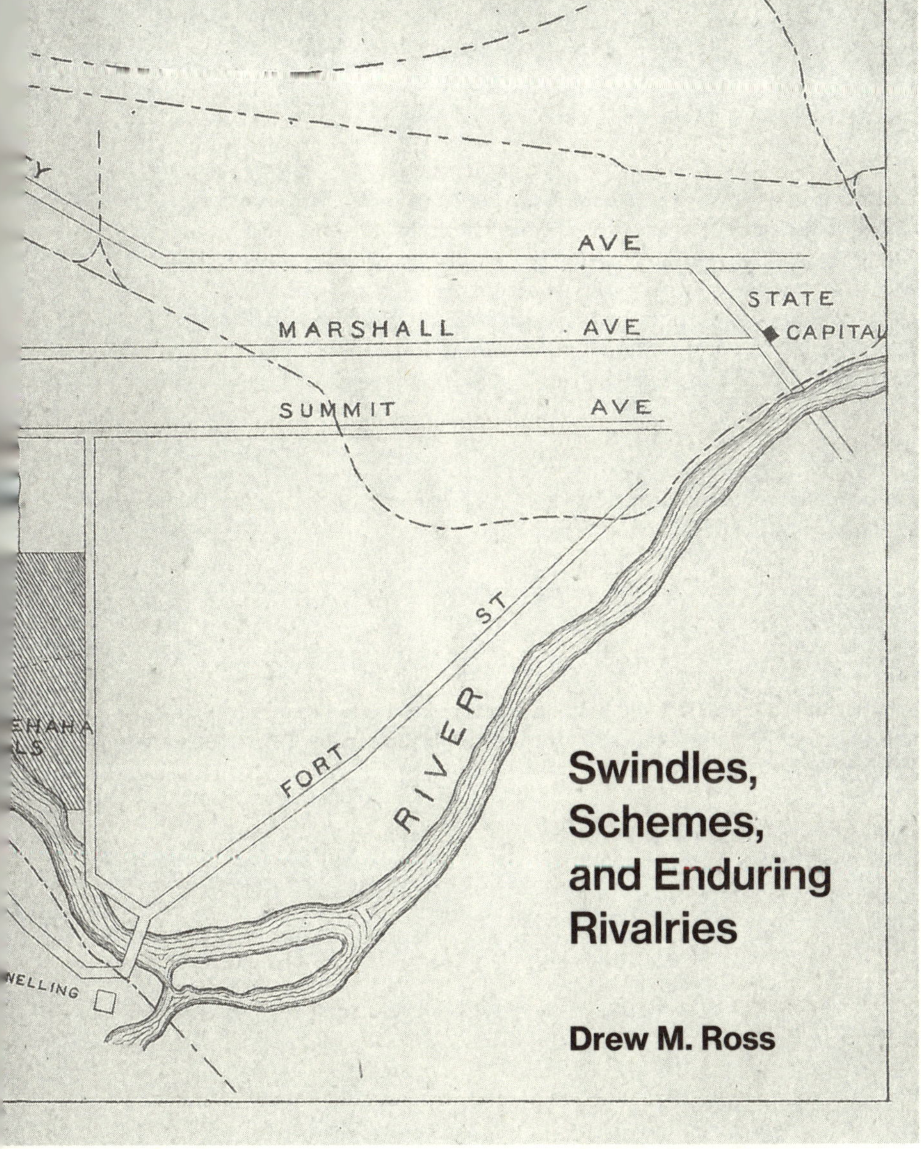

Swindles, Schemes, and Enduring Rivalries

Drew M. Ross

For information, write to the Minnesota Historical Society Press, 345 Kellogg Blvd. W., St. Paul, MN 55102-1906.

mnhspress.org @mnhspress

The Minnesota Historical Society Press is a member of the Association of University Presses.

Manufactured in the United States of America

10 9 8 7 6 5 4 3 2 1

∞ The paper used in this publication meets the minimum requirements of the American National Standard for Information Sciences—Permanence for Printed Library Materials, ANSI Z39.48-1984.

ISBN: 978-1-68134-323-5 (paperback)
ISBN: 978-1-68134-324-2 (e-book)

Library of Congress Control Number: 2025934623

"I thought I knew the story of the Twin Cities until I read this book. Drew Ross richly describes how and why Minneapolis and St. Paul stayed as distinct, unidentical 'twins.' Properly centering wild nineteenth-century land shenanigans, this vibrant history is a must-read key to understanding the Minneapolis–St. Paul metro."

—Bill Lindeke, University of Minnesota, author of *St. Paul: An Urban Biography*

"Drew M. Ross has written a poignant book on the establishments of Minneapolis and St. Paul and their remarkable continued existence to this day as separate, individual cities and not a combined city. This well-researched book deftly traces the development of the Twin Cities' distinct histories and cultures, business leaders and political officials drawn to each city, the resources shared between the cities, and the failure of efforts to merge the two municipalities into one in the late nineteenth century. *Becoming the Twin Cities* is a must-read for every Minnesotan."

—Christopher P. Lehman, St. Cloud State University, author of *Slavery's Reach: Southern Slaveholders in the North Star State* and *It Took Courage: Eliza Winston's Quest for Freedom*

"*Becoming the Twin Cities* is an important reminder that nothing needs to remain static. It is also a warning against insiders-only shaping the world as they want—whether that be boundaries on a map or policies that affect people's lives. Knowing this history is important to activate more people to speak up for the future we want."

—Tom Weber, author of *Minneapolis: An Urban Biography*

"Drew Ross's book is essential reading for anyone who lives in, loves, or visits the Twin Cities as he explores the political shenanigans that have made the cities unique in their separate and strong identities. This is an immensely entertaining book you won't want to put down. Anyone who relishes their history served up with equal parts of facts, lore, and humor will find Ross's book a delicious meal!"

—Jonis Agee, author of *The Bones of Paradise*

"This is a meticulously researched book that explains, beginning in 1805, why we have two separate cities. It is an invaluable addition to St. Paul, Minneapolis, and Minnesota history."

—Donald L. Empson, author of *The Street Where You Live: A Guide to the Place Names of St. Paul*

"Buda and Pest, Brooklyn and Manhattan—these are former separate cities bordering common rivers that merged in the nineteenth century to form greater metropolises. In this engaging, deeply researched, and well-written book, Drew Ross tells the story of how first geography but soon politics, commerce, confidence men, and outright crooks kept St. Paul and Minneapolis separate cities, not the one great city on the Upper Mississippi that contemporaries thought would inevitably emerge. Out of the rivalry of the two settlements on the river grew uneasy cooperation and eventually a *modus vivendi* of the Twin Cities, the side-by-side hubs of a twenty-first-century region of more than three million people. Ross makes a significant contribution to urban history with this important book."

—James W. Oberly, University of Wisconsin–Eau Claire

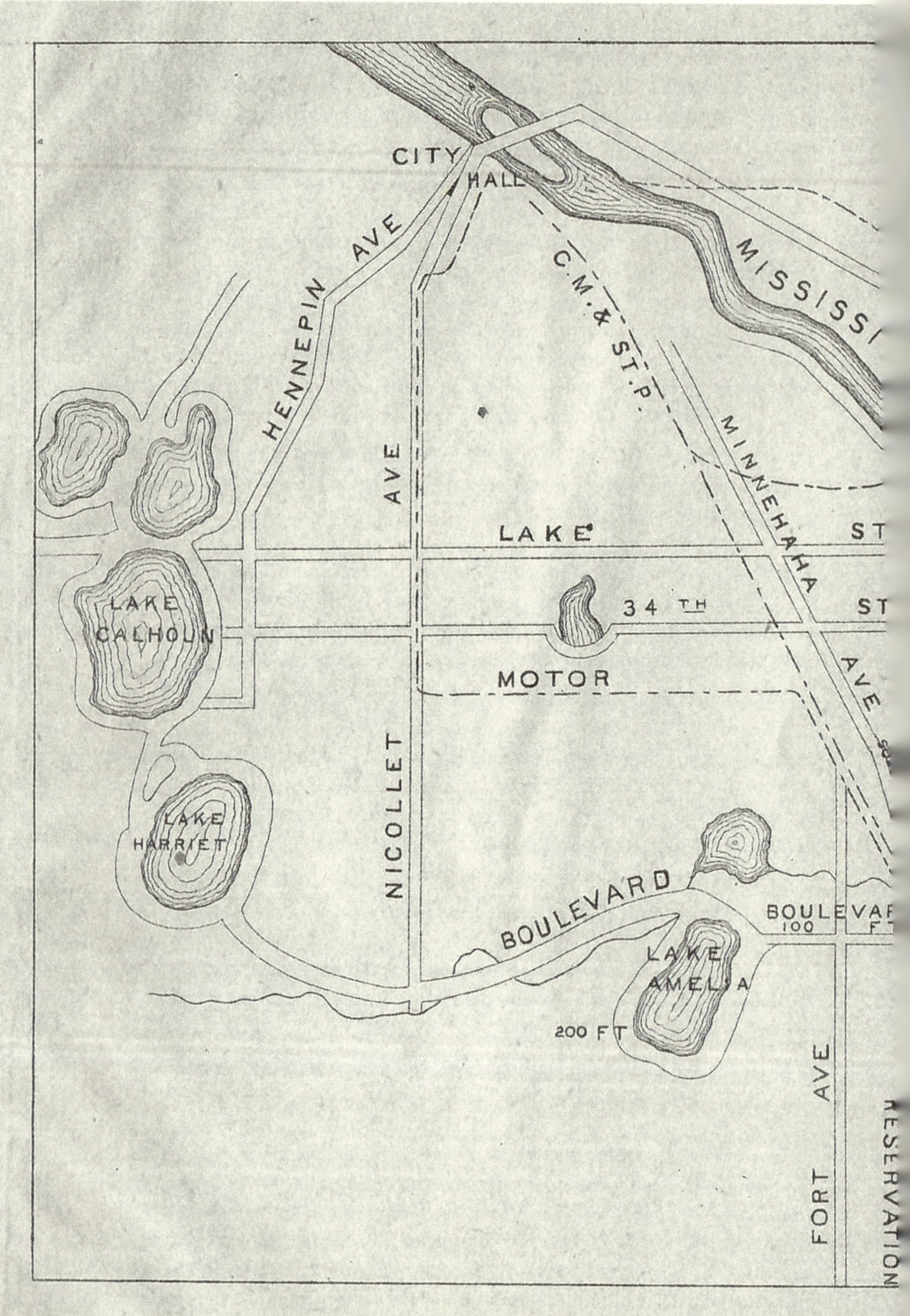

CITY
HALL
HENNEPIN AVE
C.M.& ST.P.
MISSISSI
MINNEHAHA AVE
NICOLLET AVE
LAKE ST
34 TH ST
MOTOR
LAKE CALHOUN
LAKE HARRIET
BOULEVARD
BOULEVAR
100 FT
LAKE AMELIA
200 FT
FORT AVE
RESERVATION

Contents

INTRODUCTION

Why Didn't Minneapolis and St. Paul Merge?

From the very beginning of American settlement in Minnesota, people believed the area of today's Twin Cities would be home to one great city.

The by-then familiar process of urban growth entailed rapidly expanding urban areas that over time absorbed outlying towns and villages. People pointed to the growth and evolution of other cities, such as New York City, Philadelphia, and Chicago. Each one swallowed up its competition and kept on growing. When Minneapolis absorbed its cross-river neighbor, St. Anthony, in 1872, observers and residents saw yet another instance of urban development as they were familiar with it. In the mid-nineteenth century, belief in this process was unquestioned. Most everyone assumed that eventually Minneapolis would merge with its archetypal rival, St. Paul. Regardless of political party, social status, or personal interest, people believed the two cities would become one. But it is now the twenty-first century and that prophecy remains unfulfilled.

That St. Paul and Minneapolis never united and became one city would shock all of the people in this book. So, why do we have two cities here? As recently as 2023, a reader asked the Minneapolis *Star Tribune*, "Why didn't Minneapolis and St. Paul ever merge?" How St. Paul and Minneapolis became twins—and stayed twins—is a story of an exception, the most unlikely outcome. This book tells that story.[1]

Obviously, there is nothing unusual about twin cities. You can find them around the world, from Budapest to Niagara Falls. In the United States, we have dozens of conglomerate towns and more than a few are known by the same appellation of "Twin City" or "Twin Cities," such as Champaign–Urbana, Illinois, Lewiston–Auburn, Maine, and Winston–Salem, North Carolina.

Twin City is a nickname people have used for a long time. It was already a common label used across America in the 1850s. The travels of one boat by that name tells the story. In the summer of 1855, a fast side-wheeled passenger steamboat called the *Twin City* reached new horizons when it landed for the first time at St. Paul. The boat, which began work two years earlier on the upper Ohio River, was named after its home port of Pittsburgh–Alleghany City, then known as the Twin City. (The two cities would officially merge in 1907.) This boat was a workhorse delivering people and freight to locations progressively farther away from its home port. In its travels, the *Twin City* passed through twin river towns Davenport, Iowa–Rock Island, Illinois, one of the better-known Twin Cities in the mid-1850s. (Today it goes by Quad Cities, having added Moline and Bettendorf.)

The first use of the name in the upper stretches of the Mississippi referred to Minneapolis and St. Anthony. "The twin cities of the Falls" in 1856 referred to two towns connected by the first bridge over the Mississippi. In 1858 the locals viewed the towns as intricately tied together, and the bridges as "umbilicusses which constitute them Siamese twins," said the *Weekly Minnesotian*. That was fourteen years before Minneapolis absorbed St. Anthony.[2]

St. Paul and Minneapolis didn't pick up the nickname of Twin Cities until the 1870s. By that time, people were talking about unifying the two cities into one. The newspapers, politicians, and businessmen had spent years slinging insults and trying to outmaneuver each other, and they would do so for another decade. Some began to think the rivalry might be permanent. This assumption was reinforced through the 1880s as both cities boomed independently. But then they emerged from that period and began efforts to unite amicably, instead of a hostile takeover by one or the other. The two cities never did merge into one city, and today the familiar rivalry lives on, though not so fierce as in the past.

In fact, the Twin Cities have characteristics that set them apart from other urban twins. They are river towns, but not the typical river towns that face each other. They both grew to straddle the river. Some twin cities develop along an arterial highway and share a common zone along that corridor, such as Bethlehem–Allentown, Pennsylvania or Dallas–Fort Worth, Texas. The Mississippi River might be viewed as a connecting arterial route except for its shape, a large S curve. Both cities spanned the river, yet their locations on the river put them side by side. Perhaps more importantly, their relationships to the river were entirely different.[3]

Some twin cities have shared but differently developed commercial centers, such as Jersey City and New York City. But St. Paul and Minneapolis each started for distinctly different reasons. St. Paul served as the head of navigation and developed a commercial base. Minneapolis came to life on hydropowered industry. True, Minneapolis benefited from

St. Paul's commercial business and was able to proceed with its industrial projects without attending to a commercial base. Once established, though, they each had their own business center and a commercial core with all the essentials of a city. Because of their independence, the railroads had to put a terminal yard and stations in each city. The cities had few functions intended to serve both communities. Aside from the state capital in St. Paul and the state university in Minneapolis, they replicated most municipal services, from parks to sewer treatment. The Twin Cities remained separate.[4]

What emerges from the historical record is the surprising fact that there was nothing organic or natural about the shape the Twin Cities took. Instead, a whole cast of characters—settlers, soldiers, speculators, swindlers, politicians, publishers, clergy, traders, investors, and idealists—determined the shape and destiny of urban life. Who they were and what they did has been forgotten or become the stuff of hand-me-down lore. But the archives tell a story worth resurrecting in its details, if only so that we can better see how and why these Twin Cities never united. There was nothing obvious about it. It was political shenanigans all the way.

Part I: **Creating the Twin Cities**

CHAPTER 1

Solving Nature's Puzzle

For much of the nineteenth century, American explorers and settlers faced an enigma at the Mississippi River's head of navigation. They depended on the rivers for transportation, so river confluences, such as the Mississippi and St. Peter (Minnesota) Rivers, were important hubs. And they recognized the Falls of St. Anthony as a natural and abundant power supply for industrial-sized operations of mills and manufacturing. Each feature warranted consideration for a nineteenth-century settlement. Naturally, they wanted to access both features, which combined represented a bonanza. But a rather impassable nine-mile river gorge separated the confluence from the falls. For the time being, the gorge presented a significant obstacle, rendering the head of navigation a paradise divided.

This geographic configuration was a puzzle specific to those settlers who depended on the river for transportation. The region was remote from their support and supplies, and overland travel was difficult, especially for large numbers of American settlers. While smaller vessels could ascend the river, no significant settlement was likely to occur without easier mass transport. That came with the steamboats, which worked their way upriver, overcoming the miles of shallow, previously impassable water at Rock Island, Illinois, and Des Moines, Iowa. At the Mississippi–Minnesota confluence, they met their match. The steep gradient in the gorge ran shallow and strong through an obstacle course of boulders and sandbars. For the time being, no larger boat could reach the falls.

With the gorge separating the confluence and the falls, people tried to solve the riddle of how to settle this area. Two men came up with answers for their respective times. Lieutenant Zebulon Pike and Etienne (Stephen) Desnoyer responded to this geographic puzzle in ways that reveal how they and people of their eras viewed the development of a settlement at the head of navigation. Pike understood this even before he saw the falls. His solution in 1805 was to capture the confluence and the falls for the military in a reserve. As the communities began to develop at the head of navigation and the falls, Desnoyer in 1843 settled near the midpoint of the gorge, which happened to also be at the geographic midpoint of all three settlements: St. Anthony Falls, the confluence at the mouth of the gorge, and the nascent village of St. Paul. He claimed his property would be the center of the united communities, which later became the Twin Cities.

The story of the Twin Cities starts with this geographic puzzle. How people solved it for their times gave us the shape of today's twinned metropolis.

Making the Gorge's Riddle

About 10,000 years earlier, the falls stood close to the Mississippi–Minnesota confluence. There was not yet a gorge separating them. In fact, the falls fell into a gorge at the confluence. The features unified in one location would have been a perfect arrangement for the nineteenth-century American settlers. From that point, the geomorphological forces initiated the erosion of the gorge that would complicate nineteenth-century settlement in the area.[1]

As great as the Mississippi is, it did not carve the entirety of its current path. How it carved the gorge is common knowledge, but that was the final act of a larger process. The Mississippi River makes an S-turn through the Twin Cities, with Minneapolis sitting at the beginning and St. Paul at the final curve (the S lays on its side running west to east). The Mississippi only carved the first leg of that contour. The greater amount of the excavation below the confluence was done under the auspices of its tributary, the ancient form of the Minnesota River. If that had not happened, Pike and Desnoyer would not have had a puzzle to solve.

Today people are familiar with the layer cake geology that formed St. Anthony Falls. The Ordovician bedrock was laid down by an ocean some 450 million years ago. The ocean bottom consisted of fine sand, and the waters were home to small sea creatures and coral. The dead and cast-off material from that environment accumulated on the sandy bottom and formed a thirty-foot layer of greenish-gray Platteville Limestone. This limestone is visible today in the foundations of many old St. Paul houses and the walls of Fort Snelling. That cap layer of limestone fractures into large slabs. Beneath the limestone, the ocean's sandy bottom transformed into a white sandstone. Named after the river's old name, this St. Peter Sandstone formed with a weak binding and so it erodes easily. It is so pure (ninety-nine percent silica) that Ford Motor Company used it at the St. Paul plant to make windows.[2]

The erosion process of this bedrock is simple. The water runs across the more durable limestone cap and pours over the edge. It cuts into and erodes away the supporting sandstone, an action that undercuts the limestone, causing the cap to break off in blocks. Because the sandstone layer is about 150 feet thick, the process creates a waterfall.

Over the lifetime of the Mississippi River, counted in millennia, it has carved numerous wandering courses across the Twin Cities landscape. Ravines and lakes are the telltale signs of the Mississippi's old riverbeds. On the east side, for example, the ancient river cut ravines like Swede Hollow. Trout and Phalen Creeks enter the Mississippi following old traces of the river. On the west side, the ancient river at another time formed a channel that now holds the famous Chain of Lakes—Cedar, Lake of the Isles, Bde Maka Ska, and Harriet. Then, just upriver of Minneapolis at Bassett Creek the Mississippi was diverted away from the old Chain of Lakes channel and charted a new course, mostly on its current path. It ran across the top of the Platteville Limestone, creating a new confluence at the Fort Snelling location. At the time, before the big erosion event started, the Mississippi flowed near the level of today's fort all the way to the location of St. Paul.[3]

At the end of the last glacial period, 10,000–13,000 years ago, the warming planet thawed the glaciers. The meltwater of the Laurentide ice sheet, which covered central Canada, pooled below the glacier and formed Lake Agassiz, inundating the lower parts of Manitoba, northwestern Minnesota, and the Red River Valley. Eventually the waters of Lake Agassiz broke through a terminal moraine on its southern side at Lake Traverse (on Minnesota's western border) and unleashed an episodic series of cataclysmic floods. The floodwaters came in seasonal pulses that reshaped the terrain and initiated the creation of the gorge at the heart of today's Twin Cities.

Called the River Warren, it made two turns that catch our attention, one at Mankato and one at St. Paul. The river raced down the old traces of the glacier and flushed out a large channel across western Minnesota to the Mankato area. Then, instead of turning south and following the route of the main glacier, the currents made an abrupt turn and bolted northeast toward the Twin Cities along what had been a branch of the glacier. The second unique turn occurred when the floodwater reached the site of today's St. Paul. Now running across the top of the Platteville Limestone, it came across that old channel of the Mississippi River that ran north–south out of Trout and Phalen Creeks. Though the old channel was quite deep, the last glacier had filled it with debris. A smaller waterfall, about the height of today's Minnehaha Falls, stood there near today's bluff tops. When the high volume of the River Warren floods hit this point, it quickly cleared the glacial debris in the ancient gorge that ran north–south. The floodwaters turned sharply to the south and followed that old river course.

Next it was time for the Ordovician limestone-capped sandstone to dissolve in the face of such a great force. The floodwaters poured off the limestone ledge that was level with the top of St. Paul's bluff and fell into the emptied gorge at Trout Creek where the river turns south. In no time, geologically speaking, the river ate through the bedrock, reaching today's confluence of the Minnesota–Mississippi Rivers. There, for a short time, the River Warren formed a waterfall similar in width and height to today's Horseshoe Falls at Niagara (2,700 feet wide and 175 feet high). The size of this geological event is truly difficult to fathom. The great falls of the River Warren migrated west, upriver past the confluence, and dissipated. The river flowed at the bottom of the gorge (seventy-five feet deeper than today's river), running along the freshly carved bluffs from Fort Snelling to St. Paul. In time, the floods from Lake Agassiz receded, and the Minnesota River, reduced to a trickle of its former self, swapped places with the Mississippi and became the smaller tributary river. The lower part of the S-turn was complete.

Now the Mississippi River had a waterfall—the prototype of St. Anthony Falls—at the Mississippi–Minnesota confluence. Here was the ideal for the nineteenth-century explorers and settlers: the confluence as a boat landing and the falls for hydropower in one place. It didn't last long.

The Mississippi now cut its gorge, moving north through the same geologic layer cake. Over the past 10,000 years, the falls carved the Mississippi gorge, on average, about a mile a millennium. The river flushed debris downriver, which partially filled in the lower gorge. The S-turn in the Mississippi River was complete. The mighty Mississippi, which for a time had been a tributary, had significant help in creating such a complex landscape.

It is good to remember that a number of other configurations could have developed. Had the River Warren taken another course, say turned south at Mankato, or had Lake Agassiz only emptied through its other drainages to the east and the north, the rivers in the Twin Cities area would have left a different landscape. The falls may well have remained downriver, slicing through the bedrock at a slower place. The Mississippi along with the Minnesota may have cut a narrow gorge below the confluence. Because of the lower water volume in this scenario, the main part

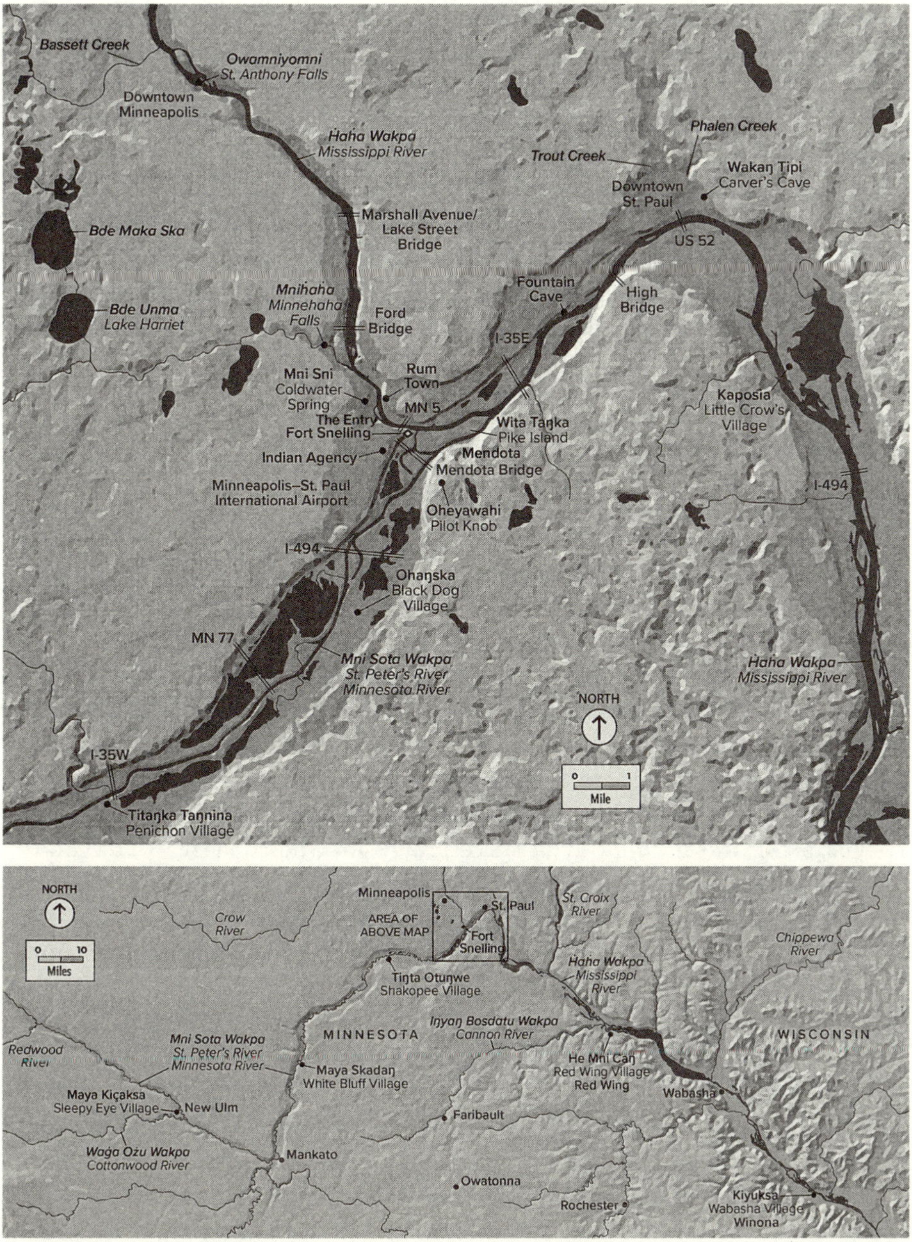

Upper map: The Mississippi River makes a large S-turn through the Twin Cities. It had many ancient courses through the region, which can be seen north of St. Paul and west of Minneapolis. Note how wide the Minnesota River Valley is compared to the Mississippi above the confluence at Fort Snelling. The lower map shows the course of the River Warren and its dramatically angular turns at Mankato and St. Paul.

of the S-turn would likely not have been as wide as it is. Without the epic floods of the River Warren, the final touch of today's Mississippi gorge would likely not have happened. Whatever shape it took, any other configuration would have created a different set of challenges for settlers—or none at all.

As it was, this glacial-melt flood formed a landscape that confounded American settlement. Those distant natural forces passing through the area hit the weak spot of the bedrock at this location and created a gorge. In this way the river generated a landscape that presented a puzzle, and in solving that puzzle the nineteenth-century settlers created the Twin Cities.

Pike's Word on the Treaty

The first person to attempt to solve the riddle was Lieutenant Zebulon Pike on his journey north on the Mississippi River in September 1805. Part of his mission was to negotiate a treaty for a US Army reserve at the Mississippi–Minnesota river confluence. Pike and his small crew had worked their way up the river to the island that was at the confluence, the very heart of the Dakota people's homeland. He had laid out his proposal to a group of Mdewakanton Dakota leaders for a reserve that included the confluence and the falls. He gave them a small down payment and promised there was more to come when the treaty was ratified in Washington, DC. He wrote to his commanding officer, Major General James Wilkinson, and announced his successful negotiation of a treaty at a good bargain. He could not have been prouder.[4]

Then, the day after his life's biggest achievement, Pike lost his flag. He thought it had been stolen. When he discovered the flag was missing from his boat he was immediately on edge and ready to fight.

Pike's flag had fifteen white stars in its blue square. The flag clearly meant a great deal to him. It flew on his boat's mast nearly thirty feet above the water and identified his crew as American. In the region he moved through the trading posts flew the British flag because the British dominated the fur trade. After the Louisiana Purchase of 1803, west of the Mississippi River, the United States was asserting its claim to the region, as well as some lands east of the river under the British flag. The land claims did not consider the large resident populations of Native Americans. The Americans would recognize the Indian title to the land, but their demeaning methods of acquiring those titles debased and insulted an ever more dependent and desperate Indigenous population. Pike's orders were multifold and in part began that process. Among other tasks, he was to find the source of the Mississippi River, which would orient the northern border of the nation's claim. Along the way he was to identify possible locations for forts and to obtain the rights to parcels of land for those future outposts.[5]

As Pike and his crew pushed up the river, they met Indigenous people mostly in canoes. Pike noticed these people avoided his party, likely when they saw his flag. When his interpreter engaged one family, they asked immediately if Pike was here for war. Others simply stayed away until his interpreter hailed them. "It is surprising," wrote Pike, "what a dread the Indians in this quarter have of the Americans." The British-aligned traders, he presumed, had impressed upon the Indians "the idea of our being a very vindictive, ferocious, and warlike people." He believed he could change their minds when they were persuaded that war was not a priority for the Americans and that instead "our conduct toward them is guided by magnanimity and justice." He was hoping that through it all, the Native Americans would revere and fear the newcomers.

He had to navigate some cultural differences. Wabasha, a Dakota leader, along with a number of his people met Pike as he approached the shore one day. They greeted Pike and his men by firing their guns three times at the boats. Unnerving as it was, the Indians were not shooting to kill. Their welcoming volleys were a competition to see who could land the closest shot to the incoming boats. The village had waited for Pike three days, and Wabasha invited Pike to stay with them. Pike declined because he had a late start on his exploration. It was September and the season was turning. His interpreter persuaded him that he should at least stop by and have a bite to eat. After all, Wabasha was giving Pike a letter of introduction in the form of a pipe. Pike could present the pipe to any Dakota people he encountered, and it would speak for his validity as a representative of the new government. The Dakota were likely interested in Pike and the Americans for expanded trading opportunities.

As he ascended the river, Pike explored promising locations for military forts, typically at high points near confluences, such as the ridge across from Prairie du Chien where the Wisconsin River flowed into the Mississippi, and Petite Gris, a hill along the Wisconsin about three miles above its mouth. Control of the major confluences would give Americans power over the reigning British fur trade. Pike reported these sites as having potential for military installations.

The American men in keelboats moved upriver through the wide, heavily forested valley bounded with bluffs. On the easy days, they hoisted their sail and listened to the fiddle players. On broad Lake Pepin, a storm blew in and raised waves that swallowed the bow of the boat as it plunged under each incoming wave. At the confluence with the St. Croix River, Pike saw the location would serve well for a fort or post and included it in his treaty.

They left the clear blue water of the St. Croix and plied up the turbid red Mississippi water with its deeper pools black as ink. As they ascended in a due north direction, they approached the bleached sandstone bluffs that had been exposed by the River Warren floods ten millennia earlier. In the last mile the river bent back on itself at an acute angle and ran along the base of the bluffs. They turned to the southwest and soon arrived at the confluence, their destination for the first leg of the trip north. The Mississippi branched to the north away from the Minnesota, which was also a clear blue. Looking upriver, the rims of the bluffs closed in on the river as it disappeared into the gorge. The Mississippi River at the mouth of the gorge narrowed to only forty strokes on the oars from side to side.

Pike's big day had come. At the Mississippi–Minnesota confluence, known as Bdóte by his Indigenous hosts, Pike used his boat's sail as a tent for shade on the island located there. Only those involved in the treaty were allowed inside. The rest of the Dakota men and Pike's crew remained outside. He gave a long speech that covered a variety of topics, and he was proud of that speech. He then introduced his proposal: He sought to buy two military reserves for the US Army, one at the St. Croix and the other at the Minnesota. In exchange for money and supplies, the Dakota, Pike's treaty said, would grant the United States "the full sovereignty and power over said district forever," and the Dakota would be able "to pass and re-pass, hunt, or make other use of the said districts as they have formerly done."[6]

Pike described a military reserve that, most importantly, encompassed both St. Anthony Falls and the confluence. He had not even seen the falls yet, though it's possible he could hear them. General Wilkinson, his commander, had requested that any agreement include both river features. To Wilkinson, the value of each of them was individually important to the nineteenth-century military, as they would be to the industrial-age settlers who followed. The treaty solved the problem of the gorge, from the confluence to the falls, by including both features. The reserve at the mouth of the St. Croix was nine miles square. The reserve at the Minnesota confluence contained the confluence and the Falls of St. Anthony and extended nine miles on each side of the river. Pike estimated it contained 100,000 acres.[7]

Of the seven Mdewakanton leaders in the tent with him, only two signed an X by their name. "It was somewhat difficult to get them to sign the grant," wrote Pike. More important to the Dakota men was that they stood on their word of honor. Pike convinced them that his need for their signature was not because he did not believe them. He explained that Americans "are a people who are accustomed to have all our acts written down," as such documents were the basis of the US legal system. Signing the treaty, he explained, would guarantee that others followed the agreement as well. "When ratified and approved of by the proper authority," he claimed, the agreement "shall be binding on both parties."

Though not the clearest language, Pike's description with the acreage suggests a rectangle of two nine-mile squares straddling the river gorge. His job was to acquire an area, not necessarily to describe its precise limits. In fact, the army never would survey the reserve as Pike had identified it. The confluence and the falls spoke for themselves. Pike's solution to the geographic problem, a treaty covering both resources, was enough. The army would not use this land until 1819, and only when prompted by the interests of the American Fur Company in the area. The need to know the exact boundaries of the reserve would not press itself upon the army until the Dakota treaty of 1837 that opened the land for settlement. When the army did survey it, the commander mentioned Pike's language, but he did not follow Pike's description. Of the nine miles to the east, the army claimed only the five miles to St. Paul. Those boundaries mattered a great deal and that decision shaped how the Twin Cities were born.

Pike had promised a commitment to the written agreement, but over the years the letter and the spirit of the law were deliberately and repeatedly broken. Settlers frequently ignored laws they found inconvenient, as this book showcases many times over. Disregard for the law also plays a role in shaping the future Twin Cities and their rivalry.

Pike solved the problem of the gorge by creating a reserve that included the two features of greatest importance, but they were at too great a distance from each other to be thought of together. As long as settlers were dependent on river travel, the separation of the falls from the confluence made these two points of settlement almost inevitable. Yet settlers always projected that it would become one city in the end.

Desnoyer Claims the Center

Four decades later, Etienne (Stephen) Desnoyer hung a sign above the door of his new tavern: "Desnoyer's Halfway House, 1843." That was the year he claimed the property. Desnoyer's parcel would become a focal point for the future Twin Cities.[8]

With his land abutting the northern boundary of the Fort Snelling

Military Reservation ("the Reserve"), Desnoyer sat atop a hill with views across the river and its gorge. He had acquired a successful business, perhaps the most popular groggery in the region around the head of navigation. His was nearest to the fort, three miles closer than that of legendary Pierre Parrant, or Pig's Eye, at St. Paul Landing. Desnoyer got the property from Donald McDonald in exchange for a barrel of whiskey and two Indian guns, common items of the fur trade.[9]

McDonald had left his home in Canada in 1818 at fifteen years old and, from what little we know about him, he wandered extensively through the north country. He was a seasoned trader and worked for both fur companies, American and North West. Known as Old Mc or Old Mack, he was eccentric, wore a plug hat—"his only remaining emblem of gentility," according to a newspaper—and used liquor to his advantage when trading with the Indians. He married a Métis woman, worked as a translator at the fort, and claimed to have built the third house east of the river across from the fort.[10]

McDonald moved north of the Reserve, three miles upriver from the fort on the east side, to a steep drainage called Rum Pitch. The name alone explains its relationship with the fort. McDonald received a shipment of whiskey barrels in 1839 at the location that would later become St. Paul Landing, and the next year acquired a license from the county to operate there. He had a popular location and stayed busy serving soldiers, voyageurs, and Indians. The Rum Pitch ravine was quite steep, a hazard for the inebriated soldiers on their return to their lodgings. But McDonald's was the closest groggery to the fort.[11]

When Desnoyer arrived, he traded for McDonald's claim and operated the groggery. He built his Halfway House in 1844, relocating his base of operation from the riverside bluff to the northeast, alongside the new land route that connected St. Paul Landing with St. Anthony Falls. Over the years the road had many different names, such as the St. Anthony (Falls)–St. Paul Road, St. Paul Road, St. Anthony Road, or River Road. Desnoyer's new tavern on this road shows changing views about the area's settlement pattern. He shifted his business to focus on the direct route from St. Paul Landing to St. Anthony Falls. The road, primitive as it was, immediately became a logistical remedy to the fort's large Reserve and the natural obstacle of the gorge.

The land for miles around was open and wooded savanna prairie that receded "from bluff to bluff, like so many stepping stones to the skies, where in the dim distance, they at last appear to meet," as one visitor described it. Sparkling lakes and streams filled with fish dotted the landscape. New residents proposed a hotel at the falls to accommodate visitors, envisioning a large resort for summer retreats that would attract all those escaping poor climates and busy lives. With more settlers in the area, people's view of the land was changing.[12]

There was more than one way to get there. In moving west, people had three choices. The northern route through the Great Lakes was blocked by the falls at Sault Ste. Marie, between Lakes Superior and Huron. That route wouldn't open until 1855. The eastern route ran from Lake Michigan to Green Bay, ascended the Fox River, crossed a portage to the Wisconsin River, and descended to the Mississippi at Prairie du Chien.

Using the third route, the Mississippi itself, people came and went on smaller vessels. The Dakota paddled dugout canoes and the Ojibwe in their birchbark canoes were faster than the explorers, the traders, and the military in keelboats or on pirogues, which were basically log rafts with rudders. The keelboat was the vehicle most often used by the army in moving troops and supplies above the rapids before 1823. But it was at times too big. When the river was low, such as when the first US Army troops ascended in 1819, they had to wade in the water and pull the boats through the sand. That 300-mile journey took six weeks. River travel was the best way to access the region, but it was not easy.[13]

The Mississippi had two sets of rapids that guarded the upper reaches from access by steamboat. The Rock Island Rapids was a fourteen-mile stretch of shallow water. The Des Moines Rapids was farther downriver on Iowa's southern border. In 1823, encouraged by government contracts to supply the remote forts upriver, the steamboat *Virginia* ascended the Rock Island Rapids and cleared the barrier once thought impossible. The US Army Corps of Engineers led by Robert E. Lee modified the lower rapids with dynamite in 1837, coincidentally synchronized with the Dakota and Ojibwe treaties that opened the land for settlement. With the steamboats, more people could reach the upper region of the Mississippi with no more effort than purchasing a ticket.

Desnoyer came up the river in his keelboat. The oldest of seven children, he was born on April 22, 1805, in Saint-Jean-d'Iberville, Quebec, about thirty miles southeast of Montreal. In 1823, at the age of eighteen, he moved up the St. Lawrence River and settled on the southeastern shore of Lake Ontario in Oswego, New York, where he worked as a farmer for four years. He returned home but had difficult relations with his father, who was possibly perturbed by his son's life with a woman who drank excessively. Desnoyer's father kicked him out and he immigrated to the United States.[14]

A trader at heart, Desnoyer used his keelboat as a home, a workhorse, and a vehicle all in one. The keelboat could be poled, rowed, towed, or sailed on still or moving water. His boat was elemental to his various business ventures. The country's first transportation revolution was by water. Networks of canals with locks and dams connected waterways with the lakes. The network was so complete Desnoyer was able to travel the entire way from his family home near Montreal to Fort Snelling in his keelboat. He traveled south on Lake Champlain, where he had brothers in Plattsburgh, New York, then through a canal to the Hudson River. In the late 1830s he was in Troy, New York, the eastern terminus of the Erie Canal.[15]

During the summer Desnoyer floated the Erie Canal with his keelboat, selling groceries and liquor. He married Mary (Marie) Jarvey, and they had a son, George Isaie. When Mary died in 1838 the infant was taken back to Saint-Jean-d'Iberville to be raised by relatives. Desnoyer moved west in his boat, first to Detroit, then likely along the Ohio and Erie Canal to the Ohio River. He turned up the Mississippi River and settled at Prairie du Rocher (Rock Prairie), Illinois. He married Maurice Doiron in 1839, and they had a son, Etienne III. Desnoyer worked the area with his keelboat, trading and transporting goods such as lumber, clothing, and grain among the river towns, primarily St. Louis. The family moved upriver to Dubuque, a small, rough-and-tumble lead mining town in the recently organized Iowa Territory. Desnoyer continued to haul lumber and lead ore in his boat. Here he met Father Augustin Ravoux, whom he would know the rest of his life. Then Desnoyer lost his family again; his wife died on May 30, 1842, at age twenty-eight, as did their child on July 1, age three months.[16]

Desnoyer continued upriver to Prairie du Chien, then to Fort Snelling. He passed the community of French Canadian voyageurs and their families settled along the river on the east bank across from the Dakota village of Kaposia, as well as the cluster of settlers at St. Paul Landing. The communities along the Mississippi River all spoke his mother tongue, French. His English was poor and heavily accented. Life would have been easy among the voyageurs working for the fur company. But the voyageurs, as laborers, were the lowest tier of the social order. Desnoyer was like Auguste Larpenteur, who also arrived in 1843, a businessman and a trader. Desnoyer likely brought goods upriver to sell and trade, as did others such as Henry Jackson, a merchant who arrived in 1842. Desnoyer was of the new vanguard coming to stake a claim. He moved past these laboring communities and set his sights instead on a unique property near Meeker Island in the middle of the Mississippi gorge, north of the confluence.

Desnoyer got his 300-plus acres of land through one of the most renowned trades of his day: a barrel of whiskey and two Indian guns. Certainly it sounds like an imbalanced trade, especially since the land came with a thriving business. Yet there is more to consider about the economic context of the time.

During these early days, values were not fixed. In a world where trade was largely based on barter, cash had a short life of utility. When cash was abundant, people were known to spend it. One man paid eighty dollars for a gallon of whiskey. And people played cards. For several years after the treaties of 1837 the annuities to the tribes arrived "with commendable regularity," according to Larpenteur. When these annual infusions of money came, traders and Indians would "play a lively game of poker."[17]

In one story, Larpenteur fondly recalled trading with the shrewd McDonald. He remembered his boss, a wholesaler, had accumulated excess coinage and saw no use for it until spring. During the dead of winter, his boss decided he would use the cash to buy some furs from the northern traders. He took his money north. He returned about ten days later without any money or furs. He only said that it was impossible to get the traders to sell their furs. And worse, tragedy struck on the return trip when a horse fell through the river ice and the metal coins were lost.

But that story, Larpenteur realized, was to cover for the fact that his boss had been fleeced by traders like William Aitken and McDonald, who moved north to Crow Wing and traded on the Red River oxcart trail. Larpenteur came to this conclusion when he himself made a similar trip and returned with nothing to show for his efforts. The traders would initiate a game of cards and "could entertain the adept and give them a percentage besides," he said. They were so much better than any able gambler that they could comfortably give the other players a seeming advantage yet still win the game. "Oh, these old traders were a jolly set," he recalled, "and whenever you came in contact with them they always left you something to remember them by." Since they got the money, all they gave in return was a bad memory.[18]

If McDonald was such a sharp trader, how did Desnoyer get his land at such a good price: a barrel of whiskey and two guns? Did Desnoyer catch McDonald in a compromised or needy position? Did he outwit him at cards? Was alcohol a factor? The trade seems extraordinarily lopsided—so much land for whiskey and guns.

In part the scenario can be explained because of the abundance of land compared to the scarcity of a sought-after commodity like whiskey. In the early years residents traded land claims "with bewildering rapidity," according to historian Mary Lethert Wingerd. With so much land available and living in a barter economy, "land claims became a sort of quasi-currency." In addition, though the 1837 Dakota treaty opened up the land east of the Mississippi six years earlier, the territory had yet to be surveyed for auction. Prior to that preparation, the sales, or trades, were for "squatter's claims." McDonald likely only claimed the land in an unofficial way and never paid for it. "We were all called squatters," recalled Larpenteur. They staked preemptive claims that gave them precedence when the government sold the land. The two seasoned traders had not actually exchanged any real estate title. Rather, they had bartered for the right to make a legal claim in the future. When the land was surveyed and Minnesota became a territory in 1849, Desnoyer paid the government $1.25 per acre for his claim.[19]

During this time of transition that would lead to a settlement, views of the land were changing. For Old Mack, his claim at Rum Pitch was the location of his business, yet it was not attached to his settling there. People often staked claims but never purchased the land. For Desnoyer, the land had value attached to its future possibilities. In their exchange, we see the changing of the guard, from the old view based on barter to a new one of permanence in the sense of appreciating land values. Indeed, Desnoyer was renowned for bragging about the value of his land.[20]

On the road between St. Anthony and St. Paul, Desnoyer's tavern stood near the center of Pike's Reserve. His tavern was equidistant to all three settlements: Fort Snelling/Mendota, St. Paul, and St. Anthony. He solved the riddle by settling in the middle, halfway to everywhere, by water or land. He either positioned himself or found himself at a local crossroads. Lucky for him the property would even be on the future Short Line railroad and have a boarding station. He believed he held the center of the future metropolitan area, what he called Bridge Square of the united cities. Indeed, his property would play a role in future efforts to unite the Twin Cities.[21]

From the beginning, people envisioned a single city. "The time will come," wrote one editor, when the settlements will grow together, and the two cities will unite: "This has been the case with other places, and we see no reason why it should not be with ours." Another expressed "no doubt" that "in a few years St. Paul and St. Anthony will become one," and "a union must follow." As early as the mid-1850s, with St. Anthony and Minneapolis in their early days, the rivalry had already begun. One editor in 1856 imagined the day when St. Paul and its rivals would be "united in wedlock and when the jealousy" will be remembered as "the play-thing of a disordered brain."[22]

The window of time when the gorge mattered for this settlement process was from 1838, when the Dakota treaty was ratified and the land opened east of the river, to 1862, when the first railroad connected St. Paul and St. Anthony. If railroads had come earlier and been more significant in the area's settlement, the gorge would have played a subsidiary role. But for twenty-four years the settlement of the area was determined by the era when the gorge stopped the steamboat.

Of course the Mississippi–Minnesota confluence below the gorge offered natural landings for a new settlement. The confluence was far better than the steep and boggy land at St. Paul Landing. Why didn't the confluence become the site of a future city, as the earliest arrivals thought it would? That story picks up where Pike's left off.

CHAPTER 2

Plympton's Original Sin

Major Joseph Plympton reported for duty at Fort Snelling on August 20, 1837, in bad health. He was so sick he couldn't perform his normal duties as commander, such as making plans and dictating messages to his superiors in Washington, DC.[1]

Plympton also had a headache of a mess to deal with from day one. The people living north of the fort had sent a letter (called a memorial) to the president of the United States. They were concerned about recent changes in the area as well as the intentions of the army and the fort's new commander. Dakota leaders were on their way to Washington, DC, where they would negotiate a treaty that included ceding their land east of the river and fort. The army wanted to evict the settlers living near the fort to create the Fort Snelling Military Reserve. Most of the settlers had lived there since 1823. They had cleared the land, built homes, and established businesses. Their life was symbiotic with the fort, entwined in the exchange of services and security. They argued in their memorial to the president that their land claims were in the public domain and they should be allowed to stay.[2]

Sick as he was, Plympton wrote urgently to reassure his commanders that he was addressing the situation. For more than twenty-five years he had worked in the frontier forts and knew their role in the settlement of an area. The walls of Fort Snelling were a personal memory from his early years there. Now he had returned, and at some point he built a cabin on the east side of St. Anthony Falls. His plans went beyond his military duties. He would leverage his position and authority to create a Reserve designed to give him and his associates an advantage in claiming the premier land by the falls. His actions in the next few years would define the shape of the Twin Cities in perpetuity.[3]

Plympton's arrival at Fort Snelling in the fall of 1837 coincided with a major transition for the area. The Dakota treaty (signed September 29) became law on June 15, 1838, and opened up the land east of the river for settlement. His problem was that the fort's Reserve, the area around the fort that held wood and pasture, lacked a defined boundary. Up until then it didn't need one. Now, before any new settlers arrived, he and the army needed to clarify the size and shape of the fort's Reserve. Pike had written a copy of the agreement, put it in a bottle, and buried it, then cut his name in the bark of a tree. According to Pike's 1805 description, the Reserve ran from the falls to the confluence and contained a nine-mile square of land both west and east of the river. But Pike never drew a map and the Reserve's contents were unidentified.[4]

People unattached to the army often settled near the forts, but this situation was different. These first settlers, dubbed "refugees of Utopia" by one early resident, arrived before any nonmilitary land was available for public settlement. They came south from a failed colony on the lower Red River in Canada (near Winnipeg). Destitute and hopeless after several bad growing seasons and harsh winters, they fled, following the Red and Minnesota Rivers. Hundreds of them passed by Fort Snelling on their way south, and some stayed. They built their homes, some of them for permanent residences and business. Now, in defining the Reserve, Plympton wondered under what conditions these settlers had been allowed to claim the land north of the fort around the freshwater spring at Camp Coldwater. He believed it should be a part of the Reserve. But he couldn't find any reports or memos in the files at Fort Snelling headquarters that described the arrangement of their settlement.[5]

The settlers were in a location that offered additional benefits. The confluence was the head of navigation for steamboats on the Mississippi. The settlers had identified the best steamboat landings near the easiest routes out of the river valley. People envisioned the landings at the confluence as a base where they could unload materials and machinery, haul that freight to the falls, and build the mills that would process trees from the pine forests upriver. They were on the prime land in the area for a new settlement that would provide access to the falls.[6]

Plympton was a unique person to supervise this transition of Fort Snelling. He had served there as a lieutenant for at least five years between 1819 and 1828. He already knew the lay of the land. He helped build the fort, gathered wood for its buildings, and prepared the cement for the stone walls and buildings. He understood how St. Anthony Falls would figure as the future economic engine of the region. Now he would determine where people could settle.

When he built his cabin at the falls in 1836, he stepped into a conflict of interest between his duty to create an adequate Reserve and his intention to capitalize on his position when the land opened up for settlement.

The Making of an Officer

Born on February 24, 1787, in Sudbury, Massachusetts, Plympton was the fourth of six boys. Though not of a wealthy or privileged background he received a good education. He was "strikingly handsome," as his family remembered him: dark, wavy hair above a high, wide forehead with dark blue eyes over a prominent nose and a large mouth. He was a Presbyterian, said to be related to the early Puritans, and known for singing psalms.[7]

A half year before the declaration of war, Plympton enlisted in the army on January 3, 1812, in New Hampshire, as a second lieutenant in the Fourth Infantry. He was immediately active in Upper Canada, just north of Lakes Erie and Huron. In 1819, in the Fifth Infantry, he came up the Mississippi River with Lieutenant Colonel Henry Leavenworth to establish Cantonment New Hope, the encampment from which they began construction of Fort Snelling. They arrived in August with half the crew exhausted from the summer heat, bad drinking water, and sleepless nights spent slapping mosquitoes. They selected a site on the south side of the Minnesota River Valley, below Mendota, the only place for boats to land on the west side of the river at the confluence. Plympton oversaw construction of the temporary log buildings they needed for the winter. Their food spoiled and scurvy ravaged their bodies so badly no one was able to tend the sickest. That winter, at least thirty soldiers died. Plympton was one of the survivors of that hellish, unforgettable season.[8]

Plympton worked with the Indian agent who accompanied the troops in 1819 and delivered the balance of Pike's treaty promise to the local Dakota people ($2,000 worth of trade goods). The size or boundaries of the Reserve were apparently discussed at those meetings. The Dakota remembered the area to be smaller, but it was not written down. Through his various duties, Plympton developed a good understanding of the rivers and the resources in the region. Trees fit for building—straight and long—were so scarce in the immediate area that the soldiers had to go up the Mississippi to the Rum River, fell the pine trees, float the logs down, and cut them into shape with a whipsaw.[9]

In the early 1820s Plympton returned east. He recruited soldiers in New York City and worked in the War Department in Washington, DC. He was comfortable both in the army culture of the remote forts and in the halls of power in big cities. On March 15, 1824, he married Eliza Matilda Livingston, daughter of the wealthy and influential Peter William Livingston. The Plymptons returned to Fort Snelling in 1825 and stayed until his regiment was rotated out in mid-1828.[10]

Officers did not make much money, but, as Plympton's marriage into New York's highest social circles indicates, they could rise to a prestigious position in society. The officer class was aristocratic and lived a lavish life separate from the enlisted soldiers. Despite the limited resources in isolated forts, they retained their social bearings from the East. They kept well-appointed households in a show of wealth. They held high society events like balls at which their wives wore elegant gowns accented with diamond and gold jewelry that would impress any visitor. "Many of these ladies would have shone in any circle," said one resident. Mrs. Plympton even had a piano brought up the river for her pleasure.[11]

In these detached assignments, the officers were self-policing and had their own style of addressing the inevitable internecine disputes. For example, duels were illegal and punishable by court-martial. Yet, among officers, their code of honor allowed an officer to challenge another to a duel. Predictably, boredom, cards, and whiskey led to arguments and illicit duels. The officers turned a blind eye to such "affairs of honor," a permissive ethos in which they intentionally underreported another officer's rule breaking. Their reports presented misconduct as a mere misunderstanding. Injuries from duels were recorded as hunting accidents. To a significant degree, what happened at Fort Snelling stayed at Fort Snelling.[12]

The commander of a rather inaccessible fort stood at the apex of military and civilian life. The fort officers, of course, acted on orders from military authorities in Washington, DC, yet the local commander reigned supreme and had little counterbalance in the realm of civic affairs. To maintain authority at such a post was a delicate operation. A commander had to establish and hold jurisdiction over the officers, soldiers, Native Americans, fur traders, and civilians. The commanders were known to step beyond their authority in matters of policy and justice, earning the epithet the "lords of the North." With that tight network, they were a regional political power in a place that had at best only nascent civil powers. With no check on their power, they were often accused of being tyrants.[13]

In the early nineteenth century the military was akin to a southern aristocracy, including many Fort Snelling officers, who were enslavers themselves (to name a few: John Bliss, Zachary Taylor, Martin Scott, John Emerson, and Plympton—who enslaved two people). Major Lawrence Taliaferro, the Indian agent at Fort Snelling, inherited several enslaved people and rented them out to officers at Fort Snelling. One of those enslaved people was Harriet Robinson, whom Taliaferro sold to John Emerson when she married Dred Scott in 1836. The Scotts' enslavement in the Northwest was not an anomaly or an isolated situation; rather, it was representative of army culture at forts across the Northwest.[14]

As an officer at a fort so far from oversight, Plympton had unchallenged authority. With the land east of the river opening to settlement, the fort's Reserve was in question, and he was in a position to shape its boundaries. His process and decisions put him at odds with the settlers. He was also aware that the army's purpose in the region was changing.

Fort Snelling's Changing Role

Ever since Pike came up the river, the army had been engaging the British in the Northwest Territory, the region north of the Ohio River and east of the Mississippi River. The War of 1812 was the beginning of the end of the British dominance in the fur trade. To keep the British trading companies out of the region, the US Army built and garrisoned forts across today's Michigan, Wisconsin, Iowa, and Minnesota. Along with defending American territory against British incursion, the army also engaged the Native peoples in the fur trade. The army located forts to protect key water routes, and most of these outposts were built quickly with logs in 1815–16. With a tight budget, too few soldiers, and rapid emigration to the region, the War Department played a version of musical chairs with the forts. The army shifted troops where they were needed, either regionally or nationally, abandoning forts and then resurrecting them as warranted. Most of the forts lasted fewer than twenty years.[15]

Fort Snelling was the anomaly in this collection of outposts. The region's largest fort, it stood on the Mississippi River at the boundary between the Northwest Territory (1787) and the Louisiana Purchase (1803) and served as a link between the two land parcels. Secretary of War John C. Calhoun wanted to extend a network of roads and forts into the Louisiana Purchase, stretching west across the Upper Missouri River basin to the Yellowstone River. The army believed they were building for a more permanent occupation. Colonel Snelling arrived in 1820 with Calhoun's expansionist vision as his orders and built a fort that was unlike any other in the western region. He transformed the seven companies of soldiers at Fort Snelling into laborers, and they worked with the most abundant local building material: the Platteville Limestone that rimmed the gorge and river valley. Plympton oversaw the preparation of the mortar. When Congress balked at funding Calhoun's greater network of roads and forts, Fort Snelling became the last fort of Calhoun's plan to be built.[16]

Fort Snelling was more like a fortress, perhaps even overbuilt. It was rarely fully garrisoned and more often run by a skeletal crew, commanded by lower-ranking officers such as captains. An army general on an inspection tour in 1827 found the fort impressive but the parade ground embarrassingly large. Further, despite its imposing view from below in the river bottom, it was vulnerable because it stood beneath the ridge behind it, leaving it susceptible to cannon fire. The assessment was harsh: The fort was conceived at a high point in activating Calhoun's plan, but the concept and design were overblown, and the fort was excessive from the start.[17]

Plympton's regiment, the Fifth Infantry, was stationed at Fort Snelling during the years 1819–28 and again in 1837–41. In those same years, the regiment also had companies on rotation at ten other forts, and Plympton served in at least five of them. He also participated in the Black Hawk War of 1832. Plympton closed Fort Dearborn in December 1836 and remained there during the decommissioning period into June or July 1837. Through all his service in the Northwest he understood firsthand the forts' life cycles, from building to decommissioning, and selling military reserve land afterward. As well as anyone, he was intimately involved in the region's rapid transition.[18]

When Plympton returned to his old stomping grounds in 1837, he was upset with the civilians' proximity to the fort. Their location—about a mile north of the fort—was typical for the times because of their desire for security, their symbiotic relationship with the fort, and the fact there was no unceded land available for them to settle on. For the most part, the settlers offered benefits to the army. A large stone house hosted a store and doubled as a school for the kids at Fort Snelling. Two blacksmiths plied their trade. Farm produce, horses, cattle, and other goods were sold to soldiers, the fort, or the fur company. The fort employed civilians such as Donald McDonald as interpreters and the soldiers' wives as servants. "Aunt Mary Ann" Perry was an experienced and trusted midwife in demand with the wives at the fort. And in return the settlers made a living and enjoyed protection. It was a commonplace and beneficial arrangement between civilians and the military.[19]

In the face of strong opposition, Plympton objected to the nearby settlement and its alleged infringement on the fort. Even though the civilian community was an integrated part of the fort community, he would destroy it. His actions were less about cruelty than about addressing how the confluence fit into the logistics of the area.

Securing the Landings

In response to the settlement, Plympton set to the task of defining the Reserve itself. He began somewhat hesitantly, seeking direction and permission from the administrative ranks in DC. He became bolder and gradually enlarged his proposals for the Reserve. All the while he gave his superiors different reasons for the expansions, including preservation of necessary resources such as wood, quashing the soldiers' access to alcohol, and subduing their boisterous noises. He never mentioned the six steamboat landings, their role at the confluence, and their relationship to the falls. In this way, he used his official capacity to protect and enhance the valuable land claim at the falls, in which he had a personal interest. In the end, it would take him two years and four maps to get what he wanted.

The first map was drawn by a talented illustrator, Lieutenant E. K. Smith, and it detailed the residences in the fort's vicinity. The Smith Vicinity map of October 1837 is priceless in its details of the area's settlement pattern, a snapshot of people's preferences in relation to the river and bluffs. Smith reported 157 people living either north of the fort (including a few dwellings on the east side of the river along the rim of the bluff) or south of the confluence at the American Fur Company trading post. This map captured Plympton's initial concern about the settlers near the fort. The civilian population may have been fifty percent of the number in the military community, so upward of 500 people in the area. That many people in a prairie setting, he argued, put too much pressure on the resources, particularly given "the sparseness of timber within the space supposed to be embraced in Pike's treaty." Wood was everybody's fuel for cooking and heating. More people diminished fuel supplies, and the soldiers spent more time farther afield gathering wood for each winter. If the army needed this fort for twenty years, the acquisition of wood would become increasingly difficult.[20]

This map gave Plympton an inventory of the steamboat landings at the confluence. In this stretch of the Mississippi, steep, impenetrable bluffs dominated the shoreline. A good landing needed calm water, a flat area, and access through the bluffs to the plateau above. These landings on the map varied in quality and offered different advantages for access in the area. The landing across the Minnesota River from the fort was at Cantonment New Hope/Mendota, the only possible landing on the west side of the river. Another landing at Fort Snelling was very good. Three of the landings, the best ones, were tucked inside the bluffs of the gorge along the Mississippi River. Known as "the Entry," the area had advantages not seen for miles downriver, possibly as far as Grey Cloud Island or the St. Croix confluence. Smith labeled two of these on his Vicinity map at Camp Coldwater with "good landing" and "best steamboat landing." These two were on the west side of the river and had good access to the top of the surrounding bluffs. They served as a point of departure for the more valuable land around St. Anthony Falls, the area's major resource. The third landing above the fort was on the east side at Rumtown (today's Hidden Falls Regional Park). This landing had distinct advantages for the near future because land east of the river would soon open to settlement. The Entry presented the best place for a future city. The final landing, which was not on this first map, was at the Cave (also called Upper Cave and later named Fountain Cave), three miles downriver from the fort.[21]

The landings were used by steamboats for the delivery of the fort's supplies, the fur trade, the Indian trade, and tourists. The steamboats provided easy access to the region. The confluence was, according to the

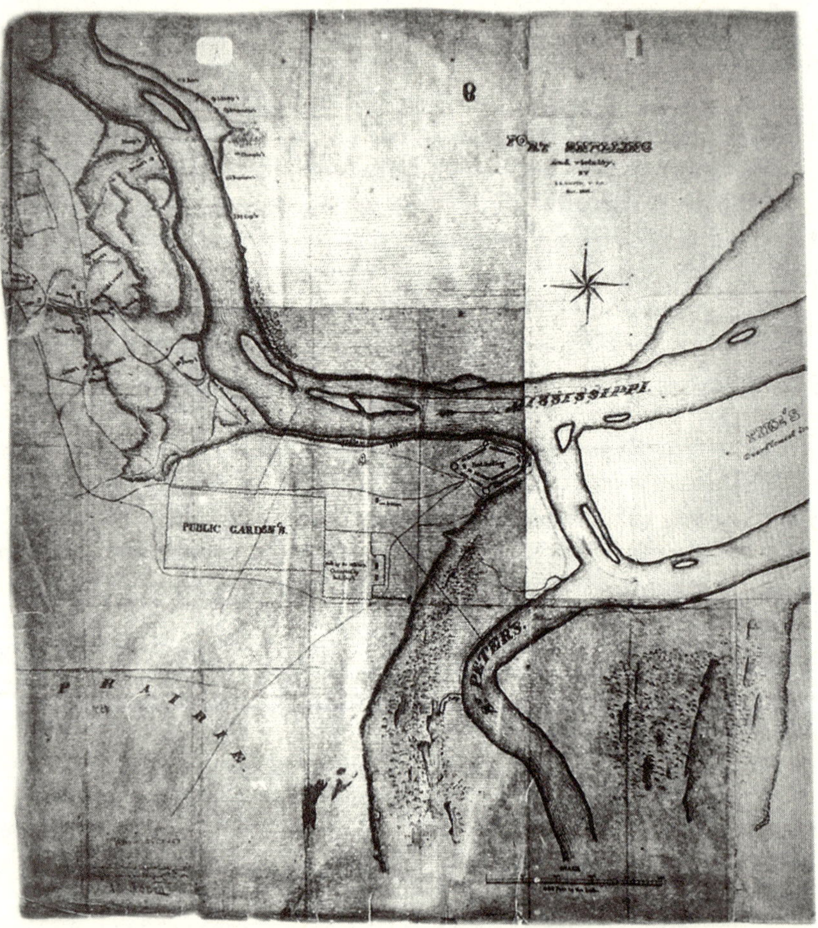

Lieutenant E. K. Smith's 1837 Vicinity map shows where people initially settled at the confluence. Upriver from the fort (upper left-hand quadrant of the map), the Entry featured the most convenient steamboat landings. Near the uppermost island, steamboats could land on each side of the river. West of the first island in the bend was the best landing. Fort Snelling and Mendota, south of Pike's Island, each had a landing.

French geographer Jean-Nicolas Nicollet, the premier place on the entire Mississippi River. And St. Anthony Falls had been an almost mythical attraction since Father Louis Hennepin had described it 150 years earlier. In the early 1830s the steamship *Warrior* delivered supplies to the fort along with "loads" of excited tourists "who were making an excursion, considered more wonderful in those days than would be a trip to the Hawaiian Islands," recalled one fort resident. The tourists disembarked at the fort and rode out on the wagon roads, one leading to Lake Calhoun (Bde Maka Ska), including the permanent Dakota village there, and the other to St. Anthony Falls, which included a stop at Little Falls (Minnehaha Falls).[22]

Arguably the most influential tourist was George Catlin, an artist with a self-appointed mission to paint portraits of Native Americans and their communal ceremonies. On his 1835 trip from St. Louis, Catlin was stunned by the dramatic change of landscape upriver from Prairie du Chien. The scenery was "continually opening to the eye of the traveller," he wrote, "and riveting him to the deck of the steamer, through sunshine, lightning or rain, from the mouth of the Ouisconsin to the Fall of St. Anthony." He proposed a "Fashionable Tour," something akin to the like-named popular sightseeing tour that included Saratoga Springs, Niagara Falls, the Catskill Mountains, Quebec, and Boston. This tour of the far reaches of the Northwest on the mighty Mississippi River took place on the deck of a steamboat, making it accessible to all types of tourists. The 800-mile trip from St. Louis cost twelve dollars and took nine to ten days.[23]

The steamboats offered easy access for tourists and, when the land opened up on the east side, it would attract the speculator and the settler. The confluence with its collection of landings would be a focal point for incoming people. Those interfaces between the river and the land were attractive as townsites. Aside from the fort's needs, Plympton used the boundaries of the Reserve as a way to control the location of future settlements and to stifle access to St. Anthony Falls. In doing so he blurred the lines between the military's needs and his personal interests.

The Town of Sintomonee

Then Plympton ran into direct competition at the confluence with one Joseph R. Brown.

Brown joined the military at fourteen years old as a fife player for the Fifth Infantry. He arrived at the confluence in 1819 and survived that first dreadful winter. When his enlistment expired, he reenlisted as a sergeant. He and Plympton likely knew each other, but they would not have engaged socially, as officers distanced themselves from the enlisted men. Brown left the army and joined the American Fur Company, across the river at Mendota, and traveled the region for his employer. A self-taught man, he owned a newspaper, was elected to the Wisconsin Territorial Legislature, and would play a prominent role in Minnesota becoming a territory. He adroitly used the political system to his advantage.[24]

By the time Plympton returned to Fort Snelling in 1837, Brown had initiated his own plan for the confluence. The coming land cession would attract settlers, and these settlers would need towns with steamboat landings, accommodations, and access to the valuable resource-rich areas upriver. Most promoters homed in on the end goal: the site of the resource, such as St. Anthony Falls. Brown's genius, according to his biographer, was to identify "townsites through which the tide of settlement must soon funnel." Brown saw the confluence as such a point of access. As people would be attracted to the falls, he saw the confluence with its cluster of landings as the focal point of through traffic. His first choice was on the eastern side of the river, opposite of Fort Snelling. He procured a county license for the ferry across the Mississippi from Camp Coldwater and laid out a townsite in the bottoms. He named the town Sintomonee, an approximation of the Dakota word *siŋtomni*, meaning "Home for All Nations."[25]

Brown knew what type of growth was coming west. He had visited relatives in Chicago and seen the rapid expansion there. He also had experience in land speculation. While stationed at Fort Armstrong, he learned the basics from George Davenport, who bought land across from Rock Island and platted the city there that carries his name. Brown had staked his own preemption claim at that site, though he let it go. These early developments in the region—Chicago, Davenport, Galena, Peoria, and Dubuque—were like a wave of settlement coming toward Fort Snelling. His town of Sintomonee at the Entry fit his style of speculation. He secured a preemptive claim and set to the task of obtaining the charter necessary for his townsite.[26]

Plympton was aware of Brown's plan. If Brown, or anybody else, was able to develop a townsite at one of the landings, it would undermine the value of Plympton's land claims upriver on the east side of St. Anthony Falls. Plympton understood that in order to preserve and enhance his claims upriver he had to control the landings downriver at the confluence. He had the army's resources at his disposal, and he knew how to apply them to achieve certain results. After twenty-five years in the army, he knew what pleased the officers above him whose permission he sought. He was a career officer, after all, and ambitious as well.

Plympton gave Washington, DC, information from Smith's census on the settlers, and then he noted there was not any established documentation that gave permission to settle there. He sent the Smith Vicinity map too, and his commanding general expressed his "pleasure and satisfaction . . . to receive information of that nature." His superiors asked for more information and encouraged Plympton to document the military resources. Plympton explained the need to expand the Reserve. At the bottom of one letter from Washington, a special postscript read, "Note: If there be no reservation already made for military purposes at your post, please to mark over what in your opinion will be necessary to be Reserved." Plympton had struck gold. His commanding officer had given him carte blanche to shape the Reserve and incorporate his own interests. Most importantly, he could seize the steamboat landings and block any settlement at the confluence by drawing the boundaries of the Reserve to include these significant sites.[27]

The second map covered the confluence area. Drawn by Lieutenant Smith, the "Map of a Proposed Reservation at Fort Snelling," dated March 25, 1838, featured a northeastern boundary on the Reserve that sloped southeasterly from a bend three miles up the Mississippi across to Fountain Cave. Plympton noted that this boundary line was "in [Smith's] survey the principal lines from river to river . . . necessarily (from the season and weather) left imaginary." The map surprised everyone, including his commanding officers in DC, because it included a much larger area than they had believed necessary.[28]

This Proposed Reserve map is, overall, a beautiful rendition of the confluence area. Notably, the Reserve boundaries straddled the Mississippi and the Minnesota Rivers and closed to the public the landings that had the best access to St. Anthony Falls. But most interestingly, it features the very thing Plympton was railing against, that being an undefined boundary. Smith, the cartographer, had drawn a number of things with precision and fine detail, including landscape features along the gorge, the settler's buildings at Camp Coldwater, and the meandering river with its sandbars. That would have required much field time. But outside of the river corridor the map is blank, lacking any landscape features. Smith was capable of excellent work and yet he didn't survey the approximately three-mile line in the northeast. Plympton blamed the season and the weather. Imaginary boundaries suggest that area was unimportant to the issue at hand. Likely no one at that time was interested in claiming that land. The map displays Plympton's intent to extend the Reserve east across the river and absorb the newly opened land that Brown and others were claiming for development of the first city at the head of navigation.

The boundaries of the Proposed Reserve map were done quickly. The upriver boundary had no stated reason, though it lay in the vicinity of

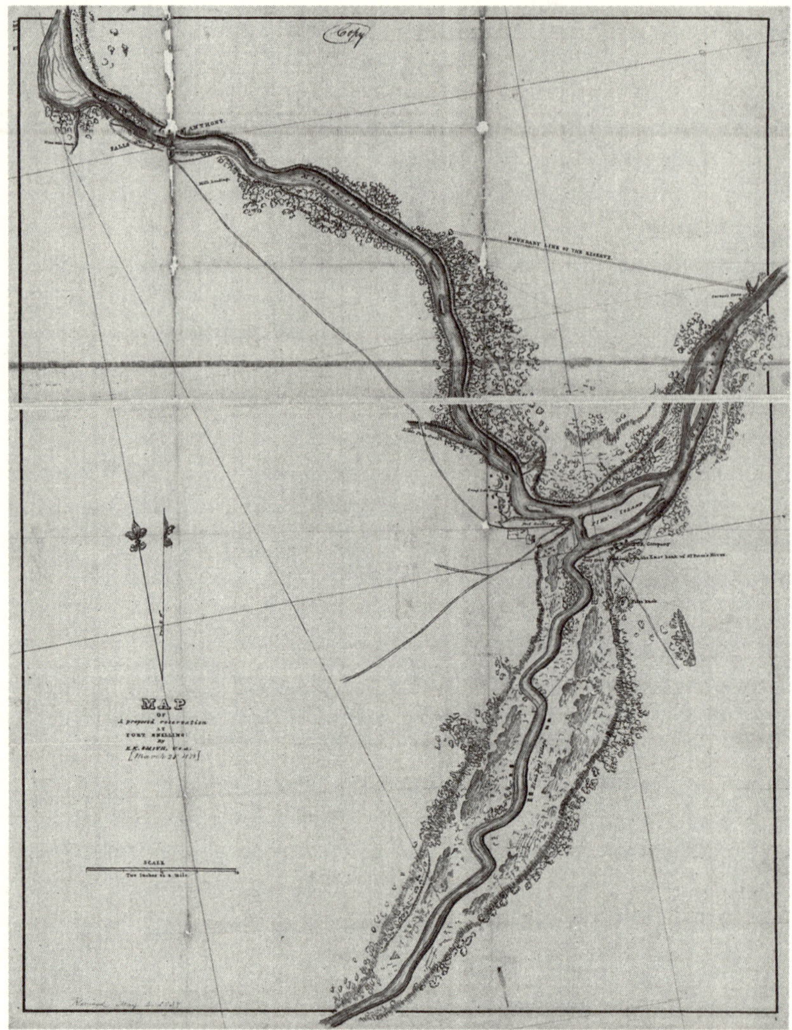

In 1838 Lieutenant Smith drew the Proposed Reserve map, the first draft of the Reserve. The northern boundary ran from St. Anthony Falls (upper left) down the middle of the river to near Marshall Avenue, then crossed southeasterly in a straight line to Fountain Cave. People could stake claims on the east side above Marshall Avenue, including Plympton's Claim at the falls.

Meeker Island, the midway point in the gorge and the extent of the rapid water. The Reserve now captured five of the six steamboat landings: the two landings above the fort at Camp Coldwater, the landing at Rumtown, the landing at the fort, and the landing at Mendota. If steamboats couldn't land at the confluence and unload their cargo, then people had no access to the land upriver. The Fountain Cave landing was the anomaly. It lay just outside the downriver boundary and may have served as a landmark. People were living in that area as well. Why Plympton placed the boundary at the Cave is unknown. But it created another problem almost immediately.[29]

Incidentally, if Plympton or the army had laid out the fort's Reserve according to Pike's description, a simple nine-by-eighteen-mile rectangle, the east and west sides would have been symmetrical. Pike's dimensions would have blocked all the land east of the fort well beyond Pig's Eye Lake. Instead, Plympton customized the shape of the Reserve. He left the land east of the river above the Reserve boundary open to claims, which included access to St. Anthony Falls. The land adjacent to the falls was the most valuable, and it was known as Plympton's Claim.

Staking the First Claim

Just four months after the second map was produced, the steamboat *Palmyra* arrived at the fort, bringing the news that the Dakota treaty had been ratified and was now law. On July 15, 1838, the land east of the Mississippi opened for claims.

The next day, according to legend, Plympton arrived at St. Anthony Falls only to find Franklin Steele, the fort's storekeeper, already there. Their meeting is legendary because there are multiple variations of the story with scant documentation and a good degree of contradiction. According to several accounts Steele had heard the news that the land was open, and he traveled to the falls in the night to stake a preemptive claim, while Plympton waited until the morning to travel. One story takes place in winter. Steele built a claim shack in the night and planted potatoes in the snow. In the morning he gleefully offered breakfast to a surprised Plympton. Some stories portray Steele as a claim jumper because Plympton had built a squatter's cabin on the site and hired a French voyageur to occupy it. Though a building is a primary rule for a land claim, Plympton had done this in 1836 when the land was still unceded Dakota territory. Aside from if and when the claim cabin was built, for many years that area was known as Plympton's Claim. In one account, Steele admonished Plympton for his moral and legal laxity of staking a claim despite rules prohibiting commissioned officers from doing so. That detail seems less likely considering their positions. Jumping the commander's claim and impugning his character would have been myopic and detrimental to their relationship. In many versions of that legendary encounter, Plympton lost out. Steele reportedly "made the first permanent claim," recalled John H. Stevens, the first settler of Minneapolis and a partner of Steele's on another claim.[30]

Other sources suggest that Plympton and Steele, along with others, collectively made the first land claims. It is more likely, as the fort's ex-storekeeper Samuel C. Stambaugh noted, that several officers and military associates collaborated in staking the claims before 1839. The people involved in the claims were Plympton, Captain Martin Scott (the commander who preceded Plympton for a little over a month, July 15–August 20), and John Emerson (assistant surgeon), who shared one section (640 acres), while Steele (the fort storekeeper), Stambaugh, and Dr. Wright (former assistant surgeon) shared a half section. In addition to this firsthand account, we will see that Plympton's continued Reserve expansion suggests he maintained some stake in these claims.[31]

The first draft of the Reserve, the Proposed Reserve map, was in place, and the opening of the land to claims spurred Plympton into action. Within two weeks of the official land opening, he issued an order on July 26, 1838, to stop all private development on the Reserve. Within the confines of Smith's 1838 Proposed Reserve map, with its imaginary boundary line, a person could not construct buildings, build fences, or cut wood for personal use. The proclamation was a red flag to the settlers. Plympton did not threaten eviction, though he asked his superiors for guidance on that point. Several settlers saw the writing on the wall and left the area entirely. Others moved downriver beyond the Reserve boundary near Fountain Cave, while some remained, clinging to the hope that something would work out and they could make their claims permanent. Refugees continued to arrive from Red River, and with the land east of the river open, they staked claims as squatters and built "cottages" across from the fort. The Fountain Cave landing remained available for civilian use.[32]

Plympton locked down activity on the Reserve to preserve resources and, now that the land cession was complete and settlement was open, he anticipated the arrival of more whiskey sellers. In November 1838, Brown, returning from Chicago, stopped in Prairie du Chien, the county seat, and made legal arrangements for a grogshop (a sort of saloon) and a ferry at the Entry. He also brought about five barrels of whiskey with him. In the spring of 1839, Brown and his associates built their grogshop at Rumtown. One of the first steamboats of the season, the *Ariel*, dropped off twenty barrels of whiskey at Brown's trading post downriver on Grey Cloud Island.[33]

The third map Plympton ordered came a year later. In October 1839 Lieutenant John L. Thompson labeled this map, "Sketch: Topographic Plan of the Military Reserve at Fort Snelling." As with the preceding

Proposed Reserve map, this Topographic Plan map has no representation of resources. Though a sketch, it does include some features such as lakes and labels such as "prairie" across large expanses. Fountain Cave is more clearly identified as being outside of the Reserve. The map replicates the boundary's river crossings seen in the earlier Proposed Reserve map, except for two differences. On the northeast boundary, instead of the straight imaginary line, the boundary line stairsteps down to a point west of the Cave, though it is unknown if this was field surveyed. Secondly, the southern boundary has been moved south of Pilot Knob and runs parallel to the river, intersecting the river farther east (encapsulating the Lilydale area).[34]

There are two other points of interest on Thompson's Topographic Plan map. For the first time Rumtown appears on a map. This appellation applied to several groggeries that popped up in that area run by Joseph R. Brown, John L. Thompson, and Donald McDonald. The other point of interest is the ravine just upriver of the northeastern boundary: Rum Pitch, where McDonald had relocated.

When Plympton included his July 1838 announcement in a letter to the Secretary of War, he acknowledged that his reasons for expanding the Reserve were changing. Initially, he filed complaints of the long-term settlers north of the fort and claimed the need to preserve resources. When the treaty was signed and the land east of the Mississippi opened for settlement, he proposed the Reserve with imaginary lines and again cited the need to preserve resources. Now, he shifted his reason to alcohol. In his letters to Washington, he set aside his contention with the settlers at Camp Coldwater (some had moved to Fountain Cave), and he no longer stressed the need to preserve resources. The groggeries were the new focus of his ire. Clearing the fort area of alcohol became his reason to enlarge the Reserve.

The fort surgeon, Dr. John Emerson, acted in concert with Plympton. In spring of 1840, Emerson wrote a letter to the surgeon general in Washington, DC. He related a difficult winter, not so much because of harsh weather but rather because they were "completely inundated with ardent spirits" that had produced "the most beastly scenes of intoxication among the soldiers" and the local Dakota. People "are pouring in upon us," bringing whiskey with them. The most egregious offender was Brown's "very extensive whiskey shop" that stood "within gunshot distance of the fort." These people defied Plympton's orders, "whose authority they set at naught," wrote Emerson. Plympton and Emerson were obviously having conversations about how to expand the Reserve under the pretext of curbing alcohol use. Emerson urged that the government expand the

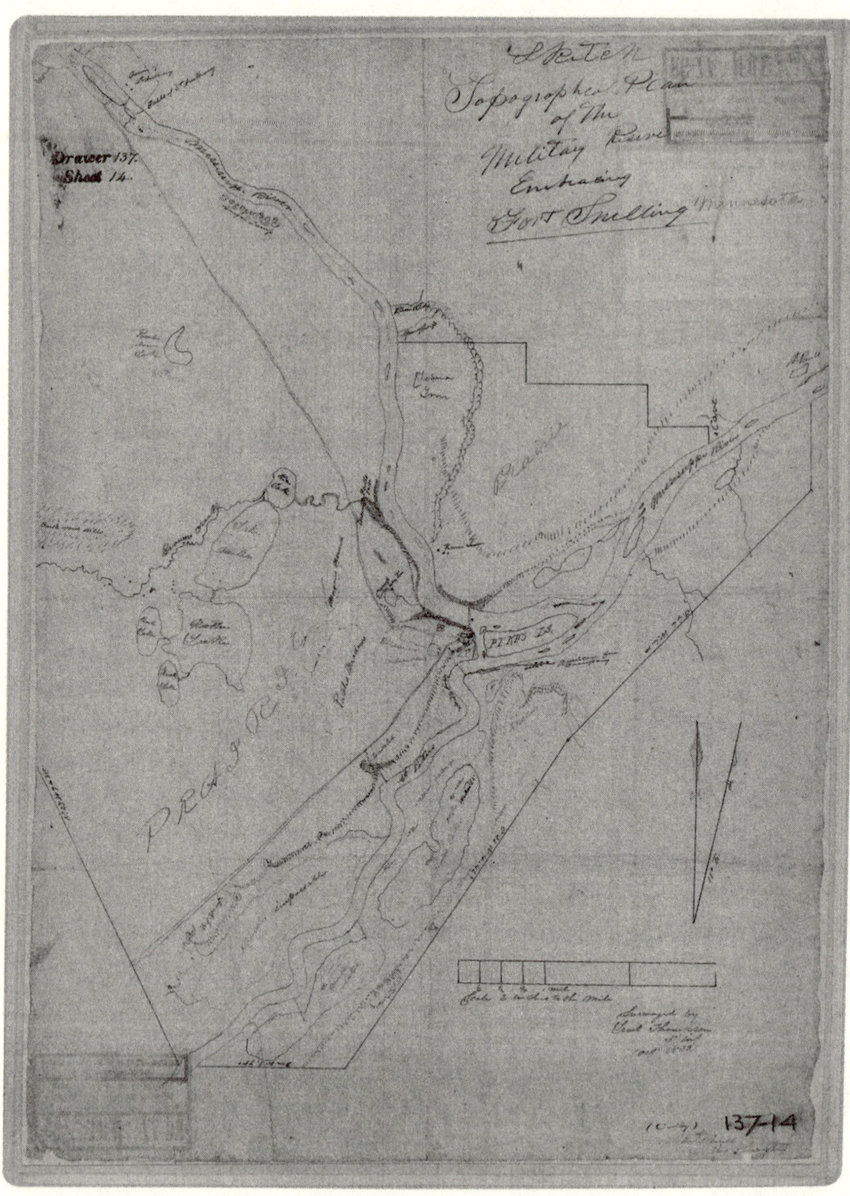

Plympton's second map of the Reserve is seen in Lieutenant John L. Thompson's Topographic Plan of October 1839. The northeastern boundary has the same end points on the river as Smith's Proposed Reserve map. Thompson alters the northeastern boundary line with a stair-step effect. The Reserve is expanded south of the river, which may have included more woodlands. This map shows the intermediary steps of Plympton's thinking between the Proposed Reserve map of March 1838 and the final map that Thompson finished the next month.

Reserve to at least twenty square miles, even to the mouth of the St. Croix River. He had specific reasons for such an outrageous request.[35]

Plympton got further support from Brigadier General John E. Wool when he visited the fort on June 2, 1839. On the second night of Wool's visit, the greatest of all sprees at the confluence erupted and ended with two-thirds of the garrison (forty-seven soldiers) in the fort's jail. It's hard to believe the spree was a random coincidence. Everyone knew the general was there as the military would have had official functions with his arrival. Whoever incited the spree may have wanted to give Wool something to write home about. When he wrote his report the next month, he recommended the same Reserve expansion as Emerson, along with prohibiting liquor on the Reserve. Wool's letter played a significant role in getting approval to further expand the Reserve.[36]

That fall, Plympton had Thompson properly survey the Reserve and produce the fourth map, Map of the Reservation Embracing Fort Snelling, which expanded the Reserve significantly. On November 27, 1839, Plympton sent that final map of the Reserve to his superiors in Washington. He opened the correspondence with the assurance that it "was in accordance with the directions of the department" and that it was "comfortable" to Smith's Proposed Reserve map, though he allowed that it came "with this slight difference," that being the principal lines of the Proposed Reserve map were "imaginary" and "upon actual survey" they crossed the Mississippi "a little further down." In addition to holding "the necessary woodland," he inserted the reason for the expansion was "to preserve the cardinal points." By drawing a line that was truly east to west—the only boundary line on the map that followed cardinal directions—he said, the Reserve boundary "might harmonize with that of the general survey of the country." He was satisfied now that the Reserve "embrace no more ground . . . than is absolutely necessary to furnish the daily wants of this garrison," but if the boundary were extended even farther to the east, "it would no doubt add to the quiet of this command."

Plympton's reasons had shifted again: Now he focused on the need for sufficient wood for the garrison, convenience of surveying, and quiet. Unspoken here is that he drew the eastern boundary several miles beyond Fountain Cave. That overlooked "inconvenient steamboat landing" was no longer available to the settlers. He now had all six landings inside the Reserve, off-limits to civilian use. He had successfully added 4,500 acres to the Reserve. What was excessive in terms of the army's needs was sufficient to protect his and his partners' claims at St. Anthony Falls.[37]

The changes in Plympton's reasons and the expanding map upset a number of people. They wrote to Secretary of War Joel R. Poinsett,

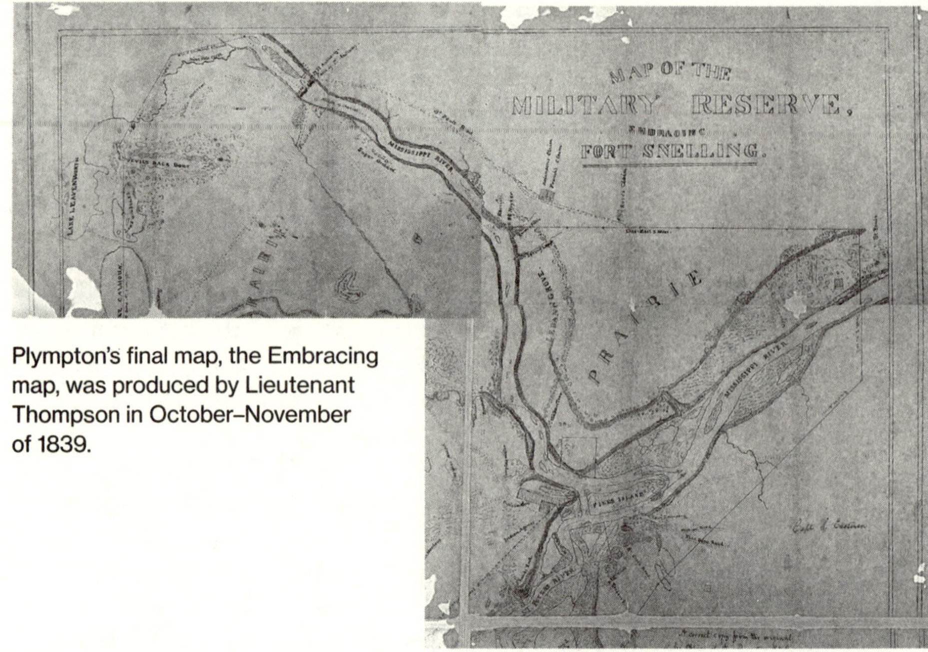

Plympton's final map, the Embracing map, was produced by Lieutenant Thompson in October–November of 1839.

pointing out the expansion made little practical sense and that Plympton had an ulterior purpose. In a letter to Poinsett, Brown, the ex-soldier, scoffed at the idea of separating the soldiers from alcohol. He knew whiskey was a mainstay of fort life. Soldiers received a daily ration of one gill, which is four ounces. They could buy whiskey and rum at the fort store. In one particularly bad year, when food was in short supply, the soldiers—some suffering from scurvy—routinely received their daily whiskey rations. Officers used the whiskey ration for punishment and reward. The Indian trade was regularly lubricated with alcohol, and it was always there for the soldiers, too, no matter the location. Alcohol was both a fact of life and a universal problem at every fort.[38]

Others argued that expanding the Reserve was contrary to the army's mission. Further, Fort Snelling's position on its bluff, noted Stambaugh, gave the fort sentinels the ability to monitor traffic at Brown's ferry and the Rumtown groggeries. They would lose that advantage if the Reserve expansion shifted the groggeries farther away. In addition, Plympton's Reserve expansion pushed settlers out of sight and out of hearing range. That abdicated the army's duty to keep the peace. If the army's mission was to protect people, why push the people away?[39]

Stambaugh is one of the most trustworthy voices in this episode. He was a newspaper editor from Pennsylvania who had spent time in Wisconsin as an Indian agent. He came to Fort Snelling and invested in land. Though a land speculator himself, in letters to Plympton's superiors he called out the major's impropriety of shaping the Reserve because he could see it impinged on the army's service and would disrupt the settlement pattern. Stambaugh's explanations meant that his own speculations might be hurt. He stands out among his cohorts—especially Emerson, Steele, and Plympton—because he was unwilling to gain at such a cost to the community.

As for the Reserve preserving resources such as wood, the additional lands were the most meager in the area. The maps indicated the area was prairie, and Brown said the timber to the east was already gone. Stambaugh pointed out that to the west the fort had limitless land and wood without having to bring it across the river. Plympton had noted that this land was still "in Indian tenure," and that by going east he was keeping in line with Pike's treaty of 1805. His interpretation was interesting considering that the fort itself was on the unceded land and the Reserve never expanded to the west the nine miles that Pike had negotiated.[40]

The civilian protest of Plympton's Reserve expansion rose to the level of political protest. Plympton was claiming land for dubious reasons—land that was already ceded and available for claims. Therefore, he was pitting the military against the civilians. A citizen's group, largely led by Brown, organized to fight the expansion. They drafted a petition to the Wisconsin Territorial Legislature, critiquing the expanded Reserve's purpose. The territorial legislature passed a resolution condemning the Reserve's extension and claiming the department was preempting land that was under the control of the Territory of Wisconsin without its consent. Legislative members submitted the resolution to the secretary of war. Congress took it up, but it died in committee.[41]

The Reserve's northern boundary left the river near Rum Pitch and ran east. This boundary placement meant the land adjacent to the falls was open to preemption claims. Stambaugh explained in his letter that this northern boundary line benefited a select group of claimants on the east side of St. Anthony Falls. Since the land cession, the claimants had been improving the property to secure a preemption. This arrangement of the Reserve principally benefited the claims at St. Anthony Falls—claims that Plympton held along with Steele, Emerson, and Stambaugh.[42]

In their letters, Brown and Stambaugh noted the primary result of Plympton's expansion of the Reserve. The new Reserve would "embrace all the steamboat landings," leaving the next available landing twelve to fifteen miles below the fort, they said, because "the country is broken and swampy nine miles below the cave." Brown, in his work with the Wisconsin Territorial Legislature, pointed out that a number of speculators, including the commanding and other officers of Fort Snelling, were set on "a monopoly of the trade of the Mississippi pine region." They employed "every possible means" to keep settlers from interfering with their plan. In essence, by blocking the steamboat landings, Plympton along with others cornered the market on mill development at St. Anthony Falls and the lumber stands upriver from the falls.[43]

General Wool had witnessed the great spree at Fort Snelling and consequently supported the idea of expanding the Reserve to the St. Croix in order to block access to alcohol. But he had played into the hands of Plympton and his cohorts. If the Reserve was expanded to the St. Croix, essentially at the other Reserve site Pike included in the treaty, they were ready. Emerson and the others had another set of claims there along with a townsite called Stambaughville (near today's Prescott, Wisconsin), which would then be near the boundary of the Reserve. Emerson was partners with Stambaugh and Steele in the St. Croix Falls Lumber Company that located in that area. Taliaferro, the Indian agent, mentions officers of the Fifth Regiment staked claims at the mouth of the St. Croix or Stambaughville. An expansion of the Reserve to the St. Croix would have left this group well situated for the unchallenged harvest of the lumber regions of both the Mississippi and the St. Croix Rivers. In truth, the timber Plympton was preserving was not inside the expanded Reserve; rather, as Brown and Stambaugh had charged, Plympton was using the Reserve to preserve access to the timber that was to the north of the Reserve.[44]

Land speculation was commonly done by opportunistic officers, who benefited from the army's permissive culture and protecting their kind. Emerson had a history of land speculation previous to his collaboration with Plympton at St. Anthony Falls. In December 1833 he was stationed at Fort Armstrong on Rock Island in the middle of the Mississippi River. He staked claims on 480 acres along the western shore facing Rock Island, adjacent to Davenport's son (today, downtown Bettendorf, Iowa). Emerson was the enslaver of Dred Scott, and he left Dred Scott in Iowa for some time to occupy his cabin. Fort Armstrong was abandoned in May 1836 and Emerson was transferred to Fort Snelling. He assigned power of attorney to a friend with instructions to bid for his claims at the public lands auction. "Our old friend Lt. J. Beach is in that land office," wrote Emerson, suggesting favoritism of some sort. Emerson aimed to "get [the land] at the government price," that is without competitive bidding. While at Fort Snelling, he mentioned another opportunity to his friend:

owning a steamboat that had government contracts. On September 17, 1839, he wrote that the *Pike* was transporting army recruits from Prairie du Chien (185 troops in two trips), bringing in $850. "You and I are to be part owner of the boat," he wrote. Emerson, Plympton's close cohort, was profiting from his position with the army.[45]

Plympton's son wrote a hagiography of him and felt compelled to defend his father at length on this point of land speculation. "His generosity and unselfishness had always been obstacles to his acquiring property," he wrote. Plympton served in locations that gave way to Detroit and Chicago, and "he lived to see them all large and prosperous cities."

Plympton was no innocent. He had tried his hand at land speculation from the beginning. At Fort Detroit, his first assigned station as commander, he purchased "the best site for a town anywhere in that district," according to his son. He and a partner had the land surveyed, laid out the streets, and divided it into lots. They called their new town Monroe. Speculators and capitalists agreed they had selected the best site for a large city. But such grandiose speculations are impossible to manage *in absentia*, and the speculation failed when others developed a nearby settlement and diverted settlers away from Monroe, promoting that site into what is now known as Detroit. His family sold his holdings posthumously for a few hundred dollars.[46]

Plympton was the last commander at Fort Dearborn. He closed the fort and remained on-site until mid-1837, when the government prepared the military land for sale. "Miles of land, in what is now the very centre of Chicago, could have been had by him for a small sum," wrote his son. But the transient life of the military made it difficult to manage real estate holdings. For the most part, this kept him from seizing on the opportunities, "even if, at the time, he appreciated them." As for St. Paul, his son claimed, Plympton was "offered, for a mere nominal sum, the present site of St. Paul, with miles of land surrounding it." However tempting the speculation might have been, Plympton was skeptical that the upper reach of the Mississippi was much of an opportunity. This family story contradicts Plympton's manipulation of the Reserve in developing advantage for the claims at the falls. Perhaps the son unwittingly confused St. Anthony Falls with the St. Paul townsite, which was so small it had no name when Plympton left.[47]

In the end, we shouldn't think that Plympton acted alone in the expansion of the Reserve. Emerson, as co-speculator, encouraged the expansion, as did others involved in laying out Stambaughville. Steele had arrived in 1837 and developed a sawmill at St. Croix Falls. He was a master of large-scale speculations. He may have been an invisible force behind

Plympton in the ongoing expansions that shaped the Reserve. He was the one who benefited the most from the Reserve expansion. In the end, he bought out the interests of Plympton, Emerson, and the officers associated with him in the claims at St. Anthony Falls and built the first sawmill with investors from Boston in 1847. Plympton never had to answer to his superiors or Congress regarding the accusations of personal gain on claims. As with officers holding slaves, the army overlooked these laws.[48]

Plympton was reassigned to the Second Infantry, moved to Florida in January 1841, and fought in the culmination of the Seminole Wars. In early 1842 he led troops in the capture Chief "Short Grass" (Halleck Tuscenuggee), a key Seminole leader. In September 1846 he was promoted to lieutenant colonel, Seventh US Infantry, and sent to Mexico, where he served under General Winfield Scott. His regiment was very active throughout the war, from Veracruz to Mexico City. He gained recognition for his part in the capture of Veracruz and the battles of Contreras and Churubusco. He achieved the rank of colonel in 1853. He died at seventy-three years of age, June 5, 1860, on Staten Island.[49]

While Plympton's military career took him elsewhere, his manipulation of the Reserve had a lasting impact. He expanded the fort's Reserve at a critical moment in the development of the region in the late 1830s. He blocked settlement at the prime location of the confluence and enlarged the military footprint which dispersed the settlement. Historians of Fort Snelling and St. Paul have long correlated the location of St. Paul with Plympton's expansion of his Reserve.

If the settlers had been allowed to stay at the Entry near the fort, "There would be no St. Paul, no Twin Cities," at least not where it is now, according to Return I. Holcombe, a St. Paul newspaperman and historian. "Had the unjust and unreasoning" Plympton not interfered, the "settlement would in time have become the nucleus of a great and powerful city." Writing in the early twentieth century, Holcombe envisioned the alternative view of the future that so many held throughout the nineteenth century, that "only one great city would now stand near the mouth of the Minnesota." He imagined that "magnificent city, larger by far and better in all respects than the aggregated cities as they now are." Instead of two city centers with suburbs in between, he saw "a solid, compact city" with suburbs surrounding it. The state Capitol building "would probably stand" on that "heaven-kissing hill" Pilot Knob, visible fifty miles away in every direction. He was confident, though, that "in due and proper time, there will be but one."[50]

Today the presumption is widespread that St. Paul offered the best possible landing site, serving somehow as the natural head of navigation for the Mississippi in the nineteenth century. But the maps of Plympton's Reserve tell a different story: The confluence of the Minnesota and Mississippi made for a far better site that Plympton managed to shield from settlement under shifting pretenses. During a tenure of just over three years, Plympton's "ungenerous and even tyrannical disposition" threw a kink in the settlement pattern, blocking access to the preferred sites, largely in pursuit of his own personal wealth. "Minneapolis might today," mused Holcombe, "or in the near future, be a strong rival of Chicago."[51]

Inadvertently, however, when Plympton kept the confluence from development, he promoted the growth of two separate cities. It could even be said that he created the Twin Cities.

Notably, the Reserve accomplished something else. The confluence of the Minnesota and Mississippi is for the Dakota people a sacred place of origin called Bdóte. The site of creation, where sky, earth, and rivers come together, remained mostly undisturbed. It and the gorge were spared from urban development, the concrete and the asphalt, which would have been the case had the confluence become the center of the city. The beauty of the confluence can still be experienced today. Never did Plympton imagine himself a preservationist.

The settlers, however, did not give up on the idea of a settlement at the confluence. There was still one possibility, and the next ten years would determine the future.

CHAPTER 3

Finding St. Paul

Father Lucian Galtier arrived at the outpost of soldiers, traders, and Indians in time to witness the birth of the town he would name St. Paul. He was impressed with Fort Snelling atop the bluff, but the twenty-nine-year-old Frenchman was intimidated by the wilderness location. His assignment was to tend the small Catholic flock in this outpost of the church diocese, 283 river miles from its cathedral parish downriver in Dubuque, Iowa Territory. The prospect of a life "of privation, hard trials, and suffering," as he described it, shook him deeply.[1]

Perched on the bench above the Minnesota River at Mendota, Galtier could look north to the fort and the small, dispersed community below it on the east side of the river. Within a week or so of his arrival, as the spring floodwaters inundated the confluence, he would have seen pillars of smoke rising on the far shore and heard shouting which conveyed the news of destruction across the water. Everybody would have known the day had come. The settlers were being evicted from the Reserve.

Galtier had come upriver from Dubuque on the first steamboat of 1840, departing on April 26. That boat stopped at Prairie du Chien and picked up Ira B. Brunson, an appointed deputy of the US marshal, who had orders from the Secretary of War in Washington, DC, to clear settlers from the Reserve. The civilian community at the confluence had grown, strung out along the eastern bank opposite the fort and extending several miles downriver to around Fountain Cave. When Brunson arrived at the fort, he gave the residents notice to vacate the Reserve, but they refused to leave. On May 6 he mobilized soldiers from the fort to execute the orders: Remove the settlers and their belongings, forcefully if necessary, and destroy their residences by fire. Brunson was at that time unknown to the residents. They would come to rely on him later in their effort to establish a town, and there they became neighbors. But charges against him over the use of violence on this day would stand for years, though he defended his actions as peaceable. The removal was a tragic moment that pitted the military against the civilian population.[2]

Plympton's expanded Reserve had an immediate impact on the settlement pattern and transportation routes in the area. The settlers—maybe a dozen families or about fifty people—picked up their belongings and moved outside the Reserve's new boundary. They could only settle on the east side of the river, and they wanted to remain close to the fort. The settlers could go upriver or downriver. If they stayed near the fort, they could go upriver to the Reserve's northern boundary at Rum Pitch (now Marshall Avenue). Or they could go downriver to the Reserve's eastern boundary at the big bend (now St. Paul). They preferred the confluence at Fort Snelling, or the Entry, as they called it. For some refugees from the Red River community, this was their third and final move. The farmers, such as the Gervais brothers, Pierre and Benjamin, and Abraham Perret, were among those not inclined toward land speculation and more interested in a place to live.

Galtier was a central character in the early years, building the first Catholic chapel on the bluff at Pig's Eye and blessing it as the chapel of St. Paul. The settlement was an unlikely gem, the location's value largely unnoticed until the new Reserve forced people to adjust their expectations. The settlers were uncertain about the area, but a church and a store gave them an identity. Some believed the settlement to be temporary, and they did not yet have a long-term commitment to this place. Over the next decade, a cascade of events driven by national developments alongside the local desire to be an independent state would make St. Paul permanent.

The primary reason for St. Paul's founding, according to the early St. Paul historian J. Fletcher Williams, was whiskey. Plympton had expanded the Reserve, Williams said, primarily to deter the soldiers from getting alcohol. The most infamous whiskey seller, of course, was Pierre Parrant, aka "Pig's Eye." Known for his distorted visage, Parrant operated a groggery at Fountain Cave, then sold whiskey by the glass at St. Paul Landing, about six miles downriver from the fort. In that light, Plympton appears to have been successful in chasing the whiskey away. However, there is more to the picture.[3]

While most evicted Reserve residents drifted downriver and relocated east of the Reserve, Donald McDonald went upriver to the Reserve's northern boundary east of the river and claimed the land above Rum Pitch. The whiskey seller opened his groggery there, likely after Plympton's cease-and-desist order of July 1838 and definitely before mid-May 1839. We know the latter date because the steamboat *Glaucus* arrived at what would become St. Paul Landing—the first known to land there—on May 21, 1839, and dropped off six barrels of whiskey for McDonald's groggery. By receiving the whiskey east of the Reserve, McDonald was able to haul it undetected around the fort and its Reserve. On October 15, 1840, he obtained a license from the county (based in Prairie du Chien) to sell "spiritous liquors in any quantity not less than a quart, at or near the Falls of St. Anthony."[4]

McDonald ran a thriving business at his groggery three miles upriver from the fort at Rum Pitch, attracting soldiers, voyageurs, and Indians. His grogshop was notorious because inebriated soldiers fell down the steep terrain as they returned to the fort. One resident at the fort recalled how some soldiers fell and lost life and limb to frost and wolves. This gruesome account is viewed as testimony supporting Plympton's claims about the problem of alcohol near the fort, but the story is incongruent with the timeline and raises a question about Plympton's purpose. Worth emphasizing is that when the soldiers cleared the Reserve, McDonald already had a successful business off the Reserve at Rum Pitch, and within six months he was running a licensed business there. It was closer than Pig's Eye's groggery downriver by more than two miles. What became Plympton's primary purpose for enlarging the Reserve—abating the use of alcohol—had failed even before his final expansion and the evacuation

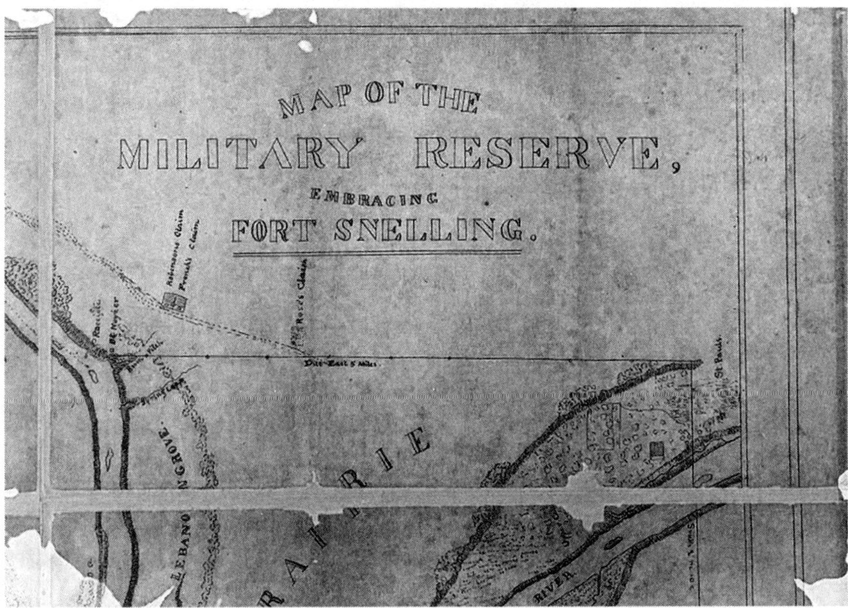

The northern border of Plympton's Reserve, as shown on Thompson's Embracing map of October–November 1839, leaves the river at Rum Pitch. Donald McDonald set up his groggery there, just north of the Reserve. The map is a copy of the original and includes notes from a later time after Stephen Desnoyer (here spelled De Noyier) had traded for McDonald's claim.

of the Reserve. Further, the anecdotes of maiming and death are undated, so they may well have occurred after Plympton cleared the Reserve. This calls into question Plympton's expansion of the Reserve to stem the tide of whiskey. If he was serious about stopping alcohol, why didn't he expand the Reserve upriver to stop McDonald?[5]

Plympton's Reserve determined the location of McDonald's grogshop, but coincidentally Rum Pitch also stood close to the middle of all points of interest at that time: Fort Snelling, St. Paul Landing, and St. Anthony Falls. Because of this centrality, it became a preferred location, leading Canadian newcomer Stephen Desnoyer to predict that it would one day be the "bridge square" of an eventual united metropolis. This idea of a central location for a united city would be attractive for decades to come.[6]

The Settlement of St. Paul

St. Paul was an improbable and impractical development. The location wasn't obvious, destined, or inevitable. The primary reason for a settlement was that it was the closest point to the confluence and the fort. The eastern boundary of Plympton's new Reserve stood about six miles downriver from the fort at St. Paul's historic "Seven Corners" (just west of the Xcel Center).

St. Paul was also the only possible place on the river outside the Reserve before the river turned south. If Plympton had set the new boundary a little farther east, the Reserve would have blocked St. Paul Landing as well as landings south of the bend. He had good reasons to set the boundary farther east and was clearly considering it. Emerson and Wool had suggested it in their letters. If Plympton used Pike's written description in the treaty, the nine miles east of the Mississippi gorge fell another four miles beyond this point. Such a Reserve boundary would have pushed the settlement options down below Grey Cloud Island and possibly as far as Prescott, Wisconsin. Not coincidentally, in the case of Emerson, Stambaugh, and Steele with their St. Croix Falls Lumber Company, that is where Stambaughville was platted. According to Indian agent Taliaferro, other officers had staked claims there as well. And not to forget the estimates by Plympton's critics that the nearest downriver landing was twelve to fifteen miles from the fort, which is in agreement with these other projections. The accumulation of evidence suggests that with or without the boundary being at St. Paul, Plympton and others did not view it as a feasible landing or choice of settlement. Their actions suggest they believed the new boundary was calculated to move the resettlement farther downriver, perhaps even to Prescott. The new settlement at St. Paul Landing must have surprised Plympton, but we don't have an account of his reaction to it. Indeed, he was transferred in January 1841 before the chapel was built.

Upstream at Mendota, Reverend Galtier began Sunday services at the fort and in Mendota, where he lived in a single room with a small, homemade altar. He realized his duties would include those families of the nascent settlement. He adapted his services and occasionally visited the freshly dispersed community along the bend in the river. As the settlement stabilized, Galtier decided to build a chapel in the area downriver from the fort. He considered three locations: La Pointe Basse on the sandbar across from Kaposia, at Dayton's Bluff (near or above Carver's Cave), and the intermediary plateau along the eastern boundary of the Reserve. The first choice would be closer to more people but it was prone to flooding. The second location was isolated and not easy to reach. He chose the third location primarily because it did not flood, it was easy for him to cross the river near Fountain Cave, and it was the closest point to the head of navigation while staying outside of the Reserve.[7]

Galtier's final selection was by no means ideal. Two farmers gifted the land, and volunteers built a chapel using tamarack, which is a bog tree. The wood slabs for the floor and benches were donated by a sawmill in Stillwater and shipped in exchange for a few days of labor by one of the men. The sawn slabs landed at Jackson Street and were drawn up the hill by hand with ropes. The chapel was a simple rectangle with a window in each wall and was finished in a few days with less than sixty-five dollars labor (probably donated).[8]

The new settlement slowly picked up the elements of a community. Pig's Eye's groggery was there at the onset, and Parrant built his first cabin at the water's edge as early as 1836. Galtier built the St. Paul chapel in October 1841. Henry Jackson came up from Prairie du Chien in 1842, rented Parrant's riverside cabin, and the next year opened the first store on the bluff, which soon drew steamboats to land there. A landing for steamboats gave reason for a name. The boat captains called it St. Paul Landing. The settlers built cabins here, initially a scattered refugee camp of a dozen or so families. They assembled loosely, without any certainty of permanence.[9]

The site proved a logistically difficult place to settle. Even though the townsite sat above the river on a ninety-foot bluff, the land was subpar—"a rough broken country, comprising tamarack swamp, sand hills, rocky ravines, and quagmires and sloughs that were the abode of muskrats and other aquatic animals," recalled one settler. If the land was flat, it was saturated, as small lakes were scattered among the otherwise steep ravines. A larger lake stood at Fort Road and Robert Street. A person couldn't travel beyond Fourth Street because of the swampy conditions. The surveyors working on the city plat were stymied because of the extensive bog. The location of the Union Depot was for a long time "a literal 'slough of despond,'" recalled one early resident. He described it as "fathomless and apparently bottomless." Early maps have no streets in that part of town. And yet St. Paul Landing was an exception along the east side of the river because it offered access through the impenetrable bluffs that lined the Mississippi there.[10]

For any river town, access to the river is the essential feature. The new location had one possible initial point of access, what would become Jackson Street, later the lower landing. But Jackson Street did not easily reach the river. Residents had to construct the access because a wide ravine ran diagonally across the slope where they planned to put Jackson Street. The ravine was thirty feet deep where Jackson now intersects Fourth Street, and rainstorms filled it with enough water to float a skiff. Building the street required extensive grading on one side and fill on the other. Jackson Street "was very steep," recalled Auguste Larpenteur, who arrived in 1843 and began a long life in St. Paul, starting as an employee at Jackson's store. He and others hauled goods from the river up to town with a yoke of oxen, each trip consisting of a single item, such as a barrel of whiskey or flour. Before the refugees developed St. Paul Landing, the site was not viewed as a natural landing by anyone, including Plympton and his associates. Understandably, it had previously "no known geographic significance," according to historian Hampton Smith.[11]

The Mississippi as a Border

In 1845 St. Paul Landing was a refugee encampment amid continuously shifting political lines. The rivers—St. Croix, Mississippi, and Missouri—had been conveniently used over the past decades to delineate territorial and state boundaries. "Westward goes the course of Empire," it was said, except when on one occasion it didn't. And the one time the westward expansion reversed direction it struck at the heart of the idea of a single metropolis at the head of navigation on the Mississippi. St. Paul Landing was small and uncertain, temporary in some minds. How the settlement became permanent was a coincidence tied to becoming a territory. And it broke a few norms along the way. The organization of the preceding states in the region—Michigan, Indiana, Illinois, Iowa, and Wisconsin—was a crescendo; Minnesota was the climax. And the Mississippi played a central role in that regional development and shaping of the state.

The Mississippi River bisects the lower North American continental landmass, draining most of the land between the Appalachians and the Rocky Mountains from near the nation's northern border to its southern boundary. The hydrological basin with its main branching tributaries, the Ohio and Missouri Rivers, has been compared to a large tree with its roots in the Gulf of Mexico. The river system was the conduit of American westward expansion into the heart of the continent. Its impact on the development of Minnesota and the Twin Cities began back in the seventeenth century because it was, as big rivers often are, a border.[12]

In 1619 Virginia acquired the land east of the Mississippi River and north of the Ohio River under a royal grant to the Virginia Company. Virginia at that time spanned the nation from the Atlantic coast to the Mississippi River. In 1784 the state was reduced to its land south of the Ohio River and the land north of that river was ceded to the United States. The eastern half of the Upper Mississippi River basin was called the Northwest Territory of the Ohio River. The territory of 300,000 square miles, created by Congress in 1787, made up about one-third of the nation's area. Nineteen years later President Thomas Jefferson made an executive decision to purchase the French holdings of Louisiana. The 828,000 square miles of the Louisiana Purchase nearly doubled the size of the United States' claims.

The Northwest Territory and the Louisiana Purchase shared the Mississippi River as a boundary, and as such it played a major role in the establishment of Minnesota and the Twin Cities. Expansive migrations of people pushed westward, but at a crucial moment the political boundaries between territories ebbed. People reacted to this, and their decisions and actions shaped the settlement pattern in the Twin Cities region. The details show an unlikely trajectory.

Becoming a state was a political process in Congress. A territory was federally managed, and after development of that territory it was transferred to the new state government, an independent political entity that complied with federal law. To become a territory, the federal government looked for a substantial population of white, twenty-one-year-old male voters in the region, usually citing a threshold of 5,000. Once the territory reached 60,000 white men, the residents could apply for statehood.

The Northwest Territory as a political compact came with a few restrictions. States that developed in that area would be "free" states without legally established slavery, and there could be no more than five states in this area. The latter point preserved the national balance between the number of free and slave states. When Ohio became the first state formed, the Northwest Ordinance ended, and the remaining land west to the Mississippi River became Indiana Territory. The same happened when Indiana became a state: The remaining land became Illinois Territory. Michigan started small, but when Illinois became a state in 1818, the Michigan Territory expanded west to the Mississippi River and in 1833 ballooned farther west to the Missouri River, which was the remnant of the Louisiana Purchase along with what would become Iowa.

Michigan Territory was reduced to its current size in 1836 and became a state in 1837, opening the land west of Lake Michigan, which became the Wisconsin Territory in 1836, including what would become Iowa. When Iowa became a territory in 1838, it included its current shape along with all the land between the Missouri and the Mississippi River (the upper Louisiana Purchase). That shift reshaped the Wisconsin Territory to include its current state boundary plus the land between the St. Croix and the Mississippi River. Again, the Mississippi was a border of the political entities, with Wisconsin Territory to the east and Iowa Territory to the west.

While these shifting political boundaries became a blur, the overall pattern was clear. A territory was always larger than its subsequent state and the remnant territory became a new state-in-the-wings. Each territory filled the remaining land and then with statehood was reduced to a smaller size, leaving land for another territory to be formed. As the states solidified and the remaining area of what was the Northwest Territory and the northern Louisiana Purchase got smaller, they ran into a problem: Political entities were at odds with the population requirements because the remaining land did not have enough voters.

Iowa became a state in 1846, but its excess territorial lands, that area of the Louisiana Purchase between the Mississippi and Missouri Rivers, did not have the required population to form another unique territory. So that part of the Iowa Territory reverted to unorganized status. This retraction had happened once before, when Missouri became a state in 1821 and vacated the area between the Mississippi and Missouri Rivers, which closed that area to white settlement. As of that time, the Dakota people had ceded none of the land and the region was known as Indian Country or Indian Territory. Most importantly, the number of Americans was not yet large enough to satisfy the population rules, and the politically organized boundary of the United States moved east. The body politic was still expansive, looking west along the course of empire, but the political reality based on settlement patterns was, for the moment, contracting. They were getting ahead of themselves.

Fort Snelling was built on the west side of the Mississippi River in the territory of Michigan, then as the territory changed it operated successively in Wisconsin and Iowa. With Iowa statehood, the United States politically vacated the land west of the Mississippi. The fort now stood in unorganized Indian Territory. To the east of the Mississippi was the Wisconsin Territory. With the land cession ratified in 1838 (Dakota and Ojibwe treaties of 1837), that land east of the Mississippi in Wisconsin Territory became available for private ownership. The problem lay just ahead with the transition of Wisconsin into statehood.

The residents west of the St. Croix River (western Wisconsin Territory) were separatists. They did not want to be in Wisconsin, so they strategically developed a separate political identity. In 1841 they formed St. Croix County, which was between the St. Croix and Mississippi Rivers, and in 1843 Stillwater organized as a town. Twice, in 1846 and 1848, as Wisconsin moved toward statehood, these separatists initiated efforts in Congress to become a separate Minnesota Territory, and both times they failed.

Then all the boundary shuffling along the rivers came to a dramatic conclusion. The population in the Wisconsin Territory was booming. In 1846 Congress passed the Wisconsin enabling act, which initiated a transition to statehood and triggered debate over the location of the new state's western boundary. As Wisconsin stood, with the territorial boundary at the Mississippi River, it complied with the original ordinance of the Northwest Territory as the fifth and final state. But things had changed since 1787. For starters, Wisconsin was centered in the distant southeast corner in Madison, which was the capital and hosted the university and the penitentiary. From St. Paul or Stillwater, Madison was nine to twelve days by mail (that's three weeks to get a reply). Those separatists along the St. Croix and Upper Mississippi, a group of fur traders and lumberjacks, squatters and speculators, did not feel at home in Wisconsin. Their business followed the river and they were economically detached from the political nexus in Madison.[13]

Further, some felt that a state line on the Mississippi would isolate the country to the north and west from the anticipated economic engine of St. Anthony Falls. That would leave the northern border country vulnerable to a British incursion. Representative Stephen A. Douglas of Illinois, the chair of the influential committee on territories, argued that moving the Wisconsin boundary east to the St. Croix would give the next state a *raison d'être*: the industrial resource of St. Anthony Falls (he had previously stopped Iowa from absorbing the falls). The reality was that if the area was annexed to Wisconsin or Iowa, the northern region would be isolated, reducing incentives for organized government. For the first time, because of the falls' promise as an industrial economic driver, the river became a center rather than a border.[14]

In the end, that the state of Minnesota straddles the Mississippi is an anomaly. Along its entire course the Mississippi constitutes a border feature, except for the ultimate state on its path, Louisiana. The Mississippi River had been used as a political boundary for the entire history of the United States, from the Northwest Territory and the Louisiana Purchase through the subsequent territories and states, including Missouri, Indiana, Illinois, Michigan, Wisconsin, and Iowa. Because of St. Anthony Falls, Minnesota became the only state to consist of these two large land accessions of the United States.

Desperate Times

Nearly everything about creating a Minnesota Territory deviated from the normal process. Because Minnesota had various nonconforming preconditions, bringing it to a territory would require creativity. The settlers "had a law unto themselves," wrote Henry L. Moss, an early settler, "which recognized the rights and claims of the settlers to be as sacred and effective as under a patent from the United States government." They weren't rebellious. They considered themselves Americans on US soil with all the rights that came with that, most importantly, perhaps, the legal system. Even as they broke those US laws to claim their land, they wanted redress through that system's legal infrastructure and judicial system. In essence, they did things illegally to become legal.[15]

Though the land cession east of the Mississippi had been approved in 1838, the federal government did not survey the area until late 1847. For ten years squatters staked their claims with no legal way to describe the land coordinates required to gain title. "We were all squatters," admitted Larpenteur. They staked their claims in the Wisconsin Territory.[16]

Meanwhile, the village of St. Paul showed signs of growth. In 1847 residents built an addition on the chapel, roughly doubling its size. Harriet Bishop opened a Sabbath school with seven students. The first hotel was built using tamarack logs. The Galena Packet Company was organized with one boat, the *Argus*. The chapel got a bell when the *Argus* sank and residents retrieved its bell. The clergy rang the bell every morning. Larpenteur built a brick warehouse and began importing lumber. Wisconsin was booming and reached a six-figure population. The residents knew Wisconsin was on its way to statehood, but their first effort to separate themselves and become the Minnesota Territory in 1846 had failed. They were approaching the height of their crisis.[17]

The settlers outside the Reserve took steps to secure their claims. "In 1847, we laid out the original town plat of St. Paul," recalled Larpenteur. They sent word to Prairie du Chien and hired Ira B. Brunson as a surveyor, the same man who had evacuated the Reserve and destroyed their homes seven years earlier. He, along with his brother, Benjamin, laid out a townsite—39 blocks totaling 398 lots—called "St. Paul Proper." This original, mostly rectangular tract was bounded east to west by Wacouta and St. Peter Streets, north to south by Seventh and Water Streets. This audacious maneuver reflects their sense of urgency. They were jumping the gun, as the US Surveyor General crew was in the area that fall. In October and November 1847 the government surveyed the land east of the Mississippi River (including Plympton's Reserve) into townships (six miles by six miles) and then those into sections (one mile by one mile). With this information, a person could precisely describe the location of their claim and therefore buy the land with a legal title. But the land in Brunson's original town plat lacked any township, section, or range information. Brunson's plat map was not a legal document. Furthermore, Brunson's plat heading read "City of St. Paul, the Capital of Minnesota." But Minnesota did not yet exist.[18]

It gave residents, by color of law, a deed on their parcels of land. They had a toehold. They had a plan. They arranged the claims themselves and prepared to buy them at the land auction the following year.

The next year, on May 29, 1848, Wisconsin became a state, and its

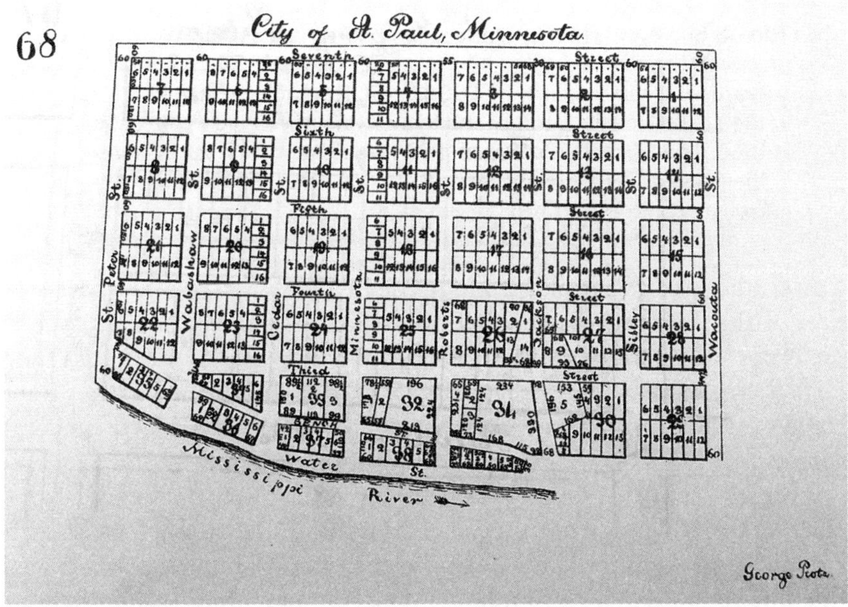

A copy of the original plat of St. Paul Proper as surveyed by Ira B. Brunson in 1847

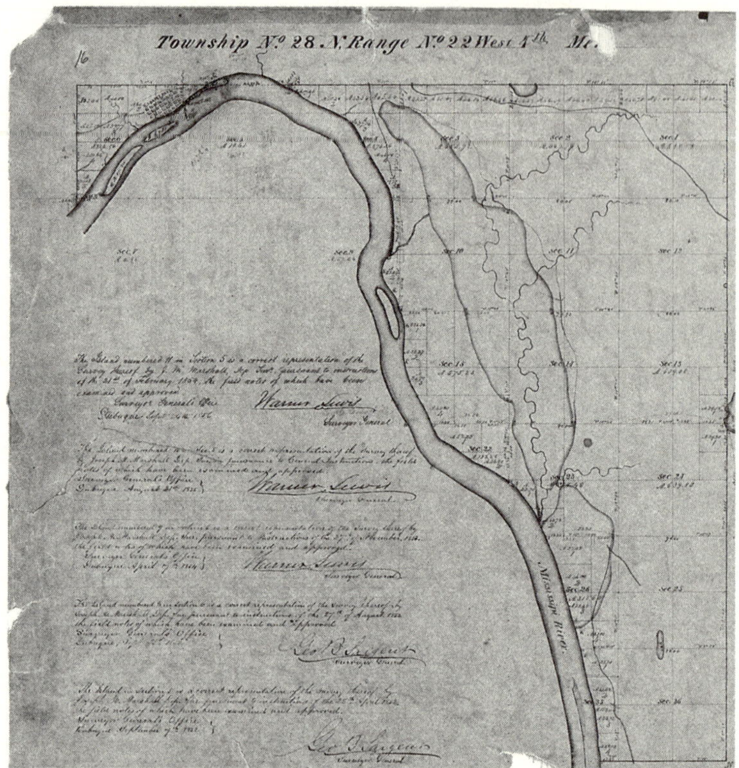

The US Surveyor General surveyed the St. Paul area in late 1847 and produced this map. Featured on it is the plat for St. Paul, the town surveyed the same year by Ira B. Brunson. The Brunson map was filed in 1849 in Wisconsin Territory and then in Ramsey County, Minnesota, in 1866. It has disappeared since then. The larger map illustrates the settlements along the river below St. Paul, around Grand Marais (also known as Ponte LeClere, Ponte Basse, and, later, Pig's Eye).

western boundary was placed along the St. Croix River. At last, the settlers of the upper reaches of the Mississippi were a separate entity, but the eastward ebb of political organization had bypassed them, and they landed in unorganized territory, albeit on ceded lands. One day they were citizens of Wisconsin Territory, a political entity managed by the federal government with representation in Washington; the next day they had no political identity. They were stateless. They had lost their political representation. No justice of the peace, no civil or criminal court, no sheriff; no government, officers, nor laws. No mail (aside from personal travel, the only means of long-distance communication), which meant no road maintenance (postal contracts were awarded with the understanding that those entities would improve roads), and no legal infrastructure through which to claim their land. Credit was tight, only possible in situations of complete confidence, and business fell. The loss of political credibility would drop the incoming migratory flow, too, as people avoided settling in an area without a political structure. These residents existed in a no-man's land. They got what they wanted—to be separated from Wisconsin—but at the cost of having nothing.[19]

Early in that summer of 1848 the small community at St. Paul Landing looked for a solution. At one point, a group of men gathered on the street in front of Jackson's store and devised a plan, which led to a public meeting in Stillwater on August 5. They understood, somehow, that Congress was not going to address their situation. Indeed, on August 14 Congress adjourned without considering their political needs as a new unorganized territory. They were in a unique situation. Normally, unorganized territory was synonymous with Indian Territory. But here, between the St. Croix and Mississippi Rivers, the land had been ceded, yet the population was not large enough to initiate the process toward becoming a territory. Congress seemed to know the population was too small, and it let the issue linger. The August 5 meeting prompted a call for territorial communities to appoint delegates and convene in Stillwater on August 26. They were going to hold an election.[20]

They called their meeting of community representatives a convention, and they sent the convention summary to regional and Washington newspapers to heighten their exposure. They signed their names to a memorial and sent it to Congress and the president of the United States, James K. Polk. They requested the organization of the Territory of Minnesota so they could be part of the United States. "[W]ithout any fault of our own, and with every desire to be governed by laws," they wrote, it wasn't right that they had "once enjoyed the rights and privileges of citizens of a Territory of the United States" but were now "virtually disfranchised."[21]

At the second public meeting they began to organize as "citizens of the Minnesota Territory," but such a place didn't exist. In a decisive moment, they changed their strategy. They planned to dispute what was assumed—yet unwritten—when Wisconsin became a state: They claimed Wisconsin statehood did not nullify the "ruminant" territory. That is, without further legal action to designate the unused Wisconsin territorial lands, that land remained legally organized as Wisconsin Territory. They claimed they still lived in Wisconsin Territory even while Wisconsin also was a state, and therefore, they had the right to congressional representation. They planned to proceed as if they were a legitimate territory and elect a delegate to send to Washington. They could only hope Congress would seat him. "If a delegate was elected by color of law," they were advised by the former secretary of the Wisconsin Territory, "Congress never would inquire into the legality of the election."[22]

"In a classic case of desperate times provoking bizarre ideas," wrote historian William E. Lass, they held that the last secretary of the territory "had succeeded to the vacant territorial governorship and had the authority to call for the election of a delegate to Congress." They organized an election that included all the settlements of the pseudo-territory for October 30, 1848. From Stillwater to Sauk Rapids and from Crow Wing to St. Paul, the election returns of white men totaled 377 votes (the largest city, St. Paul, had 73). Even though they expanded suffrage to include unnaturalized French Canadians and Métis, they were more than just a bit shy of the requisite 5,000 men needed to establish a territory. Had most men in the region been made eligible to vote, the settlers would have been in the minority and most certainly lost to the tens of thousands of Native American men in the region. Henry H. Sibley won the election, and the community representatives gave him "full power to act . . . [and] to represent the interests of the proposed Territory, and to urge an immediate organization of the same."[23]

The political class in Washington immediately saw through this charade. When Sibley arrived and asked to be seated, he met a discouraging wall of resistance. "I soon became convinced that my admission as Delegate was extremely uncertain," he said, "in fact I may say absolutely improbable." Congress largely "ridiculed the pretension" that any territorial organization remained intact adjacent to the new state. After some networking, Sibley was seated as a courtesy, without admitting the existence of an extant territory. The House eventually granted him full delegate privileges on January 15, and he was seated as a representative of the Territory of Wisconsin. The rest of Washington, DC, ridiculed the House for having sat a delegate to represent a territory that did not exist, an act that had no precedent.[24]

The Fight to Reclaim the Confluence

Simultaneously, people began to work on one of their other priorities, namely reducing Plympton's extensive Reserve. At the end of December 1847 Joseph R. Brown sought inroads on the closed landings near the confluence. Brown wrote to John Tweedy, his former Wisconsin territorial congressional representative. He proposed to build a warehouse at Fountain Cave, but he needed access inside the Reserve to land steamboats there. Brown called the Cave "the most convenient landing *below* the fort," a three-mile reduction in the trip from St. Paul Landing. He stretched for more, suggesting a landing one mile above the fort provided better access to St. Anthony Falls and the pineries.[25]

"The extension of the military reservation of Fort Snelling over so large a tract of country east of the Mississippi," he wrote, "has long been a source of serious annoyance to the business operations of the country." His own business, he said, "requires several tons of supplies for lumbering operations." He believed that a "wealthy eastern company" intended to build mills at St. Anthony Falls and projected an increase up to fifty times the current lumbering operations. The landings by the confluence saved time and money because they avoided "the expense of getting supplies up a steep and high hill" at St. Paul Landing.[26]

The logistical advantages of the confluence remained superior to St. Paul's location. As long as Plympton's Reserve blocked all the landings, it impinged on development at St. Anthony Falls. Despite the added river time to get to the confluence, the head of navigation still mattered when hauling large loads and supplies. If one was hauling machinery for sawmills, it was more convenient, efficient, and economical to avoid the climb over the hills of St. Paul. It was better to unload near the fort at the confluence. In addition, those landings had access to an established road to the falls, while the St. Anthony–St. Paul road was still in rudimentary condition.

Tweedy forwarded Brown's letter to Secretary of War William L. Marcy on February 15, 1848. Tweedy corroborated Brown's claims with "several other intelligent gentlemen," some residents and others who had traveled over the Upper Mississippi country. They "repeatedly and strongly expressed," he said, that the army did not need Plympton's Reserve, and it interfered with the settlement and development of the country, occupying "the best and most convenient ground for a landing and town site, at the head of navigation." Brown was anticipating the transition away from military life to civilian life and was likely aiming to reestablish his claims near the confluence.[27]

The army was also rethinking the value of Fort Snelling and its large Reserve. They knew the fort's role in their mission was complete and they were focused on building other forts in the more remote areas. Writing from Washington, DC, Quartermaster General T. S. Jesup believed the land was of "infinitely more importance" under cultivation by "numerous and industrious settlers" as opposed to being held by the military. The role of the fort and the military at the confluence and the region was so diminished in his eyes that he recommended "the whole territory of the Mississippi be surrendered to the Land Department for sale." The fort commander, Colonel Francis Lee, wrote to his superiors in Washington supporting the same, saying he could see the fort was no longer serving a useful purpose, and he urged that they reduce it, keeping only the land west of the river.[28]

On another front, people pressed Sibley to reduce the Reserve. Sibley brought the bill to Senator Stephen A. Douglas, who introduced it in the Senate on March 1, 1850. Though the bill went through committees of territories and public lands, with amendments, it never got a vote.[29]

The New Territory

People were anticipating and preparing for the changes. John R. Irvine was one of them. He arrived at St. Paul Landing and acquired property in 1843. Born in New York, he worked as a blacksmith and plasterer. Then he moved west via Green Bay and Prairie du Chien and became a grocer. A restless man, he was always working. He had squatting rights on a few hundred acres adjacent to the recently platted town of St. Paul Proper. His land sat upriver of the town, below the bluff, and he began to develop the Upper Landing. Much of his property was heavily wooded, and it took him a long time to cut the trees because many of them were at least 600 years old. The wood was sold to the steamboats for fuel. The rest of his land was described by another settler as "a quagmire, almost without bottom."[30]

Henry M. Rice made a business proposal to Irvine. Rice was the north country agent of the fur trading firm of P. Chouteau, Jr. and Company of St. Louis since 1834. He had recently returned from Washington, DC, where he lobbied for Minnesota's territorial status. Rice introduced Irvine to the idea of developing a portion of his claim as an "addition," a land plat surveyed into saleable lots. Irvine's property offered the small town a second landing because once the land was cleared it provided good access through the riverside bluffs up to town. In November 1848 Rice "bought in" with Irvine for eighty acres at three dollars per acre. That winter, they formed a partnership and "laid off" Rice and Irvine's addition. Their addition joined the Brunson plat to become the Town of St. Paul. Their gamble was simple: Rice was confident that Congress would accept Sibley as a legitimate representative and grant Minnesota territorial status. That declaration alone would enhance the value of real estate. Land that was subdivided into lots was more profitable for speculative investments.[31]

Back in Washington, Sibley focused on getting a bill to organize the Territory of Minnesota. He faced withering opposition from Representative Nathaniel Boyden of North Carolina. Not only was the Minnesota population too small, the critics noted, but adding a free territory would also shift the future balance of free–slave states. Douglas, a guardian of the Minnesota Territory legislation, encountered more resistance in the Senate than Sibley did in the House. Douglas, among many others, did not care at all if the new configuration of states abided by the Northwest Territory ordinance of five states. Saturday, March 3, 1849, the last day of the congressional session, finished with the typical end-of-session flurry of bills. Toward the evening's end, legislators passed H.R. 779, "A bill for the relief of James Norris and for other purposes." The funding for the creation of the Minnesota Territory was one of the "other purposes." Sibley said they ran out of time to add the territory as a stand-alone bill, but it may not have passed as a stand-alone bill. To amend bills that must pass with other unrelated matters at the end of a session is a common procedural legerdemain. Sibley did his job and found a way to get the territorial bill passed.[32]

Back home in St. Paul, after a long, severe winter, the villagers partook in their annual springtime anticipation of news from the outside world. As the weather warmed, they waited for the first steamboat to come up the river with hopes that it would bring news of Sibley's work. There is a well-known story about the townspeople catching sight of the first steamboat of 1849 coming up the river. A violent storm with strong winds, lightning, and thunder besieged the town on the evening of April 9. As darkness descended the storm paused momentarily and the residents heard an engine, which was punctuated by a sharp whistle. Despite the storm, they ran to the bluff's edge, and, in a flash of lightning, they could see the *Dr. Franklin No. 2* rounding the riverbend a mile away. As the boat approached the landing, someone shouted the news that Minnesota was officially a territory.[33]

This news was understandably exciting, though the story often lacks the context of this against-the-odds gamble to gain political recognition. The villagers no longer lived in unorganized territory. After enduring seven months of political limbo, they had regained their territorial status. In April 1849 they were again a part of the United States.

These settlers, later known as the state's founding fathers, were making the best of things, even as they had fabricated so much to become legal: the population numbers, the existence of a Minnesota Territory, and the continuation of the Wisconsin Territory. They had used these shady devices when they registered the plat of St. Paul Proper in 1847 and listed the land as being in the Territory of Minnesota. They had made a forced entry, and the consequences for the settlement of the area would have surprised earlier speculators. St. Paul Proper, once a temporary destination for settlers and squatters displaced by the Reserve expansion, was now the preferred permanent settlement.[34]

The news of territorial status fueled rumors that the Reserve would be reduced and its land would be available for claims. People rushed across the Reserve overnight, staked hundreds of preemptive claims, and threw up shanties. They carved their names in the trees or pounded a board in the ground with their name on it. In no time, the entire Reserve was claimed, on both sides of the river. Early in the winter of 1850 the fort commander ordered a lieutenant with twenty men mounted on horses to pull down every shanty and, once again, evict all the claimants. Over the next few years the army repeatedly removed illegal occupants from the Reserve and razed their cabins, only to have the squatters swarm back to the Reserve. The ongoing and routine forced removals "added bitterness and uncertainty to an already chaotic situation," noted historian Lucile Kane.[35]

Sibley returned to Washington in 1850 as a *bona fide* delegate to the Thirty-First Congress. Minnesota's first territorial assembly in its first session the previous year passed a resolution requesting Sibley to urge the war department to reduce the Reserve and secure preemption rights for the squatters. He prepared a bill, ushered before Congress by Douglas, which proposed the Reserve be restricted to the west side of the river. The first effort failed. It would take another two years before Congress passed a bill in 1852 and reduced the Reserve by three-fourths (26,023 acres). The surveyor general took two years to survey the Reserve. The land office brought it to market in 1854. Those four years were a crucial delay for St. Paul and the Twin Cities.[36]

Real Estate Seals the Deal

The first streets in St. Paul Proper ran along the river, which runs to the east–northeast in front of the town. The design was simple, and the streets were narrow. In part that was a lack of imagination. But the residents did not expect St. Paul would grow beyond this original tract. In fact, many believed St. Paul was temporary, and once the gorge was cleared to St. Anthony, that would become the head of navigation. Now, as a territory, Minnesota was attractive to outsiders. Before the Reserve could be reduced and the prime land reclaimed, people seized on what was most readily available, thereby setting St. Paul on a different path.[37]

The steamboats coming up the river were now full of people. St. Paul doubled in size that first year of the territory, approaching a thousand residents. Four steamboats per week brought people and goods from

Galena, Dubuque, and St. Louis. And even though St. Louis was some 800 miles south of St. Paul, the *Minnesota Pioneer* said, they "seem like neighbors," because they "frequently 'drop up' to make us a call." By 1849 St. Paul had eighteen stores or trading establishments whose business was as much about trading with the Dakota, Ho-Chunk, and Ojibwe as it was about supplying the settlers. The town had plenty of carpenters, blacksmiths, and merchants, but they needed farmers because importing all their produce was expensive. They had plenty of room and board, several ministers, and one school. It was "by far the largest, wealthiest, busiest, and wickedest place in Minnesota," according to the *National Era* of Washington, DC. Interest in the outpost grew, and newspapers arrived from different points of the compass asking for a copy of the local newspaper, the *Minnesota Pioneer*, in exchange. People wrote and asked: "Is your land susceptible of growing wheat generally? Can fruit be raised, such as apples, peaches, etc.? Are your winters long and severe?"[38]

Land speculators platted additions (subdivisions) at a feverish pace. Brunson, the surveyor, had taken the opportunity and "laid off" another plat called the Brunson Addition. Congressman Robert Smith of Alton, Illinois, and Cornelius S. Whitney, the receiver at the St. Croix Falls Land Office, laid off their addition in April. Otis Hoyt, the register from the Hudson Land Office, did another one in May. Samuel Leech, land office register at St. Croix Falls, laid off an addition as well. Then came Guerin and Bazil's, Randall and Roberts's, and Patterson's additions in 1850. The next year saw Winslow's, Kittson's, Willes's, and Irvine's additions. In 1852 came Bass's, Brunson's, Baker's, and Winslow's (No. 2), along with Irvine and Ramsey's new addition. In June 1853 the Warren and Winslow's cottage addition promised to deliver something beyond the ordinary: a rustic "cottage orné" experience, embracing the romantic architectural style of a thatched roof on a small cottage. The math of subdividing an addition promised rewards. When Rice bought in with Irvine, he paid three dollars per acre. The next summer he sold the lots for $75–$125, which is an increase of $300–$500 per acre in one year. It was easy money.[39]

St. Paul was notorious for its confusing street layout. In 1999 Governor Jesse Ventura suggested the streets were laid out by drunken Irishmen. The people who devised the street map were intoxicated, all right, but not necessarily with booze. Speculation fever had gripped everyone. People laid off addition after addition as fast as they could, and their plats were at irregular scales containing lots of different sizes. Streets within each plat did not conform to the pattern, size, or alignment of the streets in neighboring plats or the old town. St. Paul's layout looked to one editor like two plats had "taken a running jump at each other, like two rival steamboats," and then merged as one boat. The rapid rate of additions left an unsolvable riddle in the streets, causing people to become frustrated with the original surveyors. It's as if they felt, said one critic, that "beauty was in crooked lines." St. Paul's street map seemed to be pasted together "helter skelter."[40]

One visitor in the early 1850s liked the setting of St. Paul—the bluff overlooking the river and the hills around it—but he said its potential beauty was nearly "irremediably spoiled" by its layout. After the original town was laid off in 1847 in an orderly street grid, the rapid accumulation of additions was "so greedy" that settlers tried to plat every foot and left no "open spots for breathing holes . . . the streets of one part butt against the house lots of another part, and laid out the blocks in triangles, skew-angles, and botches without angles." The houses were built to reflect the lots. "[N]o four pages of Euclid," he said, "describe a greater variety of figures than the city of St. Paul." The place reminded another visitor of "the old French part of St. Louis, with crooked lanes for streets, irregular blocks, and little skewdangular lots, about as large as a stingy card of gingerbread, broke in two diagonally." The St. Paul settlers divvied up every last parcel, foregoing anything a city might need for comfort—no public square, no margin between the town and the river, not even a tree for shade. The visitor knew that once majestic trees stood here, as "the ugly stumps of a forest . . . now disfigure the town." He thought the residents should raze it all and start over.[41]

These beginnings of St. Paul suggest residents were uncertain about the city's longevity. One description of St. Paul noted that those who settled the town "appear to have had but the smallest possible ideas of the growth and importance that awaited St. Paul." Possibly, they still expected to return to the confluence. In 1849 St. Paul's population remained small at 200–400 people (73 voting men). Had the Reserve been reduced before they gained territorial status, their preference for the confluence may have incited different settlement patterns. There are clues suggesting that impermanence played a part in their thinking, from Brown seeking access to the confluence landings to the lack of foresight in the town layout.[42]

St. Paul "did not awake to a sense of its destiny until about eight months ago," wrote the editor of the *Minnesota Pioneer* in January 1850. It emerged from its status as a sodden refugee camp known as "Pig's Eye" with the realization that the confluence would remain out of reach. With territorial status, the investors saw the land differently, along with the town's role in the settling of the state. They quickly, with a "true vision," were wholeheartedly on board with a new certainty.[43]

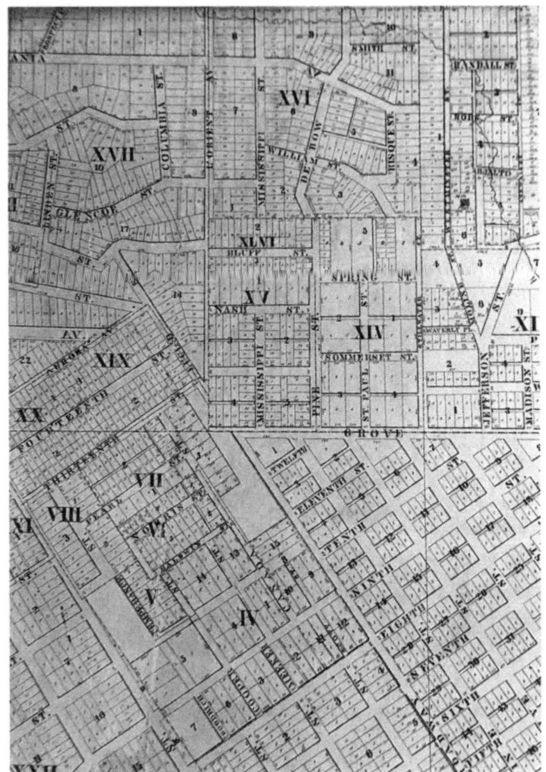

A sample of the St. Paul streets that captures the city's uncoordinated development

The vision came with a transformation of the community as well. As the population grew, residents doubled the size of the St. Paul chapel. Father Augustin Ravoux had arrived in 1842 to work with Father Galtier. He split his time between Mendota and St. Paul, where he preached only in French. Nearly all the first landowners on file had French names, but now land transfers and deeds carried names that no longer reflected Gallic ancestry. At the same time, an increasing number of the congregation did not understand French, so Ravoux switched the St. Paul services to English. By the time the Reserve opened in the mid-1850s, St. Paul had over 4,000 residents and was immersed in a speculative land fever with dozens of additions platted. The meteoric growth cemented the town's permanence, in both its layout and its priority over the confluence. By the time the Reserve and the confluence came up for sale, St. Paul had roots and its people a vision. There was no going back. St. Paul was now the head of navigation. The term had changed in meaning, from the head of the navigable river at the confluence to the commercial head of navigation at St. Paul.[44]

Plympton's Reserve boundary inadvertently created a settlement at the closest point for a land route to St. Anthony and the falls. Coming upriver, the river passes St. Paul and makes a large bend to the southwest, so a boat traveling to Fort Snelling would finish its journey by traveling southwest, away from the falls. Fort Snelling and St. Paul were each about nine miles from St. Anthony Falls. As the fort dwindled in influence and St. Paul surged in population, steamboat traffic shifted to prioritize St. Paul. It became the freight depot and jumping-off point for St. Anthony and locations beyond. With improved roads, stagecoaches initiated regular service to St. Anthony in the early 1850s. The overland route to St. Anthony became the preferred path for locals and tourists, further solidifying St. Paul's role in the area. At first glance of a map, this overland route appears more convenient than the extra travel time on the river via the fort. Just as with St. Paul's location, however, the road was required by Plympton's Reserve.[45]

Despite the substitution of St. Paul for the confluence, the settlers continued to envision a single metropolis or city. The new location did not interfere with their understanding of urban evolution. They now had a place-name and a landing, and the town of St. Paul became the storehouse and distribution center for the emerging state and region. They adjusted their vision. Now, the new metropolis would start at St. Paul and grow out to St. Anthony Falls.

Part II: **Separating the Twin Cities**

CHAPTER 4

The Reserve Conspiracy

The summer of 1854 put St. Paul on the map. The Rock Island Railroad became the first in the northwest to complete its tracks to the Mississippi River. It opened the Upper Mississippi River basin with railroad routes to the East Coast. Reaching St. Paul, the western terminus of easy travel, got easier. To celebrate, the railroad company assembled a promotional tour in Chicago and invited hundreds of prominent people, mostly from the northeast, including editors, politicians, and other renowned figures. They called it the Grand Excursion.

On June 3, people filled two trains in Chicago, then transferred to five steamboats at Rock Island, Illinois (leaving hundreds of others behind), and arrived at the far-away village of St. Paul, Minnesota Territory, on June 8. The locals pulled out every carriage and wagon to convey the buoyant crowd from St. Paul to St. Anthony Falls, across the river to the embryonic village of Minneapolis, Bde Maka Ska, Minnehaha Falls, and Fort Snelling. A New Yorker ceremoniously poured a bottle of Atlantic water into the Mississippi to celebrate the new connections. All waters flowed into one.[1]

Minnesota's recently inaugurated Capitol building was the scene: Visitors danced in the supreme court chamber, dined in the hall of the house of representatives, and heard speeches by former president Millard Fillmore, historian George Bancroft, and Territorial Governor Willis A. Gorman, among others. The festivities went late into the night. Then the passengers boarded the steamboats and at midnight launched on the return trip to Chicago, reaching Rock Island in thirty hours. The excursionists wrote about their experience and cast a positive light on St. Paul.[2]

That spring, St. Paul incorporated as a city, approved its new charter (507 votes cast), elected a mayor and city council, hired city staff, and created police and fire departments. They had four daily newspapers, seven churches, and a new cemetery. And then the steamboats came. As many as 500 people arrived every day, bringing 30,000 new people into the state that year.

But while Minnesotans embraced the growth, the Reserve was slowing them down. A person could stake a 160-acre claim anywhere within millions of acres from the St. Croix River to the western border of the 1851 Treaty of Traverse des Sioux (roughly today's border), but they could not stake a claim at the heart of the Minnesota Territory. For the previous five years, people from all fields—military, political, business, and speculator—recognized that Fort Snelling's military purpose had expired. The Fort Snelling Military Reserve would soon be "an isolated tract in the midst of civilization," said Lieutenant Colonel Francis Lee, the fort commander. It was the center that couldn't be had.[3]

One of the first things the new Minnesota Territorial Legislature did was ask Congress to reduce the Reserve. Since 1850 their territorial representative, Henry H. Sibley, had been promoting such a bill, and Congress passed legislation to initiate the decommissioning process. They parceled the Reserve into three sections and sold them off independent of each other. The first section, generally known as the St. Paul side, was the area east of the Mississippi (south of Marshall Avenue and west of downtown St. Paul). This was sold at the land office in Stillwater on September 11, 1854. The second section lay west of the Mississippi River and north of the fort and was known as part of the Minneapolis District. Initially scheduled for September 18, 1854, the sale was delayed until early 1855. The third section consisted of the fort grounds and surrounding acreage west of the Mississippi and north of the Minnesota River. This section was dispersed in 1857.[4]

The timing of the Reserve sales came just as Minnesota, along with the nation, was cresting on a heady wave of self-confidence rife with land speculation. Crop failures in Europe along with interrupted grain trade due to the Crimean War raised commodity prices. Minnesota offered up its millions of claimable acres to the thousands of migrating farmers. The hopeful newcomers were mesmerized by easy credit and fever-pitched land speculation. Locally, real estate was said to be "the only staple production" of the economy. One visiting correspondent captured the hypnosis: "My ears at every turn are saluted with the everlasting din of land! land! money! speculation! saw-mills! land warrant! town lots! etc., etc. Land at breakfast, land at dinner, land at supper, and until eleven o'clock, *land!* then in bed, until their vocal organs are exhausted, then they dream and groan out *land! land!!*"[5]

Each of these three Reserve sales was muddled and featured scandalous affairs. The government—Congress, the White House, and, especially, the military—failed to address issues in these land sales. In the sale of each Reserve section, scandals erupted that involved the highest offices in the nation and made national news. The mid-1850s was a critical period in the settlement patterns of the Twin Cities. The fights around the selling of the Reserve shaped the two cities, kept them apart, and incited the rivalry that is at the heart of their separate identities today.[6]

Squatters and Speculators

In that summer of 1854, newspapers in St. Paul and Washington, DC, ran a public notice that announced the public sale of the first section of the Fort Snelling Military Reserve on September 11 at the Stillwater Land Office. The sale was highly anticipated. In a normal sale, people bid for parcels at a live auction. If a person was on the land before the auction, they staked a preemption claim, a simple process that allowed settlers to make their claim ahead of the public auction, register it with the land office, and pay the base price of $1.25 per acre. The key to a preemption claim is that a person must live on the land and actively improve it. Preemption had been for many years the basis of land claims nationwide. If a person staked a preemption claim but had not yet registered their claim and paid for it, they were called a squatter. While vulnerable to claim jumpers, this practice had certain advantages, such as being able to sell the squatter claim to another person (as Donald McDonald had sold to Stephen Desnoyer).[7]

But things were different at this auction. Congress was initially averse to preemption claims on the Fort Snelling Military Reserve lands, and the legislation to sell them languished in committees. When the legislation for the Reserve sale passed on August 26, 1853, the bill provided no case for preemption. Then, on June 3, 1854, President Franklin Pierce signed a proclamation that set the time and the conditions for the land sale east of the Mississippi and declared the land was "not subject to preemption claims." The St. Paul part of the Reserve would be sold at auction to the highest bidder. These conditions were intended to ensure a fair sale, but the locals saw it differently. The proclamation set up a fight between St. Paul locals and the federal government, which knew the land was valuable and was seeking the best way to capture that value.[8]

By the time the exhilarating crush of tourists on the Grand Excursion arrived in St. Paul in June—three months before the land auction—upward of 400 people had staked claims across the entire Reserve in defiance of the president's proclamation. A newspaper correspondent of the *Perrysburg (Ohio) Journal* told his readers that if they were eyeing a move to the area, they were already too late. Though the Reserve land was "thinly settled," it was "tied up in illegal claims" because the land had "mostly fallen into the hands of speculators." They had seized the most valuable land and, in many cases, staked more than one claim. The Reserve was fully claimed before it was ever released. These claims were preemptive and, because they couldn't be registered, were squatter claims.[9]

A speculator in the typical sense was someone who claimed a piece of land for its price appreciation. They did not intend to build a home or farm the land. In addition to this definition, in St. Paul "speculator" status was determined by a person's perspective; a speculator could be a local or an outsider. From the outside journalist's perspective, the land was preemptively claimed, and since that was illegal in this sale, any person who staked a claim on the Reserve was considered a trespasser. It didn't matter to him that these claims were largely held by locals. He could see that they had made little effort to improve the property. They were speculators.[10]

On the other hand, the locals argued that the difference between their position and that of the real speculator was wealth. The outside speculator came in with money and could easily outbid the locals, who they claimed were cash poor. The locals presented themselves as being at a disadvantage. They said they felt pressed, even under siege, from outside speculators. A local was a settler, neighbor, or businessman. The term "local" carried a meaning that gave them priority.[11]

Local versus outsider. The definition served as a rhetorical device to present oneself as an innocent victim. The opposite was true. The locals abused the system. In these situations, squatters rarely did more than the minimum requirement for a preemption claim. They propped up a claim shanty, visited occasionally, and plowed a few furrows, if only to demarcate boundaries of their claim. "Not one out of twenty of the so-called '*squatters*' ever spent a single night," recalled one critic, "and perhaps not a single whole day upon the tract claimed by them." Their reason was pure speculation, "for the purpose of extorting from emigrants such sums as they could for their pretended possessions." Even though most everyone—outsider and local—was a speculator, the term was pejorative.[12]

The locals might have appeared at a disadvantage going up against rich, outside speculators and the federal government, but they had a method to assert what they viewed as their right to the claims. Indeed, they had done the same thing six years earlier on August 14, 1848, at the auction for the land outside the Reserve in the town of St. Paul Proper. When they settled there, the land was not yet surveyed, a prerequisite for staking a claim, so the residents of St. Paul were all squatters. When the land auction was announced, they were concerned about outside speculators outbidding them for the long-held claims they had improved. They hired

Ira Brunson,, the surveyor from Prairie du Chien, to survey the town of St. Paul on top of the bluff. They held weekly meetings to regulate and determine property lines, and a committee addressed any disputes among the squatters. They then went to the Stillwater Land Office to buy the land at auction.[13]

"We anticipated some trouble . . . from speculators, who usually attend these sales for the purpose of outbidding the settlers," recalled Auguste Larpenteur, one of the local organizers. Their plan consisted of having one person, Henry H. Sibley, place all the bids by proxy at the auction, uncontested. They ensured that no competitive bids were placed by enlisting a large, well-armed force, composed principally of Canadian Frenchmen who were also squatters. With their show of force, they could physically block any unwanted bidders and prevent competitive bidding. Sibley recalled the event nostalgically. As he called out the bids, he looked up occasionally and noticed, "I was surrounded by a number of men with huge bludgeons." The threat was real. "I assure you," said Larpenteur, "had any poor fellow attempted to put his finger in our pie, he would have heard something drop." They expedited the task in forty-five minutes because they were prepared. It was, in the end, a closed "auction."[14]

At that auction in 1848 for the town plat, the locals had united to rig or fix the sale. They acted as a combination, which was illegal. They believed they had no other option than to step beyond the federal law because the auction favored the outside speculators at the locals' expense. They took the law into their own hands in order to make their claims legal.[15]

The Claim Association

Basically, the St. Paul settlers in 1848 were operating like a claim association, a common protective organization. Claim associations were formal organizations with constitutions, bylaws, and democratically elected officers. They conducted regular meetings, posting notices on trees and in the newspapers. Each association represented a specific area. They kept records of all claims (place, date, costs, any improvements), field checked the claims, and taxed members to cover expenses.[16]

To prepare the claims for the land sale auction, members of the claim association were encouraged to settle disputes in advance and, in times of disagreement, to compromise. The *Daily Minnesota Pioneer* cautioned them that "half a loaf is better than no bread." If claimants couldn't come to mutual agreement, the claim association settled disputes through arbitration committees. The claimants presented their evidence to the committee, and the committee decided where the property line fell. The committee played the role of "a *court*, and heard counsel on behalf of the conflicting claimants, as if they had been a regularly-constituted court!" according to one critic. The association even had an appellate process to challenge those decisions. In the end, the committee issued binding decisions.[17]

According to one association's bylaws each member swore "to guard and protect the rights of each other against speculators or others intruding upon the lands of which they are the rightful owners." Another association declared that "in unity of action there is strength." The strategy was to present a united front. The claim association members were "bound by a solemn compact to carry into effect the will of the members." Their main objective was "to secure to such claimants by mutual pledges and by force of arms if necessary, all the rights recognized by the association whether in violation of law or otherwise." The tone of their language sounded like that of secret societies, which were prevalent at the time. "We strongly recommend such associations," advised the *Weekly Minnesotian*, "more especially now when so much doubt is thrown upon the legality and efficacy of the Territorial claim law."[18]

Claim associations were a formalized combination, so they were also illegal. This extralegal activity did not go uncontested. At one point, a lawyer stood in front of an arbitration committee and called the association members "*traitors*," because they were "setting the laws of their country at defiance, and openly and shamelessly violating them," according to an anonymous writer in a Washington, DC, newspaper who signed off as "St. Croix." The claim associations were extralegal organizations that provided an initial domestic order and a militia, all in one.[19]

Claimants used claim associations to stabilize ownership before standard legal ownership was available through the US system. The locals used this system to establish their claims and document improvements. The preemption claims, especially in high-demand areas, outpaced the legal process conducted by the General Land Office in surveying, recording, and selling the land (either by preemption or auction). Yet the squatters did not always register their preemptive claims with the land office at the earliest convenience. And they were frequently absent for long periods of time, so their claim was susceptible to claim jumping. The claim association offered security; it appeared to stabilize the land claim process, but in the sale of the Reserve it was a means of abusing it.[20]

A key component in the associations' declaration of purpose was to "secure actual claimants against speculators, to protect each other at the Land Sale." They wanted to eliminate competition for their claims and control the prices by keeping outside speculators at bay. The locals believed they had the right to the land because they were there first and their work gave it value.[21]

A speculator for the local, then, was anyone who would bid against someone who already had staked a preemptive claim (or squatted on a claim), a practice no different than claim jumping in their eyes. You wouldn't do that to a neighbor. Land speculation was viewed positively; you just had to be first. First to come gave claim to the title of "local," even if you beat the next guy by a day. Even if you had more claims than was legally permitted. Even if you didn't fulfill the requirements of homesteading and working the land. Just as with the sale of the lands outside the Reserve such as St. Paul Proper, if the locals had their way there wasn't going to be an open auction for the Reserve lands.

The squatters on the Reserve formally organized the Military Reserve Claim Association in 1853, writing their constitution after a regular meeting in Fountain Cave. They elected as the first president Henry M. Rice, who had become their territorial representative on March 4, 1853, and as secretary William S. Combs, a bookstore owner in St. Paul. In the 1854 land auction the claim association played an extreme role because the president's proclamation had nullified their preemptive claims. This was widely known. The claim association was not only blocking outside speculators; it was also undermining the government's efforts to get money for the land through a fair auction.[22]

The Government Detects a Combination

The day of the Reserve land auction, September 11, 1854, came with heavy rain. The crowd stood in the muddy street. The mood was muted, subdued, if not tense. Reports suggest that more than 400 people showed up, some having traveled hundreds, even thousands, of miles. Nearly 300 of them had arrived the night before from the Hennepin County Claim Association, which had joined in alliance to support and defend the Military Reserve Claim Association. The claim association and its allies wore red to identify themselves, and some were armed with rifles. Someone dumped out two wagons full of clubs on the ground.[23]

It was not a mob. The men were organized as a militia, with a leader for every ten-man squad, and an overall leader. They also docked a boat nearby to carry away anybody who bid against them. They stood in a large circle, forming a human fence around the auction to stifle any outsiders from calling out a bid. The threat of violence was close to the surface. They broadcast their message that any man who placed a bid for a tract "would not leave the ground alive," according to "St. Croix."[24]

The land office auctioneer stood in the door of the office building and called out for bids. Most striking for a public auction with so many people in attendance was the silence after the auctioneer opened the bidding at $1.25 per acre. Such a large crowd, and no one offered a higher bid. William R. Marshall, the future state governor, was the claim association agent to bid by proxy for all the individual claimants. In the end, the government sold 4,503.89 acres of land, bringing in $5,629.86. Congratulations were shared; the relief was real. They had pulled off the big deal: They got premium land for the government's rock-bottom asking price. The crowd dispersed, some pleased yet not surprised by the outcome.[25]

Then, a week after the auction, something unusual happened. On September 18, two employees of the Stillwater Land Office, W. Holcombe, the receiver, and T. M. Fullerton, the register, wrote to their boss, Commissioner John Wilson of the General Land Office in Washington, reporting that they believed "a combination suppressed the bids." A collective effort to fix the prices at the minimum bid was explicitly illegal; so was manipulating a sale by intimidation, combination, or unfair management. The transgressions were punishable with a $1,000 fine and two years in prison. Wilson replied on October 4 that any combination that interfered with the free bidding at a public sale was intolerable, and he requested a report describing the context and providing the evidence that brought them to such a conclusion. With the auction under investigation, Wilson suspended all sales.[26]

Two months later, the two agents in the Stillwater office wrote again and withdrew their claim of a combination at the sale, which they said had been based on "public rumor." The agents denied seeing deadly weapons or hearing of any threats to use them, and although there were "some half dozen more or less of cudgels or canes left on the ground after the [people] had dispersed," they did not feel those were intended for violence at the sale. In reporting the incident earlier, they did not mean to create a delay in issuing patents to the purchasers. They had not "heard a single complaint from any granter since the sale." They now believed the sale was legal and the patents should be sent to the new owners.[27]

What had prompted their about-face? Land agents were part of the community; they had to live with the people who had formed the claim association. The anonymous commentator "St. Croix" said everyone knew of the combination, "for it was a matter of public notoriety." Their duty "under these circumstances was to stop the sale; but this they *dared* not do, being themselves threatened."[28]

Meanwhile, in Washington, DC, Rice applied the pressure directly. He visited Wilson in the DC General Land Office on December 5 and requested a copy of the land agents' letter that mentioned a combination at the sale. Wilson responded to Rice in a letter later that day summarizing the agents' report of a combination and noting he had requested a detailed report from the land agents with evidence for which he was waiting. This letter exposing the agents' whistleblowing then appeared in the *Weekly Minnesotian* on December 23. In this way, the letter to Rice was leaked and outed the agents to the claim association buyers. If the Stillwater agents followed through with a report affirming the combination, the sale would have been "declared null and void," and they "might have lost their lives," said "St. Croix." "[T]hey were intimidated into silence," he said, "as they also knew that intimidation was used to prevent bidding at the sale."[29]

The agents' alert of a combination and their retraction of it raised a red flag in Washington. Such an about-face by experienced people set off concerns for government officials who were no doubt disappointed with the sale's receipts. Wilson had also received a letter of complaint from William Henderson, who had participated in the sale. Though an outsider, he was able to buy a claim a couple of weeks before the sale for $1,000, but the person reneged on the sale. Henderson called the auction "one of the greatest violations of law and justice ever committed."[30]

After another two-month delay, Wilson wrote on February 2, 1855, to say that he detected a shift in the agents' reasoning. Wilson censured the agents for having reported a rumor and then withdrawing the charge. He especially noted their oddly placed comment: "[T]he utmost harmony prevailed during the sale." To say the least, the commissioner was perplexed by the events in Minnesota.[31]

While Wilson was grappling with the Stillwater Land Office, a great opportunity fell in his lap: John Ross Browne had arrived in New York in early January 1855. On January 27, Robert McClelland, secretary of the interior in the Pierce administration, wrote to Browne and with only general instructions asked him to investigate the conduct of the public officers in Minnesota connected with the department. Browne had already accepted the assignment and was en route to Minnesota when Wilson censured the agents in the Stillwater Land Office.

A Literary Talent Vacations in St. Paul, Midwinter

On Friday evening, February 16, 1855, the stagecoach from Dubuque arrived in St. Paul with a special passenger, John Ross Browne. He checked in at St. Paul's Winslow House, a five-story brick building at the intersection of Eagle and Fort Streets, the best hotel north of St. Louis. Over the previous four months, Browne had traveled to California and the Oregon Territory, as well as passing twice through Panama to cross the isthmus. When his ship, *Star of the West*, arrived in New York on January 2, his name was mentioned as prominently as the ship's cargo of $625,885 of California gold and the other dignitaries.[32]

Browne's arrival in St. Paul made the newspapers' social column as he was a renowned author, the "immortalizer of *Yusef, the Destroyer of Robbers*," a book published just two years before based on his Mediterranean travels. His "clever book of travels" was popular, and he was viewed as "among the most gifted authors of America." People could pick up their copy at W. S. Combs's Franklin Book Store, nearly opposite Rice's American House.[33]

St. Paul in the winter was lamentably remote, with no boats arriving and difficult roads. Residents didn't see boat traffic once Lake Pepin froze up in November, and if the weather was harsh they went weeks or even months without mail. Why a traveler of the world—who had just experienced southwestern and southern climates—would choose to vacation in St. Paul in the dead of winter, traveling a week in an unheated stagecoach rattling across frozen prairie, should have aroused some degree of suspicion. Browne said he was in the territory for two or three weeks "for the purpose of picking up notes by the way-side." Locals expected his observations in Minnesota "would be one of the most popular works of the times."[34]

John Ross Browne in 1868

Browne was a talented lawyer and a stickler for detail. He had a critical eye and a mind for efficiency. He moved with an informality amongst strangers; people were comfortable in his presence and yielded information to him voluntarily. As an independent contractor for the federal government, he was trusted to act with authority in distant situations. He could audit, inspect, implement corrective actions as he saw fit, and make high-level recommendations. The US Treasury Department, Browne's primary employer, had sent him to California, which was five years into its booming gold fields. One would expect a mess and his job was to fix the problems. He fired upward of twenty-eight customhouse "loafers" and toured the state's interior with the California surveyor general to examine public lands.[35]

Browne also wrote a report on the California Constitutional Convention, an enormous accounting of the executive affairs in California for the secretary of treasury. He made a broad array of recommendations, such as rearranging departments, eliminating offices, adjusting salaries, and enlarging the San Francisco mint. One notable job was his investigation into the work of Lieutenant Edward F. Beale, the superintendent of Indian Affairs in California. While Browne approved the system established by Beale and recommended it remain in place, he censured Beale for some of his official acts, though he did not "impute" any criminality. Browne "was well versed in frontier ways," both in the rudimentary travel and in the unbridled nature of frontier politics, so he was perfect for the job in Minnesota.[36]

If the people of St. Paul had known Browne's abilities and the extent to which the government employed him, they would have been wary of their midwinter guest. What they didn't know was that Secretary McClelland of the Pierce administration had sent Browne as a confidential agent to the unruly interior territory to audit Minnesota's Indian Affairs accounts, which were managed by Territorial Governor Willis A. Gorman. In addition, they asked Browne to investigate the irregularities of the land agents' claims of a combination suppressing the prices at the land auction. In the end, Browne's reports would surprise Washington.

Browne's timing was fortuitous, and the situation played to his talents. When he arrived, the legislature was in session, and he quickly detected the territory's two embattled factions. Nationally, the Democratic Party was divided over slavery, and the local Democratic Party, known as the Moccasin Democrats because of its relationship with the fur trade, was divided between Rice and Sibley. Pierce had originally installed Gorman, his army buddy from Indiana, to avoid choosing sides in the territory's bifurcated Democratic Party. But the plan didn't work as Gorman sided with Sibley and crossed Rice on several issues pertaining to Indian treaties.[37]

Portrait of Henry M. Rice, painted by G. P. A. Healy in 1857

Browne observed Gorman without revealing his assignment and tried to understand the hostility toward him. The week before, Gorman's antagonists had presented a memorial to remove him. They had a litany of complaints, including the financial accounting of the Indian Affairs, depositing the public moneys with a private banker, delaying the last annuity payment to the Dakota, and being "deficient in dignity of character and unfit for the high position which he occupies." Rice complained to Pierce and McClelland that Gorman was ruining the party in Minnesota as he was incompetent and perhaps corrupt, especially in his dealings with the Indians.[38]

But, in truth, these complaints were partisan harassment. The real problem was Gorman's attitude toward a railroad charter for the Minnesota Northwestern Railroad (MNWR). The railroad company had legislation that would give it a land grant connecting Lake Superior to St. Paul. But Gorman had vetoed it on the basis that it gave public land to a private company, and he insisted on a three percent tax for the state on those lands. Gorman stood between the railroad and the land grant. Pierce was under pressure to replace Gorman because of his antagonism to the railroad land grant, which cost the president's friends money.[39]

To gain clarity, Browne visited the governor at home, where he was confined by a severe attack of ophthalmia (inflamed and irritated eyes). Gorman had a stern visage and a reputation as rigidly opinionated and impulsive. The eye condition must have made him intimidating. Browne showed his letters of assignment and asked Gorman, "as delicately as possible," to see the ledgers for the Indian Affairs and to count the public money at his house. Gorman produced two bags of gold coins. In the ensuing conversation, Gorman took umbrage at the federal government sending an agent to investigate him. Over the next two days, Browne conducted an audit and found Gorman's affairs to be in order. The only speculation Gorman took part in was the establishment of a town on the St. Peter (Minnesota) River, and his share cost was "but a few hundred dollars." Gorman owned an interest in the *St. Peter's Gazette* in addition to the house he lived in and a few lots.[40]

Browne began to understand the plot against Gorman, and that the complaints were designed to oust him. A delegation representing the MNWR had traveled to Washington to lobby for just that. After the audit, however, Browne could see Gorman was not guilty of the charges. The accusations by the MNWR supporters were ginned up. Those interested in removing Gorman were prominent members of the "Rice faction." Rice became adamant about replacing Gorman with someone more amenable to his projects. Presumably, Rice knew about the clandestine investigation—at least regarding Gorman. Rice would not have agreed to an investigation into the land sale. He remained in Washington during Browne's visit.[41]

Willis A. Gorman, second territorial governor of Minnesota, 1865

The Combination Confesses

On Browne's departure from Minnesota, he traveled by chance in a stagecoach with William S. Combs, the bookseller and first secretary of the Military Reserve Claim Association, as well as others involved in the Stillwater combination. They treated the renowned literary talent with deference, unaware of his undercover mission. They carried his luggage and gave him the preferred accommodation, such as the best bed at night. They passed the time buried in furs on the stagecoach disclosing to him their escapades. He had spent time with people in the community and gained their trust. He showed an interest in the claim association and the land sale. They filled the long miles and dark nights confessing openly with braggadocio the full story with ample embellishments. These self-incriminating confessions filled out his personal observations in his report.

Browne found the lands the settlers bought at auction for $1.25 per acre actually had ranged in value between $40–$300 per acre, and that the average value of the whole tract was more than $80 per acre. "St. Croix" estimated that tillable acreage was worth $150 per acre. Establishing these values, for Browne, demonstrated the existence of a combination because he found a flourish of sales took place on the black market just before the auction. This black market selling in advance of the auction matched what one would expect to see in places like Minnesota where land speculation was rife. That's because prices tended to skyrocket after the land gained a legal title, sometimes as much as doubling in an important year like 1849. These sales among the locals before the auction were at such high prices that they upended assertions that outside speculators threatened to outbid the "cash-poor" locals.[42]

What Combs and company told Browne on the stagecoach confirmed what he had seen. Local speculators had built the dozens of claim shanties that couldn't pass as primary houses well before the sale on "pretended claims." In his report, which was reprinted in the newspapers, Browne listed several people who were involved, noting their residences and businesses in the town of St. Paul. They weren't living on the Reserve and working the soil, the prerequisite to establishing a claim (if preeminent claims had been valid). They were merchants, lawyers, editors, dentists, booksellers, and real estate agents. He identified the "principal purchaser" as William R. Marshall, a merchant and future governor, who called the bids into the recording. Also on his list was Henry M. Rice.[43]

Even before Browne heard the stories on the stagecoach, he had concluded that a combination was active. If these buyers were unaware of any combination, why would they pay a high price on the black market with the knowledge that a) their "purchase" was at risk because they were not able to legally record it and gain title, and b) they knew the land sale was coming and they could bid on property starting at $1.25 per acre. All a buyer had to do, if he were a free and unencumbered agent, was outbid the others at the government sale. Why didn't they do this? Because they knew, Browne concluded, a claim association existed, and it would protect their claim. The claim association kept all the sales among the locals and at the lowest price.

Browne read between the lines of the government land agents' earlier report. In their retraction of their statement regarding the presence of a combination, they wrote the sale was conducted with "the utmost harmony." Browne viewed it as a coded message of sorts. According to numerous witnesses, the combination had the means in place—many well-armed men—ready to stifle any outside bidding. Instead, he said, without an intimidating combination "there would doubtless have been less harmony." Conflicting interests and heightened speculation at an auction usually produce "several breaches of the peace, under a system of free competition." Not to mention that the prices would have been much higher, or at the very least not uniform.[44]

This "harmony" was not a situation of being neighborly, Browne understood, but rather that most of the speculators were connected, either politically or financially, with claim associations. He couldn't believe the people would refrain from bidding on a parcel due to "motives of personal friendship." That restraint would impugn their ability as businessmen, and it didn't match "the known reputation of land speculators throughout Minnesota." One could only stretch the honor of neighborliness so far.[45]

Browne knew of other claim associations in Minnesota: Dakota County (Kaposia), the Military Reserve, Brownsville District (Lake Pepin), Calhoun, Mendota, and Hennepin County. Several of these claim associations announced their meetings and published their constitutions and bylaws in the newspapers. On trees and in public places he saw the notices of these claim associations, announcing the time and place of their meetings.[46]

"[A] strong prejudice" existed, wrote Browne, "in favor of original settlers and claimants." Yet they believed they were "perfectly justified in protecting their claims" and contended the government had no claim "in justice or equity" beyond the minimum price. It was a form of squatter sovereignty, where the citizens felt they owed nothing to their government and they had the right to take the land extralegally.[47]

If the sales were confirmed by the government, Browne estimated that the people of the United States would be defrauded by the citizens of St. Paul to the tune of $300,000 ($11 million today).[48]

O Pioneers!

Browne saw something else, an ironic twist on the myths of the frontier. He highlighted the rhetoric of the politicians who constantly spoke of "the hardy pioneers of the West," which was "calculated to mislead the public mind." Those who qualified as hardy pioneers didn't benefit from "the enhanced values," he wrote. Rather, in this case, "it is the unscrupulous speculators," he wrote, "the non-productive members of the community—who derive the advantage." Those people "have the capital and means of combination and wield the political power which enables them to represent their interests in Congress and to legalize by special enactments all violations of law in which they have a pecuniary interest."

Browne didn't pull any of his punches. His clear-eyed report is an unrecognized gem for its analysis of the claim associations' operations. In the end, Browne called for an investigation regarding the settlement and sale of the Reserve lands, recommending that the government suspend pending sales until an official report along with testimony could be produced.[49]

In an extraordinary moment, Browne was undeterred. He named names and outed people to the federal authorities. While people were happy to talk with him before they knew his assignment, when they read their names in his report in the local newspapers it became imperative that they deny his allegations or at least counter them. Along with others named in the report, Gorman pushed back on the accusations as "wholly without foundation." Though he had met Browne, he denied any consultation with Browne, "nor did he mention [the land sale] in my presence to my recollection," the governor claimed. The editor of the *Minnesotian*, a Rice organ, doubted Gorman's account. Gorman was the primary suspect for having given details to Browne.[50]

Further, the *Minnesotian* editor felt the report was a political hit job as it mainly focused its attack on the Rice faction. "It is passing strange" how Browne, "an entire stranger to our contorted, twisted-up kind of politics," could obtain the information for the report. "*Who* crammed Browne?" he asked. As he called out for the traitor to be exposed, he intoned with patriotic zeal that the investigation "violated the laws of honor amongst western people." The locals had trusted Browne and extended to him "the rites of hospitality at our own fireside and elsewhere, took him for a gentleman," but they "were most grossly deceived."[51]

The editor hit his stride in the morning edition of April 26, 1855, in an editorial, "The Secret Spy." Browne "worm[ed] himself up to the hospitable boards of our citizens, and while partaking of their 'sacred bread and salt,' meditating how best to rob them of their property—hesitating not for this end to garble private conversations, to snap up unconsidered words, to lay traps to catch the unwary and unthinking, to cog and cozzen around, to flatter and 'smile, and smile, and be a villain still.'" The comments devolved into an ad hominem attack.[52]

The newspaper was offended that the government was checking up on the Minnesota residents and looking into their "private business concerns." Now they understood Browne's midwinter visit for what it was. They had no objection to the government using "secret agents" to check on employees, but to spy on the people was "a violation of social propriety," they said. Browne had crossed the line when he investigated the people "in the secret, hidden sneaking, dirty manner." They figured he would not be back to visit St. Paul any time soon, and all for the better, in their minds, as "it would be rather *unhealthy* for him to land here at this time, or even at any time hereafter."[53]

Most everyone tried to save face by qualifying their comments and justifying their words as cited by Browne. But Rice doubled down and took it to the next level. He addressed his letter to the interior secretary, and he wasn't light on his accusation that the report was target practice. He asserted its primary purpose was "to assault the character and injure the reputation of certain citizens of Minnesota," specifically himself. Rice publicly proclaimed in his letter, which was reprinted in Minnesota, that Browne was an "infamous liar."[54]

Rice's letter was acerbic. He recounted the charges, took umbrage that his name was mentioned, and said he wasn't at the sale. He denied there was a combination (though he was the first president) and contended there were only twenty-three people attending the sale. He sarcastically derided a couple of claims in the report. For example, if there were clubs on the ground and if they violated the federal law, he said, then they should have been reported to the correct agency, in this case the timber agent. He cited Browne's claim that of those he spoke with "none denied that there was a combination." Talk to them about other subjects, suggested Rice, and if "they did not deem it important to deny" does that confirm your accusation? In this case he took Browne's writing out of context in order to disparage it. The letter offered a defensive and spiteful retort to nearly every line of Browne's report.[55]

Rice used bluster as a deliberate tactic. With bombast, overstatement, and deflection, he hoped to throw up a smoke screen so that the legal points of preemption and inherent land values could be left unmentioned. He pontificated on the meaning of honor. "The settlers themselves" gave the land value "by the introduction of industry, capital, and civilization into that new and distant region," he said. "But a sense of *honor* prevented any but the rightful claimants from bidding. There is a bond stronger than any law, which makes honest men respect the rights of their neighbors, and I am glad that that bond is so universally respected throughout Minnesota."[56]

Browne preempted Rice when he spelled out the myth of the "local" propaganda in his report. A government report is an odd place to discuss the language of politicians. But Browne had good reason: He knew that the primary defense of the sale would be conveyed in the claimants' argot.

Rice concluded by saying the landowners were being inconvenienced and it was time to settle this issue so people could get on with their lives. He urged Secretary McClelland to lift the suspension on the auction sales. The letter, aside from putting his words in the public record, was mostly a performance for his fellow claim association members. Rice was well known in the Pierce administration. Within a couple days, he walked over to the Department of Interior and demanded of McClelland: "I want the patents on those lands issued at once, and it is going to be done. I do not say this to you as Secretary of the Interior, but I say it to you as a citizen and a gentleman." The patents or land titles were issued.[57]

Rice had been had, and he was furious. His first two years as a congressman were marred by scandal. Two days after he had written his rebuttal of Browne's report, he and Stephen A. Douglas met with the president in the White House. During an extended four-hour meeting they plotted their next moves. Rather than investigate the armed combination that had suppressed prices at Stillwater on September 11, 1854, they called into question Browne's report on Gorman.

Back in Minnesota, the impact of this sale on the settlement process of St. Paul and the area was a scattered development, contrary to how many new developments were advertised for sale. One of the selling points was the promise of density. Apparently the buyers wanted to live with other people and have a city's amenities. But the new developments on the old Reserve were speculative. The buyers did not live there. The land was not developed in response to demand or a need to live there. This speculative development process left the new developments, to a good degree, as open fields.

CHAPTER 5

The Birth of a Rivalry

The Minneapolis Land Office planned to auction off the northern part of the Fort Snelling Military Reserve, the area between the falls and the fort that lay west of the river and stretched to the chain of lakes. The auction on September 18 seemed destined to repeat the St. Paul affair the week before. Like the eastern part of the Reserve, the area in Minneapolis was entirely preemptively claimed. And likewise, no preemption claims would be honored. The same antics could be expected.[1]

The Minneapolis squatters, 125 of them, had organized the Equal Right and Impartial Protection Claim Association (later changed to Hennepin County Claim Association). Like other claim associations, they recorded claims, mitigated issues, and prepared to defend their claims. They were allied with the Military Reserve Claim Association and had worn red shirts at the auction the week before. The other claim associations would assist at this auction in kind. On the morning of the sale, several hundred people gathered at the land office to safeguard the claims against outside bidders and unexpected events.[2]

In the St. Paul auction, the outside speculators had been anonymous and possibly fictitious props to give the locals good reason for their combination. In the Minneapolis sale, however, these outside speculators gained faces. They came from the surrounding region, and several of them had arrived from the South. The river offered southerners a direct conduit to St. Paul from their plantations near Natchez, St. Louis, and other southern river cities. Young men came north for the money and were encouraged by the expansive effort of slaveholders after the recently passed Kansas–Nebraska Act.[3]

The southerners at the Minneapolis sale set their sights on the highly prized property on the west side of the falls, and they developed strategies to win the bidding. The Hennepin County Claim Association members made plans to shut out the southern speculators. They knew who these outside speculators were and that they lived in St. Paul. They visited the southerners in person and warned them that their presence as bidders would provoke a severe reaction. The conflict of local versus outside speculators from the South was the onset "of the unpleasantness between the two communities of St. Paul and Minneapolis," according to Isaac Atwater, publisher of the *St. Anthony Express* and later appointed to the Minnesota Supreme Court. The Twin Cities rivalry originated, in part, over the rising tide of state sovereignty and the emboldened South.[4]

The Minneapolis land sale and its fallout ran simultaneously as a scandal regarding a segment of land that stretched from Prescott, Wisconsin, north to Lake Superior. This parcel was targeted as a land grant for the Minnesota Northwestern Railroad (MNWR). Representative Henry M. Rice, along with several prominent southern politicians and eastern bankers who were behind the MNWR, identified that land as a key link to develop a transnational transportation hub. The southern influence on Minnesota political matters at the local and national level remains largely underappreciated today.

The mid-1850s was an expansive time for the proponents of slavery. In May 1854 President Franklin Pierce signed the Kansas–Nebraska Act, which allowed local voters to decide whether slavery should be legal in their territory. The concept was dubbed "popular sovereignty," and it was at odds with the Missouri Compromise of 1820, which had sought to contain slavery to the region below the latitude of that state's southern border. People in the Northwest, one writer noted, supported slavery to such a degree that a person had to be careful what they said against it. One local predicted that slaves would soon raise Minnesota crops. Governor Willis A. Gorman, a born southerner and Pierce's personal friend, "hated any one who sought to interfere with slavery or curtail in any degree its power," according to Thomas M. Newson, an editor of the *St. Paul Daily Times*, and so the Minnesota territorial administration "was strongly pro-slavery." Newson, who knew these men personally, described Secretary of the Territory Joseph Travis Rosser, a young Virginian, as "a lover of slavery and a hater of abolitionists." Rosser was an enslaver but had not brought any slaves west with him. The expansion of popular sovereignty and the slave-supporting democratic administration made Minnesota inviting for southern land speculators.[5]

St. Paul was a democratic town. The Democrats were one of two political parties of the early 1850s, along with the Whig Party. The parties were divided within themselves on different issues, and both parties had subsets of proslavery and antislavery members, based on their region, whether North or South. When the Whig Party declined sharply after its candidate was routed by Pierce in the 1852 presidential election, a significant number of that party joined the Democratic Party. An important issue for the western territories and states revolved around self-determination, which was at the heart of state or popular sovereignty. St. Paul Democrats were not necessarily proslavery, but because of the effort to retain their preemption claims their popular sovereignty aligned them with the Democratic Party. During this time, political alliances and priorities were seemingly in a constant state of flux. The Republican Party, which was founded in response to the Kansas–Nebraska Act of 1854, was born with abolition as a touchstone part of its policy. Organized in St. Paul in 1855, it tended to be associated with St. Anthony and Minneapolis.[6]

On the morning of the land auction, September 18, the people gathered at the Minneapolis District Land Office were ready for anything. But the land office remained closed. "Owing to some reason not accounted for," a newspaper reported, the land officers had "not yet received orders to open their office." After a couple days, the sale was suspended. The absence of orders is conspicuous considering the land sale east of the Mississippi a week earlier had an identical process. The suspended sale was a red flag, a possible sign of some malfeasance. Along with claim associations stifling an auction, people sometimes threatened the land officers, resulting in postponed sales. But there was something larger at work here.[7]

The Minneapolis District spanned the ceded land of the territory, from Lake Traverse (on today's western boundary) across to the Rum and Snake Rivers. It also included the Minneapolis part of the Reserve. The railroads knew it would be impossible to remove settlers who had preemption claims. On par with a taboo, no railroad "would dare put its foot on the soil of Minnesota, and dispossess an actual settler on a valid preemption claim," said the *Minnesotian*. They were right. The law prioritized the settler with a preemption claim over railroads. Yet the railroads were important to encouraging settlement of those areas. The land had to be settled in a specific order. To avoid any conflict, Congress withdrew specific lands from sale or claims and allowed the railroads to choose from unencumbered land.

In the case of the Minneapolis District, the government withdrew the outlying areas to give railroads the first choice. The sale would include only the Minneapolis land that was on the Reserve. The Hudson Land Office also withdrew the land between Prescott and Lake Superior. But squatters on the Minneapolis section of the Reserve felt threatened by the MNWR as they believed the arrangement would "give the *illegally* organized Wall Street Railroad Company an opportunity to secure the best lands," according to the *Minnesota Weekly Times*. They asked if the squatters could buy the land in the upcoming sale or if the railroad could buy their land. A delegation of local men went to Washington, DC, to lobby for an exception for preemption claims.[8]

At the center of this real estate and railroad cyclone was Henry M. Rice, the celebrated leader and consummate speculator. He was Mr. St. Paul. During the fight to become a territory, he traveled to Washington, DC, paying his own way, to promote the legislation that made St. Paul the capital. While Henry H. Sibley, as the territory's delegate, worked inside the halls of Congress, Rice lobbied from the outside, an invaluable contribution to gaining territorial status. He was admired as well for returning before the bill was passed and initiating the addition with John Irvine that spurred St. Paul Proper to expand beyond its original plat. Rice built hotels and warehouses and enticed others to invest their capital in St. Paul. A magnanimous benefactor, he gifted land to the city for parks and to the churches for buildings. He was an enthusiastic and persuasive man. "He moved between bursts of explosive energy and periods of depression often disguised as illness," wrote historian Rhoda Gilman. In 1853 Rice won the sole congressional seat for the territory, holding that position until 1857, a period of hypergrowth. He worked with others in Congress on grandiose speculations, often based on his own ideas. These projects had a double nature. They would benefit the state and regional economy, and they would enrich Rice and his colleagues.[9]

The Towns Grow

St. Paul and Minneapolis (including St. Anthony) were on different developmental timelines because the river was a political boundary in the acquisition of land. The Dakota land cession east of the river in 1837 happened fourteen years before the one west of the river in 1851. The slow rollout of the military land further delayed the settlement in the area. As St. Paul was east of the military Reserve it had a significant head start on development, beginning in 1840 and becoming well established by the end of the decade. With territorial status in 1849 came the multiplicity of additions and a land rush. The national attention from the Grand Excursion in 1854 spread the news of St. Paul's beauty and resources, which attracted more people and money.[10]

Risen from the bogs, St. Paul was now "one of the most beautiful locations on the Upper Mississippi," said the newspapers. As one approached by river, the view of the town on the bluff was "grand and imposing." The view "has an electric affect upon the voyager," said another newspaper, referring to the yellow bluffs. In a river known for its snags and sandbars, the river in front of the town was deep, allowing for easy steamboat arrivals and departures.[11]

The steamer *War Eagle* opened the navigation season on April 17, 1855, bringing 814 passengers. The high mark that year was seven boats in one day with 200–600 passengers each. In all, 553 boats landed at St. Paul that year, double the previous year's numbers. Newcomers filled the hotels and boardinghouses beyond capacity, and people camped in the streets. Stores and saloons, livery stables and stage lines, every business tried to stay ahead of customers' needs. Carpenters could not work fast enough. They built houses and buildings of all sorts, from shanties to five-story brick buildings. The city cut trees and removed brush, filled in hollows and built bridges, and, along with improvements to prominent streets, graded Third, Fourth, and Jackson Streets.[12]

St. Paul was the gateway of the Northwest. "It is obvious to the most casual observer," wrote an editor, that St. Paul must "supply the trade of all the vast regions" from Winnipeg, the Rocky Mountains, and the Great Lakes. Looking south, St. Paul occupied "a singularly fortunate position in a commercial point of view" because it stood "virtually at the head" of 2,000 miles of river navigation including the Ohio and Missouri Rivers. Viewed as an hourglass, St. Paul was at the narrows between the top and bottom. St. Paul was the point of distribution of the Indian trade, where the annual payments were made. In addition, the Red River cart fur traders sold furs only for "coin" (cash in the form of silver and gold coins) and spent their earnings immediately on goods, everything from groceries to clothing, tools to guns, farm implements to household goods. These events infused money into the system. Money flowed through just like the river. St. Paul was the head of navigation and a depot for the exchange of goods for the entire region.[13]

Yet as early as 1849 people also asked, "Won't the great town be at the Falls?" An editor posed this as a rhetorical question, and his reply reveals how the locals envisioned the future unfolding. "There will be a great town at the Falls, no doubt, but whether it will be *the* great town, is another question. The Falls will very soon be connected with St. Paul by a railroad." While that forecast was thirteen years premature, the editor revealed the idea of single city or interconnected metropolis.[14]

St. Anthony, in comparison, was rather isolated and needed improved access. By river, St. Anthony was sixteen miles above St. Paul, but the gorge presented navigational hazards. People from St. Anthony worked to clear the river gorge of obstructions and even proposed a canal be dug to connect the two towns. They worked to improve the land route, which was in terrible condition, as well. They proposed a plank road, which would be better than prairie dirt for heavier loads, especially in wet weather. But St. Anthony was having difficulty establishing itself as a mill city. Its engine of prosperity—waterpower—was "unavailable and neglected," according to the *Minnesota Weekly Times*. "A sort of 'family quarrel'" had broken out among the claimants, and it "seriously hinders the progress of the place." About two-thirds of the real estate there was tied up by lawsuits. No one could buy or sell titles to the land.[15]

Minneapolis was bursting with excitement and energy based on the potential of the falls. "The water power here is sufficient to turn all the spindles at Lowell, as much more as you please," wrote the correspondent visiting from Perrysburg, Ohio. The shores were "monopolized" by speculators. "In the course of time this will become a Rochester or a Lowell," predicted the *New York Herald*. Everything was promise and potential. The people fully intended Minneapolis to become the head of the navigable river; they wanted to be central to all things up and down the river. Steamboats were designed to navigate the larger river below St. Paul. A few steamer captains were trying to ascend the gorge, but as one of them put it, the boats "never can if they would and never would if they could" make the difficult trip up the gorge. In 1854 the resources of Minneapolis held exciting potential but not enough to supplant St. Paul's supremacy.[16]

Still, the potential alone attracted people. Dubbed "All Saints," a pun relating the idea that this city would absorb both St. Paul and St. Anthony, the town was named the county seat of the newly created Hennepin County by the territorial legislature in 1852. The county commissioners looked for another name. They debated between Lowell, a reference to the industrial powerhouse of Massachusetts, and Albion, an ancient name for Great Britain. They chose the latter, but the citizens overwhelmingly rejected it. Charles Hoag, the resident classical scholar, came up with the idea of combining the Dakota word *minneh* (or Mni, inspired by Minnehaha Falls) with the Greek suffix *-opolis*. An op-ed published by the *St. Anthony Express* on November 5 proposed Minnehapolis. The public received it well, and the name was accepted. Since the h was silent, they dropped it.[17]

Very soon, squatters had built a dozen houses and numerous claim shanties. In 1854 the land office reported that the population on the Reserve was swelling. The rolling prairie from the falls down to Fort Snelling, according to the Perrysburg correspondent, was mostly "enclosed and cultivated," populated with "[n]ew and neat framed houses." Within a few years, more than 3,000 people called it home. The town was working on placement of the public buildings or where the center should be of "that great city in embryo, Minneapolis." The community elected county commissioners, opened a school, and built churches, schools, a

Early settlement in Minneapolis during the 1850s

county court, a masonic lodge, sawmills, and a grist mill. Yet outsiders such as the Perrysburg correspondent viewed this activity as suspect. It was "altogether a squatter operation," he said, because although the land cession had occurred, the Minneapolis District was not yet open for settlement. These residents and businesses did not have title to the land.[18]

No matter: the settlers were compelled to move forward. Minneapolis and St. Anthony felt their connection was constrained by the ferry across the river. They conducted engineering surveys for a bridge to connect St. Anthony to the town growing on the opposite shore. Two years later, on January 23, 1855, they opened a wire suspension bridge and their common interest blossomed. All this development, yet it was still not possible to have title to the land in Minneapolis.[19]

St. Anthony Leaves Ramsey County

St. Anthony and St. Paul were already in a fraught relationship. In addition to the commercial competition of river navigation versus hydropower, the two towns were politically antagonistic. But they were stuck with each other. The Mississippi was a border between Ramsey and Hennepin Counties, placing St. Anthony with St. Paul in Ramsey County. As originally laid out, Ramsey County encompassed the area east of the Mississippi from St. Paul north to Lake Mille Lacs, which included the entirety of the Rum River and its valuable pineries.

Politically, St. Anthony was roughly half Democratic and half Whig, consisting substantially of lumber men from Maine. Their temperance movement was strong enough to restrict liquor sales and hours on groggeries. St. Paul, meanwhile, remained true to its western roots as a Democratic town, seeking in part to maintain a persuasive position with the US Senate that was dominated at that time by the southern Democrats. The temperance movement had less influence there.[20]

The Kansas–Nebraska Act heightened their differences. Now slavery could be imagined in the North. The act and its influence were hotly debated in the Minnesota Territory's 1855 midterm election. The repeal of the Missouri Compromise and passage of the act represented "continued aggressions of the Slave Power," according to the St. Paul *Minnesota Weekly Times*. The upcoming election was about freedom versus slavery. Across the nation, those opposed to slavery anxiously watched Minnesota to see in which direction it would go. Their worry was that the South would "extend the area of Slavery as best suit their ends." Overall, in Minnesota the proslavery and the "out-and-out abolitionists" camps were small and of equal size. Most people in Minnesota Territory were opposed to more slave states yet were unwilling to interfere with established slave states. Small as the abolitionist population might have been, its members were concentrated in St. Anthony.[21]

For these reasons St. Anthony began to seek ways of separating itself from Ramsey County. In March 1855, with a population of about 2,000 (roughly half the size of St. Paul), it incorporated as a city far earlier than its numbers warranted. Despite the citizens' abolitionist leanings, they did not grant African Americans suffrage in municipal elections. After previously introducing separatist legislation, both branches of the territorial legislature passed an act in late February 1855, titled "County of St. Anthony," carving the county out from Ramsey and making St. Anthony the county seat.[22]

The legislators attached the bill as a supplement to a popular measure that was more likely to pass, that being the incorporation of the Minnesota Historical Society. But the bill tried to do too much. In addition to a St. Anthony County, the legislation would have created a second county, Pine County, containing the Rum River and its stands of pine trees. The separate county would be controlled by the property owners who were nonresident investors from the East Coast. They had a commercial interest with little municipal incentive. By skipping any municipal development the owners could save $5,000–$6,000 in taxes. Such a loss of revenue would be a blow to Ramsey County and St. Paul. In addition to avoiding taxes that were needed in St. Paul, St. Anthony was trying to escape paying a share of Ramsey County's debt of about $20,000. The legislation threatened Ramsey County's existence. Governor Gorman couldn't sign it.[23]

Gorman "pocketed" the bill, allowing the legislature to adjourn on March 3 without signing it into law. St. Anthony citizens were incensed, and during a grievance meeting "ripped" him "clear over Jordan." They wrote resolutions that leveled heinous accusations. His action was "a blow aimed in a cowardly manner at the prosperity and progress of St. Anthony and the northern part of Ramsey County"; he possessed "a most tyrannical, selfish and revengeful nature, showing a total disregard of the wishes

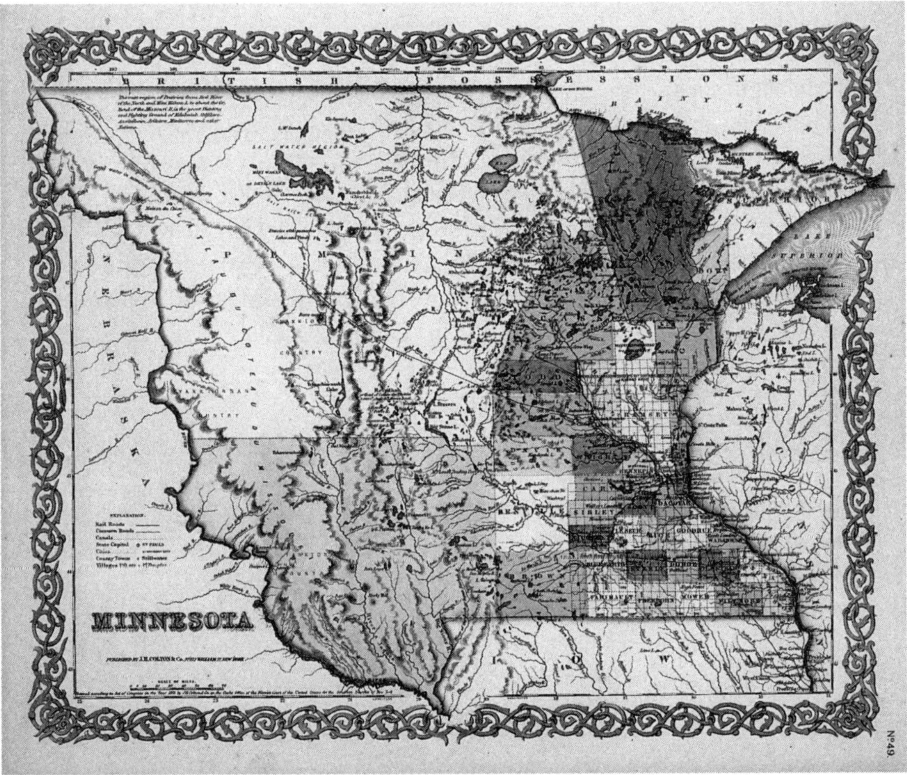

In the territorial period Ramsey County extended along the Rum River to Lake Mille Lacs. Originally Ramsey County ran north along the east side of the Mississippi River. By 1856 it had been whittled down, yet the county retained the important corridor of the Rum River, one of the main routes for transporting logs to the sawmills at St. Anthony Falls.

of the people"; and he had been "in numerous street brawls, personal encounters, and other disreputable acts," leading to court appearances. "He is totally unfit" to serve as governor, his critics said.[24]

The scenario of a St. Anthony County with St. Anthony as the county seat would have altered the course of development dramatically, according to John H. Stevens, commonly considered the first settler in Minneapolis, who hosted almost all public meetings in his house. "With two county seats at the Falls," said Stevens, "the prosperity would have been increased, but it is doubtful if there would have been a matrimonial alliance between the two cities."[25]

In the next legislative session, the separatists of St. Anthony took a different tack. They introduced legislation that would annex St. Anthony and a small portion of Ramsey County to Hennepin County. Again, the legislation would cost St. Paul in tax revenue, so they needed leverage to get Gorman's assent. They focused most of the legislation on Hennepin County's need for county buildings. The final segment of the bill extended the Hennepin County line across the river to embrace St. Anthony. The bridge across the river brought the county seat, Minneapolis, and its offices and courthouse within a few minutes' walk of St. Anthony. Even at that early date, they foresaw that the two towns might eventually consolidate. Gorman was unable to avoid this proposal because it solved a larger problem of the new Hennepin County's government buildings. St. Anthony left Ramsey County in 1856, conferring the tax burden largely onto St. Paul. It was another episode in the young rivalry between St. Paul and the towns at the falls.[26]

The Geographic Center

Minneapolis and St. Anthony were compatible because they shared the falls. There wasn't anything natural at hand to bridge the differences between them and St. Paul. Faster transportation and a big-picture perspective offered those possibilities.

In the mid-1850s the nation was in its first wave of railroad construction. Railroads reached key points, such as the Great Lakes and the Mississippi River. Minnesota was desperate for railroads. Settlers lamented the isolation of the long winters. "We are as good as out of the world five months of the year," said the editor of the *Weekly Minnesotian*. We "might as well be living in Siberia or the interior of Africa for all the practical advantages of heavy commerce, had we any produce to sell this day." The steamboat had opened up the region, allowing for two-way transportation of provisions, crops, and people. But the river was impassable after freezing, and from then until spring residents could go weeks or months without mail or resupply.

Though Minnesota had become a territory only in 1849, and prematurely at that, its residents saw railroads as a lifeline. "We must have an *outlet, and an outlet by railroad*," declared the *Weekly Minnesotian* in February 1854, "and that as speedily as possible, or we are nowhere." They were downright impatient: "Railroads first—railroads soon—are wanted and must be had." It was more than just midwinter communications, resupply, and escapes. Wheat prices, for example, were typically higher in the winter and early spring, and a railroad would allow the businesses to take advantage of that seasonality. While the steamboat had overcome the transportation hurdles in the northern landscape, the railroad would overcome its seasons and the weather.[27]

But the vision was grander than simply year-round travel and access to seasonal markets. At the time, people commonly felt the expansive nation was destined to spread across the continent. California and Oregon had secured the continent's western coast, and the war against Mexico captured Texas and the southwest region. With the new geographic outlines of the country coming into view, Minnesotans viewed themselves as its center. It was easy in the 1850s to see that the railroad would tie the continent together. In their estimation, Minnesota was destined to be the crossroads.

At the heart of this idea was the Mississippi River as a natural transportation corridor that could be amplified if it was connected to Lake Superior. The state version of Manifest Destiny appeared in the annual report of the Bureau of Statistics under a subhead, "Minnesota, The Centre of This Inland Civilization." London had been "the capital of maritime civilization." But the maritime age was past, and the inland region would replace it, the report reasoned. The natural place for the "inland civilization" to rise was in the center along the longitudinal line of the Mississippi, creating a "completed circle of continental development." The trunk line of interior transit, on land and water, was located along the hydrographical and geographical center of the continent, midway between the Atlantic and the Pacific Oceans and from Hudson's Bay and the Gulf of Mexico.

Further, Minnesota was in the middle of the temperate zone. It held so many positive attributes and it was at the center "of all the concentric circles of production and commercial movement—upon land and ocean," the report said. It was "the predestined throne of this great American Empire, which advances to the supremacy of the world." Minnesota was the center of North America and from there could rule the world. The first step was one continuous railroad line from Lake Superior to New Orleans, via St. Anthony and St. Paul.[28]

This enormous task—the responsibility of this worldly role—would resolve the rising rivalry between St. Paul and St. Anthony, giving them "a common and united interest," claimed one writer (initials J. W. N.). When completed, a great metropolis would rise between them and "the sister cities" would be the upper and lower towns. They would be "conjoined" as the heart of the Northwest terminus, and because of its central location on the continent the future city would surpass St. Louis and New Orleans. Minnesota's "brilliant destiny" was before them, and "no grander scheme was ever projected"; it was not only "possible" but "practicable" and "inevitable."[29]

The MNWR Scheme

Seeing Minnesota as the center of the nation and North America (if not the world) allowed for brave endeavors. The process for getting a railroad included state and federal government along with outside money. First, the state would incorporate a railroad company, which defined the general route of that line. Then the state and railroad company would apply to Congress for a land grant. The vision of Minnesota as the great central hub was hampered by the fact that land grants were a relatively new idea that had not yet been approved for a territory, which tended not to have the same boundaries as the subsequent state design. To make any type of railroad network happen, especially at such a young stage in the territory's development, the territory needed a good strategy and some luck.

Alexander Ramsey, the territory's first governor, mentioned railroads in his final address to Minnesota's residents in January 1853. He focused on the small link, only 100 miles of track that would connect St. Paul and Lake Superior. "Already roads are in contemplation which will unite Minnesota to the tide waters of the Atlantic and the Gulf, bringing the best market to the door" of producers and farmers throughout the year. James Goodhue of the *Minnesota Pioneer* had been proposing this connection since the territory's beginning, but now it became an official government task.[30]

The Minnesota Territorial Legislature responded to the governor's message in the first week of March 1853 by chartering four railroads. It was a bold move just four years after gaining territorial status. Railroads served as a primary infrastructure to initiate settlement, but Minnesota had a very small population to support so many railroads. The railroad companies the residents chartered illustrate the idea: a railroad in each of the cardinal directions, connecting them to networks in the east and south and connecting those networks to the Pacific Ocean and Lake Superior. The aim was to make Lake Superior a mid-continent transportation hub. The charters prescribed the railroad lines. In Congress Rice began the official process of the Minnesota Land Grant bill late in 1853 and early in 1854. The Senate passed the bill quickly in early February.

Then, as the US House debated the Minnesota Land Grant for these railroads, the Minnesota Territorial Legislature changed direction and chartered a new railroad company, the Minnesota and Northwestern Railroad Company (MNWR). The new charter repealed the previous incorporations. Advocates in the legislature pushed a new plan. They laid out this railroad to run from Lake Superior along the St. Croix River corridor, through St. Paul, and on to the Iowa border. The connection between the western end of Lake Superior and St. Paul was the priority.[31]

Rice was attuned to the possibilities of this route. Before coming to Minnesota, he had worked on the Sault Ste. Marie lock and canal connecting Lake Superior to Lakes Michigan and Huron, and that transportation breakthrough would soon be completed. The Great Lakes network was already expansive, featuring an East Coast connection and westward emigration as far as Chicago. The plan prioritized establishing a connection with a northern route for these reasons. After all, the western end of Lake Superior was a similar distance from New York as their competition, Chicago.[32]

Rice approached Robert J. Walker, former secretary of the treasury under President James Polk, who was known to be "a speculator in many lines—southern plantations, slaves, wild lands, and railroads." Walker liked the idea of the MNWR, and he brought in the banker William W. Corcoran of the Corcoran & Riggs banking firm that financed the war against Mexico. They joined Rice. The organizers offered twelve people shares in the company, including some early squatters, such as D. A. J. Baker. The rest of the shares were sold to Washington people of influence, such as Representative John C. Breckinridge (Kentucky), Senator Robert Hunter (Virginia), and Senator Stephen A. Douglas (Illinois). Rice worked with these men in platting a city at the point of transition from water to land on the western tip of Lake Superior. They called the town Superior (sometimes also Superior City), and they envisioned it as a harbor town and railroad terminus.[33]

On the face of it, Superior was a typical paper town of the time. The town plat presented a well-organized plan with finished streets and 12,000 lots. It was advertised in a newspaper as "the most flourishing new town in the west," with a store, "a commodious pier," and a large hotel. In reality, the town had about forty houses and several shanties, six families and a hundred transient speculators who resided in an unfinished, open-air hotel. Much of the town plat was still overgrown with shrubby willow. Nothing substantial existed in the town in 1854. Attaching Superior to the company's plan as the railroad terminus that would connect Lake Superior to St. Paul spurred its growth. The scheme was the means. And despite being very remote by land, the town prospered. The lots sold rapidly, and the best were flipped many times.[34]

The territorial legislature (consisting of twenty-seven representatives at that time) fought over every word in the MNWR incorporation bill. Members eventually passed it on March 4, the final day of the session. As the session came to a close, the bill idled on the governor's desk. The final hour came with no activating signature. Gorman had vetoed a previous version of the bill because it gave the railroad extraordinary powers and privileges. Without his approval, the entire scheme would fail. Gorman's signature was the missing link to getting the railroad that would connect Superior to St. Paul and the Gulf of Mexico.

Gorman was listed as an incorporator of the MNWR, meaning he would play a part in the operation and benefit from the railroad, which makes his hesitation to sign interesting. With five minutes to go before the session expired, Gorman surprised many people when he signed the charter into law. Later, he claimed he did not understand the entire bill and pinned the blame on its supporters. The proponents now had all the pieces in place. They waited "in immediate anticipation" of the land grant Rice was ushering through Congress.[35]

Only a few states—Iowa, Wisconsin, Illinois—had received such land grants, which were a swath of land with a checkerboard of sections that were alternately owned by the railroad company. In fact, the MNWR resembled the original Central Illinois Railroad (Great Western Railway) land grant that would transfer the land to a private company and the private speculators. Douglas, now a senator of Illinois, likely recognized the MNWR as the handiwork of Robert Schuyler, the Railroad King of New York, who had pioneered the idea of railroad land grants and written the original Central Illinois legislation. Schuyler was recycling that plan, and the MNWR bore an exact likeness, including having a terminus town at the end of the line. Douglas had successfully stymied Schuyler in the original Illinois land grant, yet he supported Minnesota's modified bill that gave the land to the company.[36]

Congress generally supported the land grant idea as other states wanted similar treatment. However, as representatives deliberated the land grant for Minnesota, they couldn't get past the sudden change of plans there, with the creation of the MNWR and the exclusive language that gave *the company* the land. Throughout the spring of 1854, this version of the Minnesota Land Grant bill met general opposition in Congress. It was repeatedly sidelined by procedural delays—referred to committees, overloaded with amendments—and made no headway. To break the stalemate and save the land grant, Sibley, though not in Congress, rewrote the bill in such a way that blocked any existing company from access to the land grant. This effectively denied MNWR the land grant and gave the Minnesota Territorial Legislature the duty of selecting a railroad company in its next session. The rewritten bill passed with a large majority on June 28, and President Franklin Pierce signed it on June 29.[37]

Few people saw the required public announcement the next day, June 30, in the New York *Express* for the organization of the MNWR. According to its charter, the organizational meeting had to happen by July 1. Time was of the essence. Members met at the Bank of the Republic in New York City at 10:00 A.M. on July 1 and elected a board of directors and accepted the charter. Of fourteen founders of the MNWR the most likely candidates were those who were in New York City, but the president of the MNWR, Robert Schuyler, was probably not there. He had left a foreboding note to his board of directors on his desk and left town.[38]

Considering the bill that passed, which Sibley wrote to exclude all previously chartered corporate bodies—intentionally the MNWR—from the land grant, the organizational meeting was incongruent. It would have struck people as odd when the *Minnesotian* announced that Rice was happy with the new land grant. They soon learned why: The new law still granted the land to MNWR. The supporters of the rewritten law were stumped as to how the MNWR appropriated the granted lands via a bill that was written precisely to prevent it from doing so.[39]

Now Rice and company had all the pieces in place. They had the railroad company, they had the land grant, and they had the harbor city platted as the railroad terminal. On July 4, 1854, Rice wrote to Ramsey, who was on the MNWR board: "Now in Confidence if you can buy a few lots in 'Superior' you had better do it, I had to sell all of my interest for influence." Minnesota's delegate to Congress was telling the former governor to buy land in Superior because they had got the land deal. Rice was clearly involved with the intricacies of the plan.[40]

Within a week their carefully laid plans fell apart. Schuyler had probably missed the MNWR organization meeting of July 1 because that day his scandal broke. Schuyler wrote a simple note to his board of directors admitting that the company's accounts had problems. The magnitude of Schuyler's fraud was still unknown, but it was soon revealed that he had fraudulently issued extra stock in his companies to the tune of $1.8 million. He fled the country and ended up in Italy. He died the next year, presumably by suicide.

The next week Joseph Rosser, the secretary of the Minnesota territory, arrived in DC. He conducted the normal legislative due diligence, comparing the original bill to the engrossed bill (as it passed). He soon uncovered how it was that the MNWR could be going forward with its plans. The bill had been altered. The word "future" was omitted and another word, "or," was replaced by "and." The bill was handwritten by the chief clerk of the House, John W. Forney. The absence of the word "future" would fall on him. The second alteration featured a different penmanship, so someone else swapped the conjunction. These seemingly minor edits weren't typos—they changed the bill's meaning. Someone had removed the time clause, which reverted the bill back to the original intent so MNWR could legitimately lay claim to the land grant.

Here is the language of the bill as originally written with the alterations highlighted: "And be it further enacted. That the said lands hereby granted to the said Territory shall be subject to the disposal of any *future* legislature thereof for the purpose of aforesaid, and no other; nor shall they inure to the benefit of any company heretofore constituted *or* organized."[41]

With the small change in the bill's language, the MNWR moved ahead. The organizers thought that opposition to the new law would disappear once the land grant passed Congress and the promise of a railroad was near at hand. That's not what happened. When the alterations were discovered, confusion reigned. On July 24, tempers were unleashed in the House, which formed a select committee to investigate; it began work that same day. During eight sessions, in which members interviewed witnesses, they ran into a brick wall. Witnesses gave responses that ranged from vague to evasive: They claimed ignorance or said they could not remember details. A MNWR official refused to divulge names of his associates in Congress.[42]

A key testimony presented the whole affair as an accident. Representative Hester Stevens of Michigan openly admitted to having orchestrated the alteration. He sat on the committee that brought the bill to the House for a vote. According to him, he was approached by a person who suggested the changes. (A later investigation would show these changes were requested by a director on the MNWR board, George W. Billings.) The congressman saw nothing significant in the changes and so made them. He thought the edits had been discussed in committee to reflect the changes. After the bill passed the House, he noticed the changes had not been made in the passed bill. He engaged the staff responsible for such changes, and it was decided they should take it to the chief clerk of the House, Forney, who decided the change "had better be made." The president then signed a bill that had been coyly edited to allow exactly the opposite of what the House had intended. The investigation concluded, however, that the omission and alteration were a "deliberate and intended error," and the entire process had been choreographed in advance.[43]

The scheme involved a broad scope of politicians and elite civilians, from the US president to the Minnesota governor, from top financiers in Washington and New York to members of Congress. Key people were in the right positions. Forney, who allowed the altered document to stand as presented to him, was one of the shareholders in the Superior speculation. Shares were valued from $160,000 to $222,000. The value of the Superior land depended on the MNWR's success, so Forney had a self-serving reason to allow the alterations to stand.[44]

Despite the anger generated both in Minnesota and Washington, MNWR and its allies contained the fallout because they had enough people in the right positions of power to steer the investigation into a dead end and reduce any punishment. John C. Breckinridge, an owner in Superior, led the select committee in its investigation of the altered law. The majority report exonerated all persons from willful fraud and, though it blamed Forney, he received no punishment. The minority report asked for more time to continue the investigation, but it was not granted.[45]

The Minnesota land grant alteration scandal flummoxed Congress. Most viewed it "as such a flagrant attack upon the purity of national legislation that it deserved the most marked rebuke," said Gorman in his annual Governor's Message of 1853. The House passed a bill to repeal the land grant, but in the Senate one senator objected, stopping it. Douglas (of Illinois, but also of Superior) tried to save the land grant by reintroducing it with the original language. His involvement is suspicious because he didn't protest the land grant as initially introduced by Rice, yet he surely would have recognized it as he had battled Schuyler over similar legislation for control of the Central Illinois Railroad. Now he was trying to rescue a similar land grant. If the law stayed on the books in any form, the MNWR would be able to challenge the land dispersal in court. Finally, a senator attached the repeal language to a bill that was before the Senate. With its passage and the repeal of the MNWR land grant, Congress relieved itself of the Minnesota scandal. The territory lost all favor.[46]

The political fallout was such that in 1855 Rice stood on the floor of the US House of Representatives and introduced legislation to make the MNWR "null and void." He "did not wish to have it appear that Congress has legislated for one company in the Territory and against another," he said. Eating crow on the public record was the only penalty Rice paid for the Superior scandal and the land grant fraud. Nonetheless, even without Schuyler and with the eventual repeal of the law, the MNWR challenged its right to the land in a court case that went to the US Supreme Court. MNWR lost.[47]

The scandal of the altered Minnesota Land Grant bill, which occurred largely in the summer of 1854, puts Browne's April 1855 report in a very different light. Browne's report surprised Pierce and the Superior group because it exonerated Gorman of any wrongdoing in regard to Indian Affairs or other charges. But Pierce had already moved forward with the plan to replace him. Newspapers announced, erroneously, that Breckinridge would be the governor of Minnesota.[48]

Rice and Douglas persuaded Pierce that Browne had been lenient on Gorman. In June 1855 Pierce sent Sidney Webster, his personal secretary, with Forney and others to Minnesota to reassess Gorman. Their route was via Detroit through to Superior, which suggests they had additional tasks. Webster, however, confirmed Browne's favorable assessment of Gorman, and he remained in office. The gubernatorial substitution would not have saved the MNWR or Superior, but Breckinridge would have been a dependable ally of the Rice faction. After that, the "Superior group" was not on friendly terms with the president. The apparition of Superior would dissipate with the fall of the House of Schuyler and the MNRW bill alteration scandal.[49]

As for Rice's cohorts in the Superior scheme, the southern politicians and investors engaged freely in northern speculation without any concern and little interference regarding their southern politics. The speculative investments promised greater and faster returns than they could find in the South. These "agents" of "the peculiar institution" of slavery were "quietly" buying large parcels of real estate in the free states and territories, and from that "securing princely fortunes," wrote the *Chicago Times*. They were the top planters in their home states, yet people noticed these men were not investing similarly in any of the slaveholding states. They were proud, "bawling themselves hoarse in their advocacy" of slavery "while laboring with unceasing effort to strengthen its power and extend it over new fields." They invested in large speculations that, along with significant profits, would have given them greater power in the burgeoning territory. Minnesota Territory was on the cusp of having a slave-owning congressman in the governor's office. And the Yankee bankers, railroaders, and some politicians joined them. Rice catered to these investors. He proposed, for example, another location for Superior—

inside of Minnesota—but they didn't like that because there was talk of a separate territory to the north. Rice designed the speculation according to his investors' interests.[50]

From the land auction at the Minneapolis Land Office to Superior and the land grant legislation in Congress, southerners were exploring Minnesota investments at a time when they were extending their influence over the nation. The Missouri Compromise of 1820 limited slave states at Missouri's southern border. The Kansas–Nebraska Act of 1854 allowed territories to make their own decision regarding slavery. The US Supreme Court's *Dred Scott* decision was a continuation of that trend in which southerners boldly asserted their expanding influence. With the Dred Scott decision in 1857, enslaving people became legal in the Minnesota Territory. Upon gaining statehood the next year, Minnesota wrote its constitution and outlawed slavery.[51]

The Fallout of the Scandal

Meanwhile, Minneapolis was growing even while it was stuck in a legal limbo, held up first by the military Reserve and then by the MNWR scandal. The different levels of government had moved forward in the legal processes of creating a county, designating a county seat, and incorporating a city, even though the citizens had no legal title to the land.

Minneapolis was being held back. The "postponement of sale is an injury to the settlers and to the Territory," editors opined. Minneapolis had been sidelined as suspected by giving the MNWR a priority on the most select lands. They took "advantage of the power they possessed over settlers on the Military Reserve and elsewhere," concluded the *Minnesota Weekly Times*.[52]

Observers could see the scandal's impact. "The fatal effects" of the MNWR scandal would set Minnesota back "one year, if not longer." Some wondered if the scandal would "delay the completion of the road four or five years," with every year compounding "the loss of thousands upon thousands of dollars." While this manipulation was holding Minneapolis back, it gave St. Paul more time to develop its trade advantages. "The thousands of dollars in gold which would have gone out of the Territory" for land purchases would "be retained here for the coming winter's business." St. Paul businesses would gain "thousands of dollars by this postponement," all the better to become more established and better weather the future "when the drain of coin for the purchase of lands does come."[53]

The land grabbers concocted a way to claim "the magnificent domain" but, by their overreach, "brought upon their own heads the catastrophe," concluded the *Minnesota Weekly Times*. Worse, their actions suppressed the entire territory. Minnesota had been on the fast track to be the first territory to receive a railroad land grant, a promising boost to increase settlement. The territory started fresh the next year in 1855 and chartered more than twenty railroads. But the territory had missed the first wave of railroad construction. By 1860 Minnesota still did not have one mile of railroad. Instead of getting a jump start as a young territory on the development of much-needed transportation infrastructure, the state lagged, and the first train engine wouldn't run until 1862, from St. Paul to St. Anthony.[54]

Minnesota joined a post–Civil War railroad construction boom that connected it to Chicago and brought the first trans-state lines. The Lake Superior and Mississippi line would begin running trains from St. Paul to Duluth in 1870, a full fifteen years after the MNWR scandal. The Chicago, Milwaukee, and St. Paul (Short Line) connected St. Paul and Minneapolis in 1880. A commuter line, it led to the development of the Midway and subdivisions like Merriam Park. Had the rail lines been expanded sooner, had the cities been connected sooner in their development, some other growth pattern likely would have evolved.[55]

The Minneapolis settlers petitioned Congress to allow normal preemption land claims inside the Reserve where the president had previously disallowed them. The territorial legislature sent a memo to the US Congress on February 2, 1854, saying "the pioneers who had made the wilderness bloom as the rose" should not be "exposed to the merciless cupidity of avaricious speculators." Rice worked with Commissioner John Wilson of the General Land Office to introduce a bill that honored preemption claims for the Minneapolis District; it passed in January 1855, within a month of the bridge opening.

Unfortunately for the "avaricious speculators," there would be no auction for the land on the Minneapolis section. The southerners lost out if they did not have a claim. Several of them stayed in the state and became prominent real estate promoters. The government sold 19,733.87 acres for $24,668.37, less the costs of survey and sale.

Some people were able to overlook the ways in which Rice's actions stunted development. Others, no doubt partisan, did not let Rice escape blame. "We subsequently charged H. M. Rice, our delegate, with being implicated or indifferent to the interests of our Territory. When the proceedings of the Investigating Committee were made known, his own evidence condemned him."[56]

In Rice's letter of April 28, 1855, in which he attacked Browne, he was disingenuous, if not two-faced. He repeatedly spoke of the locals as heroic, arguing they should be left unmolested by outside speculators. All the while, he operated in the background with a group of southern Democrats and Wall Street bankers, aiming to corner the market for a railroad connecting St. Paul and Lake Superior. The pioneer myth that Browne called out and Rice defended was used as cover by Rice to do the exact opposite. He was playing both sides. Despite the fraud, a majority of Minnesotans overlooked the transgressions of their politicians as long as the overall benefit served them as well. Such self enrichment projects would have benefited the values for the "local" speculator. And the "locals" might have seen Rice as fighting for them, as they believed the pioneer myth.[57]

In the end, the affair tainted the credit of the territory and delayed its ability to build at even a moderate pace.

CHAPTER 6

The Steele Swindle

In the summer of 1857 St. Paul was the fastest-growing town on the Mississippi River. The streets pulsed with the rush of a busy life. The town was expanding rapidly. Workmen labored day and night to keep up with the demand for new dwellings and stores. Another small army was engaged in grading streets and laying gas pipes, and the air was continually shaken with the concussion of blasting rock.

Sixteen to eighteen steamboats could be seen at St. Paul's landing at one time. And they brought hundreds of passengers on each trip. Immigration rose steadily through 1853 and 1854, then exploded with growth as astonishing numbers of immigrants poured in. By 1857 the territorial population had nearly tripled from 53,000 to 150,000. Most new arrivals to Minnesota remained near the head of navigation and the falls.[1]

These throngs of new residents were not coming to Minnesota for cheap, abundant natural resources, such as gold or silver. Minnesota's magnetic draw was land, the promise of property at a low price. The expansion of the nation and the certainty of a "Manifest Destiny" were underwritten by easy credit and a lot of land. The land was the vehicle for speculation, and the land boom was nationwide. People made such quick profits they were said to have "coined money." In this speculative environment, the third and final parcel of the Fort Snelling Military Reservation came to market. It would be the prize for the top speculators, and it stoked the idea of a central city at the confluence.[2]

St. Paul was also known far and wide as the *fastest* and liveliest town on the Mississippi. Asset speculators were gamblers. They bought as much as they could at current prices believing that in the near future they could sell for a much higher price. Stories circulated of people making shrewd deals and reaping enormous profits. One of the biggest was $23,000 in a single sale. The land was the hard asset, but making money from the other speculators was just as lucrative and often faster. In the summer the city filled with tourists, speculators, and conmen, a floating population of 2,000 or 3,000. Minnesota, fresh off its extralegal fight to be legal, became a hotbed for the con artist. It had hardly learned to walk and now it was running with thieves. “We had almost too much to offer and it went to our heads,” recalled one.[3]

Everyone was buying real estate, and every other office in town had a real estate sign offering services in the window. Prices soared. Interest rates soared. Everything and everybody soared. Money flowed like the water in the milltail: fast horses and fast women with whiskey and cards. Wine and liquor came upriver and spiked the mood. Dinner tables sparkled with antique silver and fancy wine glasses. They feasted on wild game, local and imported. Horses and carriages on par with those in New York City coursed through the local streets—the main street measured a mile long. And everybody had that look on their face because they knew they would soon be a millionaire.[4]

The people believed in real estate and really nothing could distract them. Even while the value of dirt rose like a balloon, they couldn’t feed themselves. With all the excitement, the basics of life were neglected. Farmers left their plows to make money in the real estate market. Food had to be imported from Galena or St. Louis. Why work when in one year or in a couple of months you could change one dollar into four with a land investment? The choices people made were extravagant. Horses were their primary source of transportation and needed to be fed. A few miles away the Minnesota River Valley had millions of tons of naturally growing hay. Yet, instead of taking time to cut some hay, they imported hay bales from Dubuque, the additional cost of shipping being immaterial. Their choices reveal how the land rush distorted economic perceptions. They produced nothing and yet everything was available to buy.[5]

D. A. J. Baker offers a good example of this feverish speculation. He came from Maine and was an early settler, arriving in 1848. He was a member of the committee that framed the Minnesota constitution, was appointed a judge, became the county superintendent of schools, and taught in the first public school in the territory. After one year, he left for law and real estate, opening his office in Merchants Hotel on Jackson Street. He had seen other cities grow up from nothing. In fact, he knew from personal experience what there was to be had. In 1853 he staked a preemption claim in Superior, and six months later flipped it for $80,000. It was hard to keep teachers and farmers in such an environment.[6]

People of good repute lost track of their reason and joined the fray. If you were there and you were smart, if you wanted to make money without breaking your back, you had a townsite map and carried it with you at all times. “Paper towns” were developments that appeared on paper to have been platted for the sale of lots. Countless townsites and additions to towns were laid out and peddled as investment opportunities. Maps of these towns showed them to be everywhere, but many were never surveyed and didn't really exist. Even so, a paper town could be worth a lot of money in the right hands. One could sell a town lot multiple times over. One could sell the lots wherever one went. The parceled lots in these paper cities were sold on the streets, on the steamboats, and by the hundreds in the East. The nation was land mad. And the center of this craze was St. Paul.[7]

Minnesota was so lucrative that it attracted "big time" gamblers, swindlers, and fly-by-nights who had emptied others' pockets in the California gold rush. They were known as sharpers, perhaps for their "sharp maneuvering" as "confidence men." Street sharpers were everywhere, conducting their business on the sidewalk with a supply of townsite maps and blank deeds. They would overwhelm an unsuspecting person on the street, selling them lots for several hundred dollars, fleecing them while making them feel good. The sharpers would perch on the levee as a steamboat approached, then board the boat even as it docked and home in on a naive investor. The objective was the newcomer, the one looking for a great deal on a piece of real estate. In truth, if there was any real land behind the paper deed, it was worth a fraction of the asking price. Some people were relieved of their money before they got off the boat at St. Paul. These types of cons happened so often and for so long that St. Paul gained a nationwide reputation for swindle.[8]

Minnesota came of age amid a national fever that climaxed in 1857. The speculation was a "mad, crazy, reckless spirit," according to one resident who estimated that St. Paul's real estate mania was wilder and more extravagant than in any other city in America. Those who lived through the height of this speculation period were later at a loss to describe the frenetic experience. In the first ten years of Minnesota's existence people made decisions in a state of mind that was beyond the pale of rational thought. If rampant fraud walked openly on the sidewalk, then one can expect to find it at the highest levels as well. If we combine all the themes of the 1850s, we can see the grandest scheme of them all in Franklin Steele's purchase of the final part of Fort Snelling.[9]

Reviving the Center

In the midst of this economic spree, the heart of the Reserve which had blocked the premier landings and preferred settlement locations finally came on the market. Franklin Steele had been busy collecting the claims on the east side of St. Anthony Falls and Nicolett Island. He was active

Franklin Steele, circa 1875

in the tumult of the Military Reserve combination in St. Paul though he remained in the background. Whether he was in Stillwater on the day of the sale, dressed in a red shirt, holding a club, we don't know. He did feel unable to make a claim on the Minneapolis side. Instead, he recruited an assistant, John H. Stevens, and together they arranged for a large claim in the Minneapolis District sale. Steele was also an incorporator or stockholder of the Minnesota Northwestern Railroad (MNWR). Now he aimed for the final fruit the fort would bear, the parcel above the confluence. He planned to build the long-awaited city and the center of the great new metropolis.

Minneapolis was catching up to St. Anthony with more than 2,000 people, growing over ten times in two years. Within one year of the 1857 boom the number of buildings doubled, approaching 500. The town had the basics, including dry goods, groceries, hardware stores, drug stores, blacksmiths, liveries, and banks, and it had the specialists, such as watchmakers, tailors, milliners, shoemakers, harness makers, bakers, butchers, and painters. It also had the requisite population of real estate dealers, surveyors, and lawyers.[10]

Ever since the bridge connected Minneapolis and St. Anthony, and especially after St. Anthony became a part of Hennepin County, people assumed the two villages would consolidate. The relationship was organic, based on their mutual interests at the falls. They knew the shared stakes heightened the impetus to coalesce. It prompted people to ask: What could tie together the interests of St. Paul with the villages at the falls? Already they were vying to be the dominant center of the future city.

The fort sat at the junction of the Minnesota and the Mississippi Rivers, and by river miles was a bit closer to St. Paul than the Falls of St. Anthony. The Reserve had dominated the area and, after the sale of two parcels, the last section of about 7,800 acres remained. The rolling, fertile plain on top was prime property. Elevated above the confluence, the Fort Snelling site "is one of the most eligible and beautiful on the Mississippi river for a town," wrote the DC–based *American*. The confluence was "the natural site for a great city, and St. Paul would unquestionably have been built there had not the Government held the point for military purposes," said the *Chicago Democratic Press*. The army had built a protective fort to ensure safe settlement, yet did so at the most desirable site, displacing and distorting the usual settlement pattern. Now the city builders had returned. Every speculator envied the man who got a piece of that bluff.[11]

Steele hatched a plan to right that wrong, as residents saw it. He aimed to buy the fort property and start the city anew, with St. Paul and St. Anthony/Minneapolis as outlying satellites. Steele's plan was to return to the birthplace of the region, the place all had assumed would be the center. Bdóte, as the Dakota call it, was the place where the rivers come together. A sacred site of origin for the Dakota, it became the site of imagined prosperity for Steele. Fort Snelling would be the bridge between the rivals.

Early in 1857 rumors were afloat, according to the *Daily Minnesotian*, "that some grand scheme of speculation was on hand" at Fort Snelling.[12]

Steele had worked with a number of other prominent people, including Congressman Robert Smith of Alton, Illinois. They had collaborated on different parts of the Reserve, and they both were engaged in the Minneapolis District sale. Smith was like Stephen A. Douglas of Illinois—an out-of-state politician who repeatedly dipped his hand in the speculative stream of Minnesota. Smith laid off one of the first additions of St. Paul's lower town and donated what is today Mears Park. He used his congressional position to access government officials in DC and got select properties in Minnesota, usurping locals such as Henry Sibley and Franklin Steele. As Smith left Congress in 1849, he got the lease on the government mill on the west side of St. Anthony Falls, saying he planned to live there. More valuable than the mill was the location. He leased it out, never living in Minnesota himself, and he leveraged that toehold on the west side of the falls into a substantial claim on prime property. He knew Minnesota and liked it for its money-making opportunities. Smith had discussed

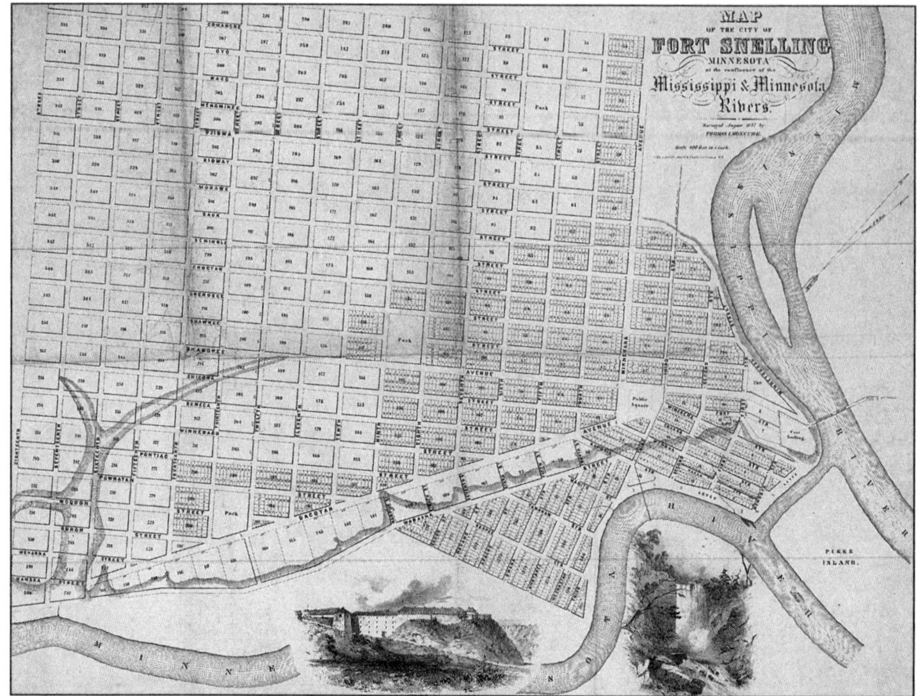

Franklin Steele's plan for the new city at Fort Snelling in 1857. Earlier that year, Steele purchased the final section of the Fort Snelling Military Reserve, which consisted of the fort area.

with Steele the development of a city at the confluence. He would have liked a share in the fort's purchase.[13]

When Steele initiated his plan to buy the remaining portion of Fort Snelling Military Reserve, he moved on without Smith. He passed a note via his territorial representative, Henry M. Rice, to the secretary of war, offering $75,000 cash for the property. The secretary rejected the offer without considering it, believing the fort remained essential for military activities. With the change of administrations in March 1857, John C. Breckinridge of Kentucky, who had nearly become Minnesota's territorial governor, was now vice president, and the Minnesotans had a close ally near the top of the US government.[14]

Steele knew the government was failing to capitalize on the liquidation of military properties. In auction after auction, the government had lost to the squatters. Claim associations successfully shut down the public auctions on the two other sections of the Fort Snelling Military Reserve as well as at other forts in Iowa, Wisconsin, and Illinois. At the same time, land—millions of acres in Minnesota alone—was coming on the market and flooding it. The federal government's executive branch was overwhelmed. They generally believed auctions were the best method to level the playing field for the public, rich and poor alike. But the General Land Office and Department of Interior seemed aware the claim associations would interfere. Steele developed an alternative solution for the government. He set out to gather a crew to guide the land sale to him.

Next, Steele arranged with Rice for legislation that would allow the secretary of war to sell the remaining section of land around the fort without a public auction. By precedent, under an 1819 law, the land was to be sold at a public sale. Rice crafted nuanced language that granted the secretary the power to sell at his discretion any military sites that he deemed had become useless. Such an item, appearing to be only a small adjustment, did not need a stand-alone bill. As a territorial representative, Rice could not introduce a bill or such language. He recruited others to amend it to the army appropriations bill. Newspapers reported that Senator John B. Weller (California), Representative James L. Orr (South Carolina), and Representative John A. Quitman (Mississippi) "were uncommonly zealous in sliding [the] paragraph into the Army Appropriation Bill" that would allow the secretary to make such a decision.[15]

In the Senate the idea met resistance. Opponents got Weller to adamantly confirm, regardless of the slight changes introduced, the land would be sold: "At PUBLIC SALE." Weller's antagonists, like most people, wanted the government to sell for the best possible price and to avoid favoritism, which meant a public auction. But because of the known antics of squatters and claim associations, what appeared to be common sense did not match the reality on the ground. Auctions were easy to manipulate. The language Steele and Rice were inserting was trying to avoid that trap. The army appropriations passed the Senate on March 2, 1857.

As the House debated the bill, the southern Democrats managed to suppress news of the bill's amendment. The normal procedure is to have a bill read into the record twice, along with assignment to committee, so representatives can hear and discuss it. When the first request for a reading came, Representative Quitman discouraged the reading and got it dispensed to committee by vote. After a contentious debate in committee over these new powers for the secretary, the bill returned to the full House. A member requested the reading of the amendments, and Quitman again asked for a vote, this time on the whole report at once. Representative Orr, the speaker of the house, declared "that was the only way it could be done." After several rounds, they successfully blocked any reading until the final bill. Then Quitman clinched by motion the passage of the army appropriation bill.[16]

Some newspapers saw this maneuvering for what it was. Congress generates bills that have hundreds of items in them, and it's easier to use such a bill "to get something done which ought not to be," said one newspaper in reference to Rice's amendment. There was simply "no time for examination," the editor noted. This bill passed and it would have been successful but for the question that made it into the Congressional Record, "at PUBLIC SALE." That's why a senator had insisted Weller say explicitly the sales would be public. But the general and vague wording of Rice's amendment disguised the amendment's particular purpose. It was meant specifically for the sale of Fort Snelling.[17]

The Plan Unfolds

Steele and Rice wasted no time in applying the amendment. On April 7 Rice wrote to the Secretary of War John B. Floyd, the former governor of Virginia, and recommended the government sell the remaining part of the Fort Snelling Reserve, except for about forty acres for a depot. His setup seemed neutral. Now that the secretary had the discretion to sell military lands, Rice advised a survey for Fort Snelling, dividing it into parcels not exceeding 160 acres, a sale at public auction at or above a minimum price, and that the equities of occupants be respected. This last note referred to Steele. For about twenty years he had lived adjacent to the fort property near Minnehaha Creek, where he built a house and raised a large family. Two days earlier Rice had written to Alexander Ramsey from Washington saying the plan was ready.

The next phase was to help Floyd gather information on Fort Snelling. Dr. Archibald Graham of Lexington, Virginia, a friend of the secretary, paid Floyd a visit in DC. Graham said he was traveling to Minnesota and wondered if there was any public business he might do that would contribute to his travel expenses. Floyd was new to his job and had positions to fill. Primed by Rice's letter, Floyd's to-do list included having the fort assessed by commissioners to estimate its value and make recommendations on how best to sell the property. Floyd offered Graham the job of commissioner to oversee the land sale, but Graham declined because he wanted to buy some land.

Soon after this meeting Graham ran into John C. Mather, a New York state senator. They "fell into conversation" about the western lands and opportunities to make money on those lands. Mather learned about the

Fort Snelling sale and the two made "a tentative agreement . . . towards an operation in the Snelling reserve." Richard Schell, Mather's neighbor and "a regular speculator," claimed to have read about the land sales in the newspaper. Within weeks Graham, Mather, and Schell became what would be known as "The New York Company." Floyd appointed Mather to audit claims at Fort Ripley, another federal property northwest of St. Paul, with an eye to its future sale. They knew the secretary had discretion to sell the land through a private sale without a public auction. They aimed to buy it in a private sale.

As soon as the New York speculators agreed, Graham departed for Minnesota. As the story goes, the New Yorkers were in search of a local person to operate as a front man. Toward the end of April Graham met Steele and recruited him to be their purchasing agent. Graham returned to New York and with his report the "combination" was ready to proceed. Their maximum price was $120,000 for the remaining Reserve parcel of 7,800 acres.

Back in Washington, Floyd had found commissioners who would prepare the fort for sale and determine how it would be sold, either through a private sale or by public auction. The first commissioner was William King Heiskell, an acquaintance from Virginia. As Floyd prepared Heiskell for his trip to Fort Snelling, he cautioned him about Minnesota: "Keep your eyes skinned; you are going among a parcel of sharpers and speculators." Graham and Heiskell coincidently bumped into each other in Washington and decided to travel to Minnesota together. Graham said he didn't know Heiskell, but Heiskell admitted to having known Graham for five or six years.[18]

The other commissioner was Major Seth Eastman, a former commandant of Fort Snelling, who would oversee the survey of the fort and preparation for its sale. Floyd directed the commissioners to establish the current status of the Reserve and decide if the buildings should be kept or sold. If they sold the land at public auction, they were to survey it into forty-acre lots so people of small means could make a purchase. Otherwise, they could sell the whole parcel at private sale. Floyd gave them latitude to make the decision on their own, but no sale could be less than $7.50 per acre.

Mather of the New York combination was already in Minnesota conducting his assignment at Fort Ripley. After he finished, he arrived in St. Paul on the same morning as Graham and the commissioner Heiskell, May 31, and he went to church with Heiskell. The two commissioners, Heiskell and Eastman, went to the fort, evaluated the property, and discussed the best way to sell it. To the locals they were strangers (except for Eastman), as the streets were filled with new arrivals. They did not announce their business and were casual in their approach. Traveling incognito, as they did, allowed them to gather information informally.[19]

In St. Paul, Heiskell heard about the sale of Fort Snelling land everywhere he went. People talked about it around tables and on the street. "The plan of operation appeared to be settled," he observed, "that the lots should bring from $1.25 to $1.50 per acre." As we have seen, the locals could adroitly rig a sale. People claimed the last section of Fort Snelling shouldn't sell for more than $50,000. Floyd's lower limit of $7.50 per acre amounted to $58,500, but with news that a combination had been formed, Heiskell believed the locals would prevent any open sale.[20]

Heiskell came away with the impression that the locals all valued this land the same. A "great prejudice exist[s] in the public mind against the sale of any land belonging to the United States at more than $1.25 per acre," he observed. "[E]ven the best and most respectable men will unite to prevent the sale" above the minimum. It didn't matter to the buyers that a person could turn around and sell it for $50–$80 or more per acre. Residents thought this extreme distortion of valuation and the handing of wealth to the locals was not unethical. They "considered the government only a temporary custodian of land which should be turned over to them as soon as they needed it," observed historian Lucile Kane.[21]

The following Friday, June 5, commissioners Heiskell and Eastman met at the fort. There were so many land speculators about and such an eagerness to get possession of this prime piece of property that they feared an open public competition would fall to a combination and fail to bring in money above the minimum. The commissioners therefore decided to sell the fort and its acreage as a whole at a private sale.[22]

The conditions of the buildings at the fort played a role in their evaluation. Designed for military purposes, the structures were largely useless to a residential or commercial development. Built in part with "rude" materials, the fort and outbuildings were dilapidated, and their "value had departed." But the fort, constructed with local limestone, retained military value. Whoever got the fort would have a property that could accommodate military use, if the situation were to arise in the future, a significant asset that would come into play as the final irony of this scheme.[23]

The commissioners debated who should receive the offer of the fort. They estimated the "extensive improvements" made by citizens were greater than $30,000. Mostly that was Steele's investment. Those improvements did not entitle Steele to preemption rights, however. He made the investments but "without any legal claim to the title beyond that of mere squatter." Also, he had made an offer to buy the fort, the only one most people knew about. The commissioners offered Steele the fort parcel for \$90,000 (\$11.54 per acre), which Eastman had fixed upon as its lowest valuation.[24]

In response Steele renewed his previous offer of \$75,000 (\$9.62 per acre), which the commissioners rejected, and Steele agreed to their asking price. Mather wrote up the agreement and the sale was made on June 6, 1857. Everything here can be defended as being in accordance with Floyd's directive and the amended 1819 law. Despite the likelihood of the buyers (Steele along with his New York associates Graham and Mather) being in contact with the commissioners Heiskell and Eastman and influencing their evaluation, the price was better than could be gotten in any other way.

How Steele Stole

When the news broke, the private sale of Fort Snelling ranked nationally as "one of the astounding events of the year," according to a DC newspaper. The private sale of a military reserve was scandalous because it was exclusive to a rich person or party and it cut out the local settlers. People followed the story in newspapers across the country. From Maine to California, papers reported on the sale or more often reprinted articles on it, sometimes adding an editorial by way of introduction. Beyond the scandal, people were watching because other states had similar parcels of military land that would eventually come to market. The issue in Minnesota would set a precedent.[25]

For many observers, the point of greatest concern was the amount of money the government lost by selling for \$90,000. Outsiders viewed the swindle as taking the government for anywhere from \$650,000 to \$2 million (from \$24 million to \$3.6 billion today). Others questioned if Steele pocketed the profit, or if others in the department also made out with some money. If the land was sold in such a way, they said, the transaction had the stench of corruption. The private sale was attacked for eliding any sort of open competition for the land. "Mr. Steele, or Stole" they suspected was merely the front, a small person in the chain: "the purchaser, is but a go-between." The "real buyers are gentlemen of high position, and everywhere known in the political world," said a Washington, DC, newspaper. Reporters and others may have suspected Floyd, but they didn't know for sure.[26]

People began to look into the details of the sale and under what authority it was made. "This little sly, stealthy, cat-paced piece of legislation," said *The American*, a DC paper, was only discovered by chance by a

Minneapolis attorney. He happened to read the amendment in the army appropriations bill that changed the 1819 law and rightly surmised it was intended for Fort Snelling. He confronted Steele, who denied it. The lawyer described the situation clearly in an anonymous letter to the *Weekly Minnesotian*, published on April 4, 1857. The amendment would allow the sale, and it could "be excluded from pre-emption by actual settlers." If the War Department offered the entire tract as one parcel, the sale would exclude all but a few. The price would be at a discount "for much less than its real value." He suggested Congress pass another law that would retract the amendment. He signed off with a Latin saying, *Verbum sapientiae sati* ("A word to the wise is sufficient").[27]

People had known the last piece of Fort Snelling would be sold soon, and every speculator had an angle to get some of it. Locals had already formed claim associations, which suggests they had been staking claims in the area. *The American* concluded that "this cautious, clandestine, stealthy legislation was part and parcel of a plot to get possession of that valuable property for a song." Steele had repeatedly been in Washington intending to get Fort Snelling sold and had declared that he intended to be the owner of it. He initially denied the plot, deflecting by pointing to other reserves that would be sold soon. But when his critics were unpersuaded, Steele flipped his story. He admitted that the amendment to the 1819 law was indeed written for Fort Snelling. In fact, he said, the fort had already been sold under that authority for $11 per acre. The fort was already his. There was nothing they could do, he claimed. In truth, the sale wouldn't happen for another three months. But Steele's distractions put off the inquiries until the deal was completed.[28]

The scent of scandal in one area raised suspicions that the entire operation was rotten. "Everything about the transaction indicates that there was some deep corruption at the bottom of the enactment under which the sale was made," said a Vermont newspaper. The newspapers across the nation bemoaned the wrongs like a Greek chorus. They highlighted the low price in a private, presumably partisan deal. The private sale had cut out locals interested in purchasing property on the Reserve at market value. The local settler never had a chance because the land was "disposed of *secretly* and *in the dark*, to a single individual" at a fourth or fifth of its value.[29]

Some people, though, knew the agreed price wasn't bad. An Iowa newspaper called it one of the best sales the government had made. They pointed to other recent sales of Osage, Oklahoma, and of Fort Crawford at Prairie du Chien, Wisconsin. They questioned the value of the stone ramparts and barracks. Where could a person buy 7,800 acres of unimproved land for $90,000? "The land is undoubtedly valuable," agreed the *North Iowa Times*, "but the talk that parties stood ready to bid $200 and $300 an acre on it is all *bosh*." Others agreed. Judge Charles Flandrau of St. Paul estimated the price was more than the fort was worth.[30]

The newspapers were misled by these big numbers and attitudes related to squatter sovereignty. Speculators, opponents, and squatters talked up the lost value that the market might bear, but given a chance at a public auction, as Heiskell said, they would have coalesced their combination to depress the price to a minimum. The protesters were either unaware of or favored the power of claim associations to shut down a public auction.

For a good number of editors, the main focus was Minnesota's reputation for scandalous land deals. The Superior/MNWR spectacle orchestrated by Rice and Douglas was a recent memory, that "magnificent speculation" by "certain leading politicians" at the head of Lake Superior in which the major players "feathered their nests." Newspapers of the day were certainly partisan themselves. In their calls for an explanation of the Fort Snelling sale they accused Minnesota's politicians of abusing their positions:

> The Administration cannot be too prudent and vigilant in watching the maneuvers of certain speculators, who, in the mask of Democracy, are in fact "ravening" depredators and speculators. There are men, who stand high at Washington, who entertain grandly, and succeed in deluding some of our high functionaries, and yet who, in fact, are openly employing political position and place to enrich themselves at the expense of the people, by various devices of peculation and swindling. Minnesota has been a favorite area for these speculators.[31]

The issue became so hot and apparently became associated with the Superior/MNWR debacle such that Senator Douglas published a disclaimer that appeared in many newspapers saying he had nothing to do with this particular scandal.[32]

Scandal was the point. "Talk of 'Galphinism!'" declared *The American*. "Galphinism" was political slang for swindling the government. "Here is a fraud that throws all former rascality entirely in the shade. Hereafter, let stupendous frauds be known by the expressive term of 'A STEELE.'" The new scandal was outdoing the old scandal. "Fort Snelling is likely to become as famous in the history of national swindling as the Galphin and Gardiner frauds," predicted the *Raftsman's Journal* in Pennsylvania.[33]

The scandal was also partisan as the people involved were Democrats. Steele was a prominent Democrat, and the president's administration was Democratic. Many leading Democratic members of Congress visited Minnesota that summer from Georgia, South Carolina, Alabama, and other states. Opposition newspapers couldn't help but needle the politicians. "We suppose Douglas has gone to Minnesota," projected the *Utica Herald*. They suggested the scam was "by a few leading Pro-Slavery politicians." Along with Steele and Rice, they directed their criticism at Orr, Quitman, and Weller, and some extended it to Floyd and Pierce.[34]

Meanwhile, back in Minnesota, Steele had drawn up a map of the new city on the bluff at the confluence of the rivers. The townsite was laid out and surveyed into lots. The plans replaced the entire fort and all its buildings. He had the first road graded. He sold a small portion of the Reserve (1/27 or 290 acres) to three developers for twice the original purchase price. This was the beginning, they thought, of the new center, a great metropolis with St. Paul, St. Anthony, and Minneapolis as its suburbs.[35]

After a few years off, Robert Smith of Illinois was reelected to Congress. In the interim he had tried to be a party to the purchase of Fort Snelling. He had partnered with Steele previously, and now Steele had got that land, leaving Smith out of the deal. Smith had written letters to the secretary of war asking specifically about the sale of Fort Snelling. The administration claimed the letters had not been received. He may have sensed he was being shut out of the sale due to some other scheme. With the press asking such questions as, "Where, when and how was [Fort Snelling] sold, and what parties were permitted to compete for the purchase?" Congress was prompted to investigate. As the temperature rose in the protests, Smith called for an investigation into the private sale.[36]

It turns out the sale had generally followed the legal framework, and the government did sign a deal that, if carried out, would yield more money per acre than anything previously. Steele and Rice did sneak in the amendment that allowed them to funnel the sale to Steele, which was self-dealing to be sure. The alternative was a public auction, which would most likely have been shut down by a claim association. Rice would have supported that too, at least in public.

Floyd would later be accused of playing a central part in the sale. He was protected in Congress by his partisan allies and never proven guilty by historians, but Congress censored him severely and removed the powers of the amended 1819 law that enabled him to sell the Reserve land to a private party.[37]

It seems impossible for Steele to be simply a pick-up agent or a local front man. His past and the results of this operation both suggest that it was in part, if not entirely, a plan he had hatched and developed while in Washington the previous winter. In fact, the results suggest Steele was the principal mind behind it.

Yet the deal had other serious problems. The terms the government gave Steele via commissioners Heiskell and Eastman were in fact unprecedented. They sold the property to him on credit. Steele paid $30,000 on July 10, with two annual payments of like size to follow. Further, they gave him the credit with no interest. Going rates in St. Paul's real estate boom were 2.5–5 percent *per month*. The commissioners later testified that they had forgotten to include any security or interest payments on the installments. The congressional investigating committee, after accumulating a great deal of testimony, found that the purchase was effectively a combination against the government. They recommended that the sale be vacated. But nothing was done.

The Scandal That Got Away

In the upper town of St. Paul, on the sidewalk in front of W. S. Combs's bookstore, a group of men gathered, friends from the recent 1854 land sale. Combs had been an officer in the Military Reserve Claim Association (with Rice as president), and the others likely stood in red shirts with clubs to shut down the public land auction. These men walked the streets with posters that displayed plats of townsites and additions. These were not paper towns; they were real plats on the old Reserve. The men spoke of the beautiful locations, the likelihood of densely populated additions, and the all-but-guaranteed rise in values of 500 percent or more. They were selling the only staple production in town: real estate. In truth, settlement under this type of surplus was erratic and dispersed. Houses and neighborhoods were built sporadically. Because of the speculative hold across the landscape the area grew in an aberrant way. Instead of selling as a result of demand for living, they were selling an idea. And that idea died in October 1857.

Shortly after these men had acquired such promising real estate through the Reserve "auction," a market crash deflated the values. The crisis started in late August when the New York office of the Ohio Life Insurance and Trust Company closed its doors. The crisis rippled across the country, hitting Minnesota in October. Bank doors closed, as did the stores. All works of improvement ceased. In a remarkably short time, the speculators went from having visions of soon becoming millionaires to the reality of being flat broke. Accounts describe a general gloom settling on the community. Speculators could not "buy a meal's victuals with

160 acres of wild lands," said the *St. Paul Daily Globe*. They were desperate enough that they would have sold their land for less than the original purchase price of $1.25 an acre (not including any black market pricing), but no one was buying.[38]

The impact was brutal. The crash of 1857 distorted everything they knew about the economy. Many of the basic arrangements of life were upside down, especially compared to the speculative atmosphere they had known. The implosion across the economy was broad and deep. Minnesota had been a magnetic draw ever since the day it was squeezed into a territory. It was a speculator's dream with plenty of land and an endless supply of buyers. While the crash crushed everyone, those with more debt fared the worst. Everybody's fiefdom had been built on credit. Speculators might begin with loans to buy land at three percent per month, and when they needed a bit more their interest rates would rise to five percent. Then, like simply tipping over a line of dominoes, one bank ran out of money, and it called in its loans, leading another bank to call in its loans, and so on. The crisis reversed the flow of credit. The money needed to be returned to settle accounts. But when everyone was working on credit there wasn't enough money to keep banks solvent.[39]

In Minnesota, people were reliant on the eastern creditors, who now demanded repayment of loans. The speculators could no longer extend their loans at any rate of interest. They paid until they were out of cash. In the aftermath, the residents of St. Paul, St. Anthony, and Minneapolis had little or no money for basic trade. Businesses failed at rates estimated at fifty to seventy-five percent. Upward of fifty percent of the people left the north country promised land.

Some estimated St. Paul suffered the direst consequences, more than any other city in the West. Like anywhere else, values were inflated and unreal. Browne's 1855 report listed the owners of the property on the former Reserve. The list included a broad spectrum of business owners. Everyone was in debt holding speculative land. Some of their properties in St. Paul sold before the crash in 1856 at a price that was not reached again before the end of the century, forty-four years later. In the wild speculative ride, they locked up the land. The crash of 1857 solidified the settlement pattern in the Twin Cities, one that we know very well today and mistakenly take as somehow obvious. The result was that a centralized metropolis did not materialize and, except for St. Anthony and Minneapolis, the settlements remained dispersed and separate.

The crash forced Steele into a difficult position. His plan was to make his payments to the government as he sold off parcels and lots. After the crash, sales ceased to exist and he was not able to make the following two payments. The government tried to extract the money from him in a lawsuit. Though the government held the title to the property, Steele, for unknown reasons, retained possession of the land. Then came the rebellion of the enslavers. In April 1861 the army commandeered the fort for the use of federal troops, beginning with the First Minnesota Infantry Regiment, and then the government operated it for several years after the war as well. Later, Steele sent a bill to the War Department for eighty-one months of rent at $2,000 per month for a total of $160,000 minus the $60,000 he still owed from 1857. In January 1871 Steele received the title to a reduced amount of territory, 6,400 acres. All told, it ended up being a successful speculation for him.[40]

Steele would bolster Minnesota's reputation for corruption and grift. Nationally, his name was synonymous with swindle. And though he would sometimes fail miserably at what he set out to do, he showed how easy it was in those times to swivel from an imploding scam to another lucrative scheme. He was quite gifted in this arena.

But it was the last chance for a city centered at the confluence. The birth of the new city at the Reserve had failed. It became something more than a paper town, but it was never enough to be a ghost town.

Part III: **Uniting the Twin Cities**

CHAPTER 7

The State Fair Wars

The State Fair of 1878 was larger than life. "The present State Fair is admitted to be the finest and most complete ever held in Minnesota," reported the *New York Tribune*. Considering the state was only twenty years old, the journalist felt the fair was "surprising and really noteworthy." That year's fair had two headline attractions, the nation's top racehorse and the president of the United States.[1]

First, the "celebrated" trotting horse Rarus was called "king of the turf." A rare exception that broke the rule of "blood will tell," Rarus was "of ignoble stock." He was discovered on the street pulling butcher carts and bought for less than $300. He had no pedigree, but he won the genetic lottery. A street horse, he blossomed into a trotting champion. In two years he cut his time in the mile from 2:20 to 2:13¼, a new record that "electrified the trotting world" as it bested the previous record by three-quarters of a second. Some 25,000 spectators came to see his first race in Minnesota. Rarus "leaped at one bound from comparative obscurity into the very first rank." His story—a Dickensian rags-to-riches tale—mesmerized everyone. It touched on the fantasy that lay at the heart of land speculation.[2]

The next day, President Rutherford B. Hayes became the first president to visit Minnesota. Upward of 50,000 people crowded the fairgrounds, with the *Daily Globe* describing "a great mass of humanity" in the grandstands with some 20,000 people.[3]

The 1878 "Hayes Fair" was put on by St. Paul, but it was not the only fair that year. Minneapolis hosted its own fair. The two cities competed for the best features and the highest turnout. Though competing fairs might seem a jovial sport, the 1870s were perhaps the most vicious period of the Twin Cities' rivalry. The two fairs were at the forefront of this competition, which was as much about city dominance and political feuds as it was about entertainment. When St. Paul booked both the country's top racehorse and the Republican president, the resentful Minneapolis fair organizers planned their next move.

RARUS, THE KING OF THE TURF.

Rarus was a Cinderella story of the 1870s. He rose from pulling carts through the New York City streets to become a trotting champion. Horse racing was one of the greatest attractions at nineteenth-century fairs.

The 1878 "Hayes" Fair

Early on the morning of September 5, people filled the streets of St. Paul, on time for the president's 5:45 A.M. train arrival. As with other stops along his tour, such as in Madison, Wisconsin, a special salute was fired, though in St. Paul the honor was done from guns above town on the bluffs. After breakfast President Hayes left downtown in a large parade from Union Depot along Third Street (today's Kellogg Boulevard). St. Paul was the main stop of the president's tour of the Northwest, which started in Ohio and ended in Bismarck, North Dakota.[4]

"The city is in holiday dress," reported the *New York Herald*. The streets and buildings were ornamented with flags, streamers, and bunting. A decorated triumphal arch stood over the street near Bridge Square for the procession to pass under. It said "St. Paul, the Metropolis of the Northwest, welcomes the President." Festoons spanned the street bearing the president's portrait and, on the reverse, the words "Union Forever." On the sides were smaller shields bearing the words "No North, No South, No East, No West."[5]

The signs weren't referring to St. Paul and Minneapolis. The Union had defeated the Confederate states in the Civil War thirteen years earlier.

The work of reuniting the country remained a prominent task in the president's administration. In Minnesota he encountered a local schism of a smaller scope yet of a somewhat similar psychological nature. The rift between the Twin Cities had grown to a "violent animosity" in a "struggle for supremacy," and the two were quite stuck. The president knew of these political lines. Perhaps his presence might give the cities a day off from their enmity. Hayes's appearance alone inspired the headline: "He Unites St. Paul and Minneapolis as One Loving City of 200,000 People." That was a St. Paul newspaper, which clearly inflated the number (each city had about 40,000 people at the time). Some in Minneapolis took umbrage.[6]

As the presidential caravan moved through St. Paul, the crowds clogged the streets. People filled the windows, and young boys hung from lampposts. As the president passed, Minnesotans waved handkerchiefs, removed their hats, and stood in silence to show their respect. Hayes had easily won Minnesota over Democrat Samuel J. Tilden in the 1876 election by nearly twenty percent. He was well liked, and the Republican Party had blossomed in Minnesota. After the short parade of six blocks, the president's entourage boarded a special train at the Sibley Street depot and rode to the State Fairgrounds, Kittsondale, a million-dollar stable and racetrack just west of the city limits (near today's University and Snelling Avenues).[7]

At the fairgrounds, the crowd was much larger, and the grandstand was standing room only. The day featured that special Minnesota hot, a humid

President Rutherford B. Hayes was the first president to visit Minnesota. He gave speeches at the 1878 St. Paul and Minneapolis state fairs.

ninety degrees in the shade. The wind brought waves of prairie dust that covered the perspiring people.

The president arrived at the fairgrounds with the most prominent citizens: St. Paul Mayor William Dawson, Governor John S. Pillsbury, and George R. Finch, president of the State Agricultural Society, which ran the St. Paul State Fair. He had a high forehead topped with light hair and deep-set eyes set above a Roman nose. Hayes's full, graying beard covered his mouth, so the only expression rested in his eyes. From the stage, and without a microphone, he intoned about the facts and figures of economic recovery and his administration's efforts to pay down the country's enormous wartime debt to reduce the interest payments. He stressed the need for a stable currency.

One note of levity during his presentation came at the expense of the early Minnesotans and, at the same time, exposed him to his critics. In his speech, the president called out Alexander Ramsey, the ex-governor, who was also onstage with him. He recalled that thirty years prior, in 1848, the Stillwater Convention had skirted the population requirements for territorial status in which 5,000 voters were needed. Minnesota had produced an inflated number "by the trickery of counting," he said.[8]

The idea of fraud was an interesting topic for him to raise. The presi-

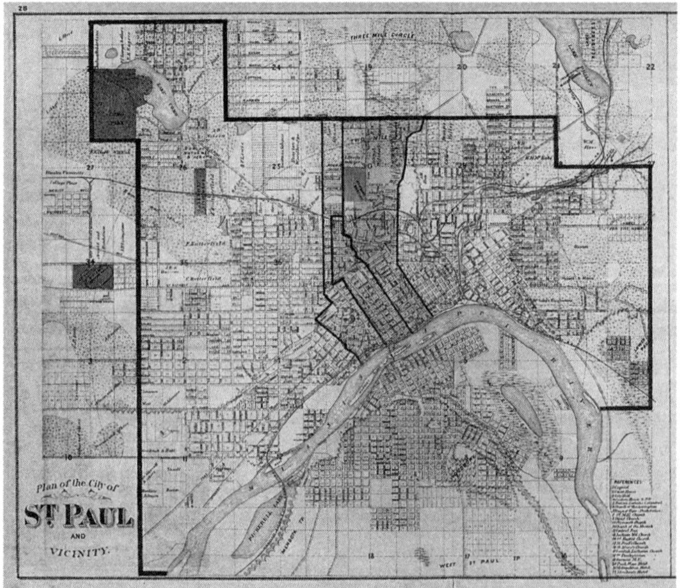

In the 1870s the St. Paul State Fair was held at the Kittsondale racetrack (the dark gray rectangle below Como Park and left of the city limit on Lexington Avenue).

dential election of 1876 was besieged with controversies of voter fraud and stolen elections in Florida and Louisiana. It took months to settle the election, and a congressional committee would find that Hayes's campaign had committed fraud. One New York editor made note of the irony and differentiated the crime in degrees: "Minnesota, however, even as a Territory, was never disgraced by the sort of counting done in Louisiana for Hayes."[9]

Hayes concluded his speech with a return to his effort to unify the spirit of the country. He referenced the hard times in the South and donated the proceeds of an auctioned Bible to a Confederate soldier in need. As the banners announced, Hayes was trying to unite the country in spirit. But he made one mistake. That he stopped in St. Paul but skipped over Minneapolis deeply insulted that fair's organizer and the city's residents.[10]

Why Two Fairs

The battles between the fairs of St. Paul and Minneapolis began earlier in the decade. The St. Paul State Fair of 1871 got the decade off on the wrong foot. The word got out that, as of that year, St. Paul would be the State Fair's permanent home. The idea irritated the Minneapolis contingent and set off a bitter rivalry between St. Paul and Minneapolis over the location of the State Fair. The fair quickly took on symbolic meaning, signaling the power relationship between the two cities. The older St. Paul considered itself the natural location for such events. Minneapolis, smaller but growing, wanted to prove its worth. People in both places had sensitive egos and were easily offended.[11]

People called it the St. Paul State Fair although St. Paul, as a city, did not run the event. The State Agricultural Society was based in St. Paul and produced the annual fair. The statewide organization pursued the mission of promoting the state's agricultural appeal and dispelling concerns about the northern climate. The roots of this organization were in the agricultural societies of Ramsey and Hennepin Counties, which had begun the effort before statehood in 1854.[12]

The St. Paul fair was more meat and potatoes; it featured education about agricultural innovations and networking opportunities for farmers. The fair was the social event of the year for dispersed and isolated farmers and included the latest innovations of machinery, educational programs, and competitive exhibits of farm produce and livestock. Through the 1860s the fair moved around, entertaining people in St. Paul, Owatonna, Fort Snelling, Red Wing, Minneapolis, and Rochester. Like today's state fair it was a favorite event, but back then it could be interrupted by economic hard times or war. Sometimes the merchants and businesses in the city stepped up and supported the fair and at other times they completely abandoned it. The fair organization received state aid of about $1,000 after 1868, but it was perpetually teetering on bankruptcy after each event.[13]

The Minneapolis fair, by contrast, was run entirely by private operators. As the fairs became symbolic proxies of each town, they served as instruments in the battle for superiority. Minneapolitans were more the fair enthusiasts, it seems, as their participation and attendance numbers at *both* fairs at times exceeded those of St. Paul. This statistic also suggests that the two fairs were different enough to merit attending both. It may have been that St. Paul's fair included exhibits and entries from a broader range of the state.

King's Fair

The Minneapolis fair offered one man a natural platform. William S. King, the fair's sponsor and promoter, was an incurable showman. A newspaper editor and publisher, an antislavery Republican, and a Minneapolitan, he used the fair to promote his interests. He was "one of the most energetic and public-spirited" men in Minneapolis, wrote a political biographer. He was a man of the times who fit the needs of Minneapolis and its rise "by nature and by disposition," recalled an editor of King's newspaper, the *Minneapolis Journal*. A Renaissance man more commonly known as Bill King, he was controversial and sometimes difficult to understand as a peacemaker or antagonist. He embodied the Minneapolis fair to such a degree it was called King's Fair.[14]

King was born in upstate New York in 1828, the fifth child of an itinerant Methodist preacher. His father was a radical, reform-minded man and was one of the early antislavery agitators in northern New York. King in his mid-twenties became a political organizer and publisher. He organized the Young Men's Republican Club, published a partisan newsletter, and was involved in the initiation of New York's Republican Party.[15]

At the age of twenty-nine, in the summer of 1858, King moved to Minnesota, explored St. Paul, and settled in the village of Minneapolis, then with a population between 1,800 and 2,000. His good friend Horace Greeley knew something about the political layout of the new territory and had advised him to settle on the west side of the river. Greeley invited King to write for his New York *Weekly Tribune*, the foremost antislavery newspaper of the day, and King did so under the pen name "Hennepin."

The political makeup of the area would have played a role in King's decision to live in Minneapolis. Up until that time, the Democratic Party was dominant in the Minnesota Territory. The Republican Party of Minnesota was only a few years old, having started in 1855, just months before the national party in 1856. St. Paul, which had the higher density of people, remained a Democratic stronghold, while Republicans tended to be centered in the newer St. Anthony, which at that time was more important than the nascent Minneapolis. The collection of abolitionists at the falls had no newspaper, and though a few Republican papers had come and gone, they sought a newspaper that better expressed their views on temperance and civil liberty.[16]

King was opinionated and a talented wordsmith, and he quickly became one of the loudest voices of Minnesota's Republican Party. He purchased the *Minnesota State News*, likely for its printing press, and in May 1859 began publishing the *State Atlas*, a weekly newspaper promoting the Republican agenda. "With impetuous zeal" he applied his "trenchant pen" to the political scandal du jour: the $5 million loan, an ill-conceived railroad subsidy that cost Minnesota taxpayers millions of dollars. On the issue of slavery King took "the most radical position" and "wielded a caustic pen" in shaping public opinion. "No editorial writer in the state has ever equaled him in warmth of expression or bitterness of denunciation," wrote a biographer. The democratic platform, King wrote, "can be summed up in a few words. It is a railroad swindling, bogus banking, and heavy taxation structure, moulded and adopted by the railroad swindlers and their Attorneys." King was in his prime as an influential newspaperman.[17]

In the early years the Democrats held all the elected offices: governor, legislature, supreme court, congressional representatives, and senator. This monopoly changed some in the county and legislative elections of 1856 and 1857. But in the election of 1859 the Republicans won majorities in both chambers, taking control of the Minnesota House (58–22) and falling only one seat short in the Senate (23–13). The 1860 election for the third Minnesota Legislature was "a political revolution," resulting in overwhelming Republican majorities in the house and senate (the Democrats held two seats in each chamber).[18]

After the Civil War a new brand of Republicanism took hold. The *Chronicle*, a Minneapolis weekly, began to challenge the *State Atlas* for readers. While the *State Atlas* remained undiluted and principled in its stance, the *Chronicle* became a popular daily. In March 1867 King and other investors combined the *Chronicle* with the *State Atlas* to become the *Minneapolis*

Tribune. King's stock in the enterprise gave him a dominating influence. Newspapers were clearly partisan, but news was partisan and partisanship was news, and King used it to his utmost advantage.[19]

King had several interests that played a role in his development of the Minneapolis fair. From the beginning, even before the technology was available, people laid plans for linking Minneapolis and St. Paul by rail. One of the first efforts had the futuristic name of "The Air Line and Hour Line Railway." King seized on this idea and established the Minneapolis Street Railway Company in Minneapolis in 1873. The company purchased a steam motor and laid a track on Second Street, from Hennepin Avenue down to Cedar. The track remained unused, and the company collapsed.[20]

In 1875 King revived the transportation project, this time promoting the vision of a complete railway system in the city. He turned again to a group of investors who supported his vision, a part of his deep-rooted ties to the east. They were from Ilion, New York, on the Erie Canal, near his hometown and where both his first and his second wife were from. In September 1875 the first car, pulled by a horse, began service on Washington Avenue (near the passenger station of the St. Paul, Minneapolis, & Manitoba Railroad). King's enthusiastic leadership resulted in several more lines in the following two years. Thomas Lowry, the vice president of the corporation, bought a controlling interest in 1877 and became renowned for his development of the street railway system.[21]

Another interest of King's—it bordered on passion—was farming. He

William S. "Bill" King in 1878

assembled a 1,400-acre farm from other smaller farms, calling it Lyndale Farm, where he raised premier breeds of cattle, such as shorthorn, Ayrshire, and Jersey. He was known nationwide for this exotic livestock. He loved his farm a little too much, and his expenditures exceeded his income. He had to use the land as collateral for loans to cover his expenses. But property prices began to rise as the city expanded, and, to balance the books, he sold lots for residences as well as the 128-acre plot for the Lakewood Cemetery. The rapidly rising land values caused a dispute with the manager of the loans, and King sued, a famous case that was settled in his favor. He received nearly $2 million in securities and properties.[22]

But King lacked fiscal discipline and was "generous to a fault," according to one biographer. King paid his attorneys amply, started new ventures "with more zeal than prudence," and happily shared his good fortune with others. Within a few years his remarkable wealth had dwindled to nothing. He followed his instincts more than his reason, and without overthinking whether he would win or lose. His wins were able to outpace his losses; his good luck struck often enough to keep him ahead of his bad luck. If there was a secret to his magic, it was that he failed in ways that befriended people. Minneapolis was his city, and the citizens loved him. Outside of money, Bill King was used to getting exactly what he wanted. He was a micromanager—so intensely that his health suffered. He had vision, he had a city, and he had competition.[23]

The Epoch of King

All of King's interests—the large farm, exotic cattle, a bighearted run through $2 million, the street railway, and the newspapers—came into play in producing the fair. Minneapolis was not large—it was referred to as a village. But the people rallied behind King and were zealous about having the best fair. He used a sixty-acre field, then on the outskirts of Minneapolis (Matthew Park in Seward neighborhood). King's Fair was something special to the city's residents. As a showman, he wanted speakers, exhibits, and competitions. King placed large advertisements in the newspapers that featured in-demand speakers and horse races, perhaps the number one attraction. His cattle illustrate what set him apart from his contemporaries. King's preference for the exotic breeds of livestock shaped his take on the fair. He wasn't using regular market cattle. King wanted a unique fair. He had the idea of a fair as entertainment, one that engaged the emerging urban population. He used the fair (or exposition, as they also called it) to promote Minneapolis.

People called him "Old Thaumaturgist," which was an odd word even in the nineteenth century. It meant a magician or miracle worker, and his fairs were such wonders that it would seem to be the reason for the name. The word carries a nuanced meaning that tells us more about him, that being his penchant for the legerdemain, a sleight of hand, or intended deceit. The antics King used in his battles with the St. Paul fair highlight this meaning of his nickname. The city of St. Paul was still run by Democrats, and he used the fair as a tool to combat those politicians. King would go to all ends to deceive the rival fair with the intention of crushing it.

In 1878 King's fair ran simultaneously with the St. Paul State Fair, and he threw his all into getting the main attractions. One thing drove a good fair: horse racing. But he missed out on Rarus. And the president—*his* president, a Republican—would prioritize a stop at St. Paul's fair, giving Minneapolis a consolation prize with a speech on his return from the Red River Valley on the final day of King's fair.

How to Fuel a Feud

The fair competition began in 1871. When the State Agricultural Society announced its fair for the end of September, King retaliated by scheduling his fair two weeks earlier, September 12–15. The entire community put their best effort forward. King exhibited his varieties of thoroughbred cattle. His friend, Horace Greeley, came west to deliver the annual address. And it was well known that by holding the fair so near in time and place to the State Fair, Minneapolitans intended to do more than just compete with St. Paul. They wanted to deliver a blow to its fair.[24]

This effort put St. Paul businessmen in an uproar. Immediately after the Minneapolis fair, the people of St. Paul responded. The larger of the two cities with a population of 20,030, St. Paul publicized the State Fair in resounding fashion. Letters and news stories appeared in print, and promotional materials made the rounds. The resulting fair was a huge success. For the first time, farmers exhibited products raised along the line of the Lake Superior and Mississippi Railroad, running from St. Paul to Duluth, including a 120-pound squash, seventeen-pound beets, and thirty-pound cabbages. Even Minneapolis contributed to the happy results.[25]

The next year, the fairs were similar in this style of competition. Instead of exhibiting at the Agricultural Society's State Fair, King shipped his best cattle specimens to the Illinois State Fair. The close relationship between the fair and the railroads was a new development. The expanding rail lines became partners with the fair, facilitating promotion and offering special fair rates to people who lived far away. The general public seemed less particular about the fairs as they enjoyed them both. When the two fairs were running at the same time, the organizers might have been trying to undermine each other, but for fairgoers it was like a holiday. Both fairs were good, and visitors benefited from the rivalry with twice the fun.[26]

Trouble started in 1873, when another economic panic drove the country into a depression. As the country recovered, a grasshopper plague struck, ravaging the crops year after year. In 1876 the economy was improving, giving people hope for a return to normal. But the wet spring caused a late planting, followed by a drought, and then the grasshoppers returned and laid waste to the crops. It was all finished off with a devastating hailstorm. Minnesotans were determined to have the fair and scheduled it for October 3–7, but the weather turned early and ugly, itself "a freak of nature." Every day was cloudy with gusty, cold winds. Only small crowds gathered at the most popular events: the horse races and ball games. People rode to the fair on wagons against cold, driving rains; a silent, solemn sight akin to a funeral procession. The merchants and businessmen of St. Paul and Minneapolis dropped out of the exposition, leaving exhibition buildings empty. The 1876 fair was a failure from beginning to end.[27]

The silver lining of that experience was the hard times brought a conciliatory mood among the competing fair organizers. Through that failure, it appeared they might have resolved themselves to collaborate on the state fair. At the Agricultural Society's meeting in early 1877 King announced that he thought a permanent site should be selected for the fair. Then, the debt-ridden State Agricultural Society merged with the Minnesota Stock Breeders' Association, of which King was the head. King was elected president of the newly combined Agricultural Society, causing some St. Paul members anxiety that they would lose control of the organization to him. As a sign of the times, society members also approved the executive committee to meet with the Minneapolis Board of Trade and St. Paul Chamber of Commerce to work on a permanent location for the fair. King, who also served as secretary on the Minneapolis Board of Trade, would be instrumental in choosing the site.[28]

In 1877 the rivalry between the two cities was spiking again. The issue this time was crime, and each blamed the other for its problems. Therefore, it's odd that the 1877 fair proved to be a high point in collaboration. The fair was held the first week of September at the Minneapolis fairgrounds, and King led the planning, promoting, and directing of the "great combined exposition" according to ads. He was in ill health that summer and overwhelmed, and though he resigned organizers refused his resignation so he continued to plan the fair. A Bill King fair included many attractions, ample buildings, and a crowd-pleasing racetrack. His fair also featured plentiful beer stands, numerous "side shows," and a variety of other so-called attractions. It received glowing reviews for the displays ("large, valuable, and attractive"); the livestock, poultry, and agricultural products; and the exhibits of manufactures and the fine arts ("most excellent").[29]

The fair was boosted by good crop yields, fewer grasshoppers, beautiful fall weather, and an improving economy. People were able to have a hopeful outlook for the future. Additionally, the residents of the then small city of Minneapolis rallied themselves to make the exposition a success for the town's reputation. Nearly every manufacturer and merchant in the city had an exhibit. St. Paul and the Agricultural Society pitched in, and other towns connected by rail did too. The street railway with horse-drawn cars had four lines that brought people to the fair, thanks to King's initiative with the street railway company. The Milwaukee Road brought St. Paul passengers over the river for twenty-five cents. In the most extreme contrast to the previous year, the cars and coaches were overfilled with a celebratory mood, the people singing and laughing along the way.[30]

That fair of 1877 attracted the largest crowds ever assembled in the state for a single occasion: 20,000 on one day. The organizers made a lot of money. After the fair, they summarily dissolved the partnership and split the profit of $6,398 between the two organizations, which brought the Agricultural Society out of debt. The fair of 1877 was truly King's greatest success in production and profit. The union of the two cities had shown they could work together to the benefit of each. They didn't have to compete to be their best.[31]

But after that one moment of successful unity, everything devolved to the familiar one-upmanship. St. Paul expressed interest in collaborating on the 1878 fair, but King "indignantly rejected" the offer, according to the *St. Paul Globe*. A dispute arose regarding the location of another combined fair, but also King believed he could make the money for himself. King, recalcitrant, was outraged. He vowed revenge and decided to hold his own fair in Minneapolis with his new statewide organization, the Minnesota Agricultural and Mechanical Association, designed to compete with the Agricultural Society. He was determined to force the Agricultural Society to "abandon the field," the newspaper reported. Astonished, the Agricultural Society resented his attempt to destroy them and resolved to go head-to-head with King's fair.[32]

King went all out. He produced a much larger fair with the same features of livestock, fast horses, parades, and renowned speakers. Minneapolis had record attendance, with estimates of 150,000 visits. Generally, the people felt the Minneapolis fair was the better of the two, due to the number and scope of exhibits. It had total receipts of $30,000, nearly unimaginable, and nearly triple what had been made before. It succeeded at a premium, however, as expenses exceeded income. As with King's farm, his numerous ventures, and now his fairs, King's success in numbers and reputation was at the expense of his finances.[33]

Then the Agricultural Society scheduled Rarus and President Hayes. St. Paul was elated with the president attending its fair. But both exhibitions were successful, attracting thousands of people each day. The large attendance was due to the local pride and public spirit of St. Paul and Minneapolis, which moved people to turn out for both fairs. The rivalry did not lead people to boycott a fair.

Hayes, in concluding his talk at the 1878 St. Paul State Fair, referred admiringly to the condition of the Twin Cities. He used the lighthearted ribbing of counting people for a territory to make a specific point. He employed the story to heighten the contrast of how few people were in Minnesota thirty years ago to congratulate residents on their current population: "[I]f you are not a million in Minnesota you soon will be," he said. And with that he could say the hard part: St. Paul and Minneapolis "are one in interest, one in the future, one great city, in spite of present difficulty," reported the *Daily Globe*. The crowd laughed and gave him "prolonged applause." His mission was to "conciliate," whether nationally or locally, and he forecast in ten years a city of 100,000–200,000, embracing both the cities of St. Paul and Minneapolis, which drew "great applause."[34]

For the readers of the New York papers a correspondent broke down the situation. The Twin Cities' rivalry was "constant," like that seen between New York and Boston or Chicago and St. Louis. A significant difference, he noted, was their relative position to each other. They are rather close, which meant the rivalry could be personal as well. The president's visit left one of them jilted. "Minneapolis was jealous of St. Paul, and the President had given the former the go-by," he reported.[35]

At some point the president's entourage was informed of the need for him to appear in Minneapolis. He was advised to "pass one day at least in each of the rival cities," attracting visitors to both fairs. Then both cities would have "the same cause for congratulation and boasting," noted the New York reporter. However, if one fair were preferred to the other, then "existing jealousies would be intensified."[36]

Hayes had one day to visit, Thursday, and he was scheduled to speak at the St. Paul fair. King was very angry and urged the presidential party to stay longer in Minnesota to promote his fair. When they wouldn't, King requested the president skip St. Paul and attend his fair instead. "Much telegraphing and letter writing has been concentrated upon this point," but the presidential party kept the schedule. St. Paul was to be "exceptionally favored." The citizens of St. Paul "chuckled," reported the *New-York Tribune*, while those of Minneapolis "felt aggrieved."[37]

At some point the president altered his schedule to visit Minneapolis on his return from the Red River Valley. By that time, the Minneapolis fair was winding down. Hayes spoke on the fair's last day to about 20,000 people in the amphitheater of the Minnesota Agricultural Fair Grounds, about the same number as at St. Paul. He gave a more substantial speech at Minneapolis than was reported at other stops, though he did not give a dissertation on economics as he did in St. Paul. The salt in the wound was in the opening of a story covering the incident: The *New York Herald* placed the wrong city in the dateline, stating that the events took place in Indianapolis.[38]

In closing his Minneapolis speech, the president again tried to reconcile the differences between the cities. Hayes thanked listeners for their reception of his ideas, "some of which, doubtless, they [the audience] do not altogether agree with." He highlighted this feature in American public life. Whatever is said "in the angry discussion of political strife," the American people, regardless of political party, "seem to have the sagacity" to realize who they are talking and thinking about, and despite "ever so many mistakes," if they find the person is "honest and patriotic and means well, they will treat him as you treat me." Hayes's efforts to reconcile the nation's divided spirit found a local application in Minnesota.[39]

Life in the Twin Cities was a scrappy competition within a nation that was trying to put its deadly conflict in its past. A more optimistic view of the rivalry appears repeatedly. "There can hardly help being a spirit of rivalry between these two cities," said the *Daily Globe*, "but this rivalry has been to the advantage of both and neither one has lost by it in the estimation of outside sections of the country." A divided metropolitan area was viewed as competitive or enriching, whereas no one could say that about the Civil War. War was Hell. Rivalry was merely Purgatory.[40]

The Road to a State Fair in the Midway

Through the ensuing years, the fair associations continued their antics. Call it a chess game or—lacking strategy—a game of chicken. Each tried to bait the other into collaborating through a compromised position. When that didn't work, each tried to ruin the other. King never produced consistent returns, and in some cases lost a great deal of money. St. Paul ran hot and cold, year to year, with great community buy-in during some years and a lack of interest in others.

In 1877, the year of the profitable combined fair, city representatives initiated a formal search for a permanent location in the Midway between St. Paul and Minneapolis. Then, in 1879, a year after the "Hayes" Fair, they offered "to abandon the fight," according to the *Minneapolis Tribune*, and work together in promoting their shared interests of agriculture and industries. King along with other citizens met with representatives of the Agricultural Society and St. Paul. They began to plan a union exhibition prioritizing grounds midway between the cities with easy railroad access from each. This unified fair buoyed people's hopes, as they believed it would reflect their true potential in working together. But something derailed the efforts to unite the fairs. The sides couldn't agree on a location. The Agricultural Society pulled a fast one and got surprised by the response. It delayed scheduling the fair until Minneapolis announced its dates. Then the Agricultural Society promptly scheduled its fair for the same week as Minneapolis, setting up a head-to-head competition. In response, Minneapolis capitulated—offering St. Paul a union fair, giving them choice of location, full management, and so on. St. Paul declined several similar proposals.[41]

St. Paul never trusted King's offers, which were almost too generous. He would describe St. Paul as "the post of honor" and allow a St. Paul man to run the show with supportive work by King. Minneapolis men would do most of the work and raise funds, allowing a surplus to go toward expenses. Yet there would be a caveat. Due to prior obligations, the fair needed to be in Minneapolis. The Minneapolis fairgrounds were widely viewed as the most complete and convenient to access. And it may have been that Minneapolis was angling for its fairgrounds as the permanent fair site. Time and again, St. Paul declined the overtures. And this refusal upset Minneapolis.[42]

Such concerns aside, King seemed to be done with fairs. But there was too much bad blood between the two cities. "And so we may at any moment hear the formal declaration of war," said the *Tribune*. "Minneapolis evidently anticipates it, and with her usual spirit and vim provides for it. Her propositions for peace being rejected, she loses no time in preparing for war." The Minneapolis businessmen rallied and pledged $10,000.[43]

King was the best at public fanfare. His newspapers, his politics, and his fairs had his unmistakable brand of outlandish embellishment, exaggeration, and showmanship. But he couldn't squash the St. Paul fair because St. Paul had something Minneapolis didn't. St. Paul was the capital, and the people who didn't live in the Twin Cities generally had some state-level association with St. Paul. Minneapolis boosters craved that top-tier title, but until they got it, it was Minneapolis versus St. Paul and the rest of Minnesota. Often overlooked in the rivalry is that the nonmetro communities were watching and had a say in what happened in state-level events like the fair and the capital location. Without the communities of Greater Minnesota, the two cities would have been deadlocked on issues.

When the failure to unite was evident, the *Daily Globe* collected newspaper headlines and comments from around the state in the spring of 1879 under the headline: "The War Which Minneapolis Makes Upon the State Exposed," adding that "All the State Will Rally Except Bill King." The collected clippings exposed another theme about how people viewed the two fairs.[44]

Most of the newspapers of communities beyond the metro viewed the issue as King's problem. "Bill King wanted it all his way," the *Hastings New Era* said, "and because St. Paul would not consent he declared war." The *Wabashaw Herald* agreed, writing, "St. Paul and Minneapolis are again on the war-path on the fair question." St. Paul had agreed to a random selection for the hosting, but Minneapolis said it was all or nothing. That wasn't all bad in the eyes of the *Farmington Press*, which looked for the silver lining, noting that the rivalry of last year would again provide a "stupendous display." So be it, the writer concluded. "Everybody will want to visit both as usual, and we shall probably witness another grand carnival."

"Bill King, or Minneapolis proper, seems unwilling to bury the hatchet and shake hands with St. Paul," said the *Zumbrota Independent*. "Although opposition is the life of trade," the commentors also thought it could be overdone. They cut a joke at King's expense regarding the money he lost at fairs: "If Bill King feels disposed to donate to the State a portion of the proceeds of his Canada trip in this manner, we have nothing to say." (King, as a congressional representative in the mid-1870s, spent an extended time in Canada to avoid a subpoena from a congressional committee.)

Combining "the two great fairs . . . turned out a miserable failure, as everybody expected it would," the *Northfield Mail* expressed a bit fatalistically. "If the two cities can stand the throat cutting game," said the *Delano Eagle*, "the rest of the State can stand it to look on." But the *Eagle* made clear its preference was the Agricultural Society's fair. There would be two fairs come September, noted the *St. Cloud Times*, with "the old jealousies, strifes . . . and discords between the two cities." Its writers encouraged people to patronize the St. Paul fair. And here is a notable point: Regardless of the failed collaborative fair, said the *Le Sueur Sentinel*, "it is impossible for sober-minded farmers not to see that their duty is to exhibit their products" at the St. Paul fair. The life of the Agricultural Society "is at stake in the coming struggle."

Time and again, these towns and cities outside the Twin Cities expressed their allegiance to the Agricultural Society's fair. Despite King's exotic livestock, the St. Paul fair reportedly had the better livestock show and was more representative of Minnesota at large.[45]

That year of 1879 Minneapolis wanted to strike a fatal blow to the St. Paul fair, and in many ways it succeeded. The fairs were held on the same days, and Minneapolis had a competitive verve. King's fair was better attended. Its organizers had plenty of money and "a spirit of liberality." Some thought St. Paul should not compete, not to mention the Agricultural Society's enormous debt of $4,000. Rumors said the organization ceased to exist.[46]

But the St. Paul fair returned in 1880 in Rochester, and it was successful financially with good attendance. King announced "a great Northwestern fair," but it rained. The Agricultural Society broke even, while King lost an astounding $18,000. This continued in the coming years as King tried to outdo the society and, from a numbers point of view, he did. His fair attracted multitudes of people to view the expensive exhibits, but for promotional purposes organizers distributed thousands of tickets for free admission. With no financial report ever published, people speculated that he had lost money.[47]

The two fairs had been engaged in their frenemy tactics since 1871. The finale was reached in 1883. Again, an offer of a united fair; again, a rejection. This time King proposed to hold the fair on new grounds between the cities, in the Midway. But St. Paul was skeptical of his motives, afraid such a site would benefit Minneapolis more than St. Paul.

In revenge, King lived up to his nickname of Old Thaumaturgist and "opted for trickery." He announced he would hold no fair, hoping the Agricultural Society would be lulled into complacency and plan a mediocre fair. When the society announced its fair would be in Owatonna, King sprung the news that his fair would be held one week earlier in Minneapolis. Again he aimed to outclass the other fair, the hope being that the Agricultural Society would wither and die. The exhibits and advertised products at King's fair were a success, but the fair in general was a failure. It never was repeated.[48]

The most significant event of 1883 was that King tried to pull a double cross. It seemed to be the last straw and ended his fair activities. The organizers had beat around the bush for so many years, no one was happy. Exhaustion was apparent, but the two organizations were unwilling to quit. The consensus was that a permanent home would lead to mutual profit and benefit, but all the potential locations, such as Minnehaha Falls or a Midway spot, were too expensive, running about $10,000 per acre. A more reasonable price was available at the Ramsey County Poor Farm, but Minneapolis rejected it.[49]

In the end, Minneapolis woke up one morning in 1885 to learn that Ramsey County had offered the grounds of its poor farm for the state fairgrounds and the Agricultural Society had accepted. The legislature supported the incorporation of the neutral territory and passed an appropriation of $100,000 to construct buildings for the State Fair. Ramsey County formalized its offer and donated to the state 200 acres for a fairground. The State Fair had a permanent home.

Minneapolis felt jilted, once again, but the stalemate was broken.

St. Paul, as the capital, showed its greater political influence in this legislation of the land transfer and appropriations. In addition, the legislation extended the St. Paul city limits west to the Ramsey County line on the Mississippi. The Twin Cities were now contiguous, and the river a boundary twice over at the county and municipal levels. This expansion would irritate most everyone in the Midway and Minneapolis. A crafty maneuver, it shaped future conversations and caused problems in efforts to unite the two cities.[50]

The State Fair's new location happened to be about halfway between the two city centers. A railroad spur track was run into the middle of the fairgrounds for easy access across both cities. The animosity seemed to diminish, and the two associations worked together for the fair's success. After thirty years of fairs, in September 1885 the modern State Fair was born.

CHAPTER 8

Navigating the Gorge, Negotiating the Capitol

The Minnesota Capitol was full of business for an evening session of the legislature on March 1, 1881. At about 9:00 P.M., a young page ran into the Senate chamber chased by falling embers and billowing black smoke, crying, "Fire! FIRE!" Everyone soon discovered the building's center dome was filled with flames. People went to the doors and found the flames blocking the stairs. All the exits were inaccessible. The smoke began to come down through the ventilator in the center of the chamber's ceiling, making "the imprisoned" uneasy. Everyone had become "completely unnerved." People shouted orders at the top of their lungs and cursed. The president of the senate violently rapped his gavel and called for order. He vaulted over his desk and "with stentorian voice" ordered people to stay cool, saying, "for God's sake, gentlemen, be still, there is plenty of time." But his actions only stirred the confusion because nothing indicated that they had any time. Someone motioned to adjourn the session.

Senators rushed to the windows and smashed them. They looked down from a height of about thirty feet for a safe place to jump into a foot or two of snow. Flames appeared in the gallery and now glowing embers began to spit down from the ventilator. Gas lines exploded and fueled the inferno. The open windows supplied more oxygen to the fire but also helped the smoke to lift, so the senators returned to the stairs and made their escape. As the last members left the chamber, the large chandelier fell "and everything was wreathed in flames." The building's dome fell at 9:40, and the center of the Capitol became glowing embers. The fire began to burn out by midnight, with only spot fires remaining in the ruins a couple hours later.[1]

Incredibly, people managed a bucket brigade–style rescue of the building's contents and saved books, files, papers, paintings, and furniture, throwing these items in the street in a shoulder-high pile. The governor, clerk, state auditor, and historical society all had safes that survived and protected records. The greatest loss was books, over 11,000 of them, which included most of the law library. The most iconic scene was a man carrying out an enormous globe on his shoulders like Atlas.[2]

"The capitol was never a very handsome building," said the *Daily Globe*, "but last night's ordeal did not improve its appearance." The next morning dawned on an aggressive effort to remove the capital city designation from St. Paul.[3]

Minneapolis business leaders tried throughout the 1880s to become the capital city. They had done the same with the head of navigation just as St. Paul leadership had wanted to capture the waterpower. An interesting twist to the rivalry between the cities was their mutual jealousy. Each city coveted the other's natural gifts—river access versus river power. Minneapolis had a jump start in its manufacturing and milling development because it could use St. Paul's established commercial development. Utilizing that advantage, Minneapolis leaders pursued their metropolitan ambitions. They wanted to be a center of trade, which came with the head of navigation. And they wanted to be the capital, which meant power and being center stage of state affairs. If they couldn't be the capital, the consolation would be to bring the Capitol building closer to Minneapolis. The fight for the capital city and the location of the Capitol building rose to a climax in the 1880s.[4]

In 1875 the two cities were as close as they would ever be to identical twins in terms of population, with Minneapolis (including St. Anthony) at 32,721 and St. Paul at 33,178. Both were in the process of doubling in size in that decade, leading to the expectation that they would soon grow together "whether or not they maintain separate municipal organisms," according to the *Minneapolis Daily Tribune*. As they filled the physical space between them, they anticipated uniting the head of navigation and the waterpower. The consensus was that the two cities would someday become one city. When viewed from outside as well as from within, the two cities were beginning to look like one metropolis.[5]

The rivalry was decidedly juvenile as "they had stood for years like two boys with chips on their shoulders." Their separate development was their birthright and at the heart of their rivalry. In 1877, while they stood equal in numbers, the spirit of their rivalry was at its most pitched and feverish. They harbored "a feeling of animosity as bitter as it was intense," said the *Daily Globe*. And the citizens, like true fans, were on board.[6]

St. Paul had a jump start on development, with upward of 6,000 people before Minneapolis had a post office. As the head of navigation, it was the focal point of the exchange of goods, including storage and transportation of those goods. It was the starting point of stage lines to the north and west. As the capital, it was the center of political and business affairs for not only the state but the region as well.

St. Paul's economy underwent a transformation during the period of 1870–90. Its early economy was based on the exchange of goods for the Indian trade and the fur trade. The Indian trade disappeared after the Dakota were forcibly exiled from the state following the US–Dakota War of 1862. But St. Paul remained a top fur trading city as the region for harvest expanded. The military contributed to the economy, as did the growing wholesale trade. In 1869, as the commercial center, St. Paul had sixty-two jobbing houses, which imported goods and sold them to retailers. Between 1877 and 1881, the jobbers almost doubled their wholesale business volume to $47 million. The river remained important for transportation, although St. Paul was the hub for railroads, which were now growing steadily in the nation's second railroad boom.[7]

Through the Civil War, St. Anthony and Minneapolis were reliant on St. Paul, which had an unquestioned supremacy into the mid-1870s. Then, Minneapolis absorbed St. Anthony in 1872, as had been expected since the village was annexed to Hennepin County in 1855. The thirty-eight percent population increase along with additional milling power made the community more resilient to the 1873 market panic and following economic depression. A series of technological breakthroughs in addition to the development of railroad infrastructure brought Minneapolis to realize the manufacturing and milling potential of the falls and challenge St. Paul's supremacy in population and wealth.[8]

The innovations in flour production were unforeseen, and they played to Minneapolis's favor. Because of the northern climate, Minnesota farmers raised a hard spring wheat variety. When ground between two millstones this wheat yielded a brownish flour (like today's whole wheat flour), which at the time was less desirable. The first breakthrough was when European millers developed a milling process that crushed the wheat kernel between iron rollers (instead of grinding it). After multiple passes, the rougher bran husk fell off the starchy, glutenous middlings (today called the endosperm). The second breakthrough was the ability to remove the rough bran pieces with forced air. When this was done, the middling yielded a white flour. Introduced in 1870, these technologies launched Minneapolis flour into a premier product in world markets.[9]

Meanwhile, farmers had a simultaneous leap with the invention of the self-binding harvester, which saved labor, reduced their costs, and allowed them to increase their acreage. The railroads were rapidly expanding their network, reaching new fields such as the rich soils of the Red River Valley. That in turn attracted droves of immigrant farmers. All these factors increased wheat production for mills that were ramping up their flour production. By 1880 the largest mills were churning out 4,500 barrels of flour a day, nearly eight times more than previously. The nineteenth-century industrial mind had finally captured the promise of St. Anthony Falls. The innovations transformed Minneapolis.[10]

Running the Gorge

The industrial verve of Minneapolis had captured the falls, but proving that the city was the head of navigation was much more difficult. Between St. Anthony Falls and St. Paul downtown the river drops over 100 feet, most of it through the confines of the steep-sided gorge where the river was choked with blocks of limestone debris. When Plympton and Steele first staked claims near the falls, the river was actively cutting the gorge, eating away the underlying sandstone and collapsing the limestone cap. The result was hull-splitting rapids and shallow channels. Aside from the falls themselves, the gorge was the most impassable point on the Mississippi. The gorge already played a big role in the creation of the Twin Cities, and from the 1850s on it became a part of the struggle for superiority between the cities.

In St. Paul's early days people predicted the settlement would never survive. They expected it would be bypassed when the river channel was cleared to St. Anthony. The most viable landing was about a mile below the falls, called Cheever's Landing, near today's University of Minnesota. People expected that location would be the "head of navigation." The towns at the falls wanted that claim.[11]

By road, St. Paul was nine miles from the falls. By river, it was nearly sixteen miles on a steamboat, with the gorge adding time and uncertainty. When viewed through distance alone, the geographic layout suggests St. Paul was a shortcut to the falls, an obvious solution to the problem presented by the river's winding route and the challenging gorge. And yes, the settler, tourist, or speculator had several travel options. They could ride on one of the two stagecoach lines queued at the steamboat landings or rent a buggy at the livery stables. But it wasn't the answer for every purpose.

Hauling freight to St. Anthony or Minneapolis, on the other hand, gave one a different perspective on the river route and the gorge. Steamboats could carry 350 to 400 tons of materials such as bags of grain, steel slabs, bundles of sheet iron, hundreds of boxes of glass, dozens of boxes of axes, hoes, spades, and pitchforks. All that freight was unloaded at St. Paul, stored, transferred to wagons, and hauled over the hills of

The view looking upriver at St. Anthony Falls. The steamboat on the right shore is at Cheever's Landing (today East River Flats).

St. Paul, which raised the cost. It made practical, economic sense to find a way to navigate the gorge.[12]

In 1850 no boats had tried to ascend the gorge so the issue was still unsettled. St. Anthony coaxed steamboat captains to try the ascent with offers of cash, extra insurance, and exclusive cargo rights. In early May 1850 the *Anthony Wayne* came up from St. Louis (about a two-week trip), and Captain Rogers announced he would continue up to the falls. A large party of people joined them, including Governor Ramsey. The captain made the navigation look easy and ascended the gorge faster than expected.[13]

With the first "steamer" reaching the falls, celebration was in order. The passengers danced on the decks late into the night to the music of the fort's Sixth Infantry band. The town leaders called out for Captain Rogers and rewarded him with the premium purse of $250. They held a meeting and passed resolutions that celebrated the captain for having shown how practical and easy it was to navigate the gorge. The town pledged to patronize the *Anthony Wayne* with their business. The next day the boat pulled into the current, and within twenty-four hours it was hundreds of miles downriver.[14]

It repeated the run on June 28. Again, with a large party on board, the *Anthony Wayne* left St. Paul at 9:00 A.M. and left Fort Snelling at noon. The current was calculated at eight miles per hour. The *Anthony Wayne*'s engine in ordinary current could make ten miles per hour. In the gorge, the captain opened up the engines to clock two or three miles per hour.

By midafternoon the boat and its passengers landed within view of the falls near the village. At dusk they left and were in St. Paul by bedtime.[15]

In those first years, the steamboats *Anthony Wayne*, *Lamartine*, *Dr. Franklin No. 2*, and *Nominee* made the climb, allowing St. Anthony to claim to be "the head and foot of navigation." Businessmen built warehouses below the falls near Cheever's Landing that would receive, distribute, and forward cargo. The steamboat *Governor Ramsey* ran upriver from the falls to Sauk Rapids. In short order, the community assembled the infrastructure and with a determined confidence called St. Anthony the natural depot for the goods that came up and down the Mississippi River.[16]

The boats that made it up the gorge in the early 1850s, however, carried more people than cargo. Often a boat needed to drop part or all of its cargo before ascending the gorge. "It would never pay to run up there," said one captain considering such difficulties. The captains faced a paradox: For a steamboat to ascend the gorge they needed high water to get over the boulders and sandbars, but that meant the current was too strong for them to make a reliable ascent, especially with cargo. For a boat that did try, one captain guessed, he had "two chances in three of being stove in pieces in trying to back out of a bad scrape." The risks increased the cost and, in the end, hauling overland from St. Paul was more reliable. Unloading at the confluence would have been an alternative option as the shippers could access an easier road on the west side of the river. But at that time they couldn't unload any freight there because the Reserve closed the landings.[17]

Despite St. Anthony's rising confidence, few steamboat captains were interested in the adventure. People in St. Anthony accused their rival of interfering, by exaggerating the dangers and the cost of insurance. But it was no secret that only boats able to face the risk of destruction made the run. Three of the boats that navigated the gorge, *Anthony Wayne*, *Lamartine*, and *Dr. Franklin No. 2*, were older boats. By 1852 they had all sunk or blown up (though not in the gorge). "Really, it would appear [running the gorge] is death on a steamboat," chided a St. Paul editor.[18]

Enticed by those early steamboat ascents, advocates organized companies to build boats of special design for the falls trade. The St. Anthony Falls Steamboat Company had their boat, the *Falls City*, customized for the gorge by premier steamboat builders in the Pittsburgh area. A sternwheeled boat over fifty yards long and nine yards wide with four and a half feet of draft, it could carry 400 tons. Based at St. Anthony, it was scheduled to run from Rock Island or Dubuque to the falls through the season. The captain promised the owners he would "dip her bow in the spray mist of the cataract." He was aware of what was at stake, that this boat was "a final test" of the gorge. If this customized boat successfully skimmed over the boulders, the problem was solved. However, if it failed, he said, "we may bid a long farewell to steam navigation to the Falls."[19]

The *Falls City* reached St. Paul in July 1855 and dropped its freight. On its first run it reached Meeker's Landing four miles below the falls and faltered. In turning around, the stern struck a ledge of rocks and the current swept the bow against the riverbank. On this maiden voyage it sustained damages of fifty percent of its production costs. Once repaired, the *Falls City* made regular trips from St. Paul to Galena, but it never again tried to run up the gorge. The boat was sold before the close of its second season.[20]

Minneapolis interests would keep trying. In the spring of 1857 a Pittsburgh line of steamers was contracted to run the gorge. From the beginning of May to June 18 it recorded twenty-seven arrivals at St. Anthony. The steamers delivered 3,000 tons of goods. The spring runoff was the secret to their success. But the risks remained, and many businesses continued to haul overland from St. Paul.[21]

The river had stopped the *Falls City* in 1855 at a predictable spot. Moving upriver from Fort Snelling to the falls, the gorge became progressively more difficult to navigate. The lower half had deeper water and few obstructions. At a dogleg bend near Rum Pitch, the river gorge narrowed, and the water became steeper, faster, and rougher. Steamboats had more success ascending the lower section and landing there at Meeker's Landing. The advocates adjusted their goals.

"The '*Head of Navigation*' is discovered at last!" declared the promoters of St. Anthony. They announced that the steamboat *Hindoo* sat at Meeker's Landing waiting to unload its St. Anthony–bound cargo. This was only the beginning, they said, as the *Hindoo* could reliably navigate to this point and planned a weekly run. They called for donations and volunteers to grade a short road from "the future levee" to St. Anthony. They rang their bells and shouted. St. Paul laughed at its "sister city" and its boosterism for a new landing. It simply wasn't a threat to St. Paul.[22]

St. Paul editors were always there to tease the St. Anthony gorge runners when they failed. "Lost, some time this summer," read the *Daily Minnesota Pioneer*, "a stray 'Head of Navigation,' supposed to have belonged at some very recent period, (the date of which is not certain,) somewhere in the vicinity of 'Meeker's Landing.' Last sightings were of the stray floating downstream." The newspaper mockingly offered a reward for the Head of Navigation's "safe delivery at the Lower Landing" in St. Paul.[23]

The midpoint in the gorge near Meeker's Landing continued to attract people's interest. It was where Plympton had placed the Reserve boundary, where Rum Pitch gave soldiers access to Donald McDonald's groggery,

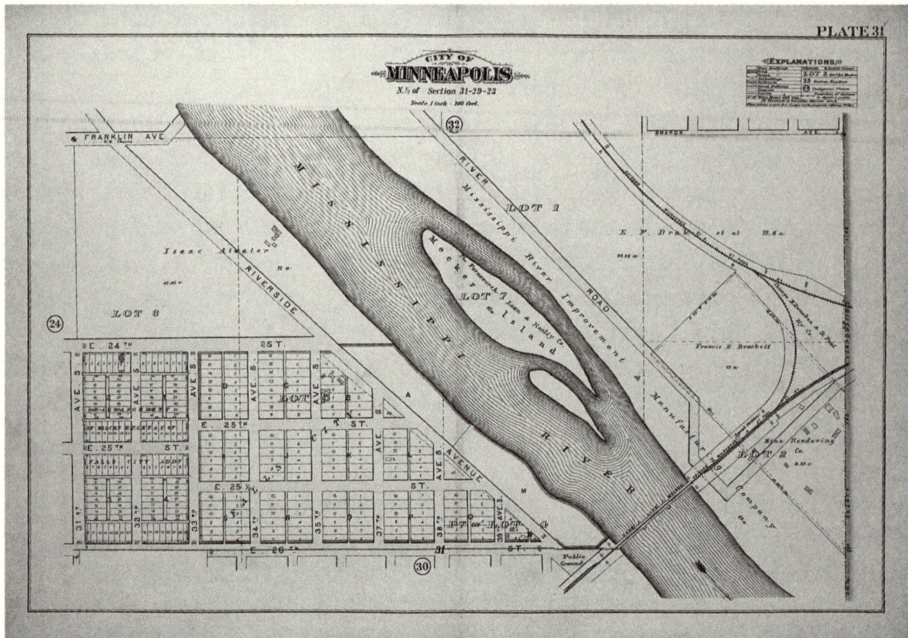

Map of Falls City on the west side of the Mississippi River gorge just above the Short Line Bridge and across from Meeker's Island and Landing. Stephen Desnoyer's property was on the east side and south of the railroad tracks. This "paper town" was drawn in 1856 and never developed.

and the site Stephen Desnoyer had declared to be the future city center (today's Lake Street–Marshall Avenue bridge). In the 1856 real estate boom, Henry C. Keith, a farmer on the west side of the river, laid out the town of Falls City, a paper town opposite Meeker's Landing and just upriver of Desnoyer's property. Keith's development assumed that this area of the gorge would be the head of navigation until the river channel above was cleared of obstructions. The plan was to build a warehouse, develop a landing, and grade a road into the gorge.[24]

In 1857 a group of Minneapolis men, headed by Bradley B. Meeker, began an effort to tame the rough waters of the gorge. They organized the Mississippi River Improvement and Manufacturing Company and began planning a lock and dam at Meeker's Landing. The benefit was obvious for St. Anthony and Minneapolis as it would make navigation to the falls easier and reliable. The drawback, however, was that such a system would gift St. Paul with waterpower. In 1867 St. Paul investors gained control of the company, and they prioritized developing hydraulic power for manufacturing. This led Bill King's *State Atlas* to react by saying Minneapolis would absorb any developments, such as factories or mills, by extending the Minneapolis city limits. The braggadocio aside, the battle over the gorge and its promise as a resource was important to both cities and their plans for growth. The western edge of St. Paul's city limits did not yet extend to the river, though the land east of the river was in Ramsey County. Some people in Minneapolis viewed the land in Ramsey County as available to them despite its political designation.[25]

The highest use of this navigation improvement idea was brought forward in 1879, as people from both cities discussed uniting. The Meeker dam was promoted as a power generator that would merge the interests of the two cities. In 1882 a joint operation by St. Paul and Minneapolis capitalists planned to revive the Mississippi River Improvement and Manufacturing Company to build a common manufacturing area. Importantly, the plans were now more about power generation and less about navigation.[26]

The two cities ended up on either side of the gorge and its potential as a resource held both a cure and a curse for both. Claiming the head of navigation was important for a variety of reasons. Minneapolis leaders wanted to establish the claim in order to bring associated commercial development. Businesses wanted it in order to lower their shipping costs. St. Paul wanted to develop the waterpower there. The industrial age mastered the development of the falls but failed to navigate the gorge by boat or dam. The various interested parties were unable to bring ideas to fruition until the twentieth century. By then the development had little impact on the area's economics.

The Capital City

After fire destroyed the Capitol in 1881 Minneapolis people made efforts to shift the capital city. Governor John S. Pillsbury moved quickly and refused to consider the question. Like the river and the gorge, the capital city and the Capitol building were points of conflict between the two cities. Politicians and businessmen considered the capital location an open debate.[27]

The capital location for Minnesota was an ever-grinding problem. Minnesota came of age in the antebellum period, and its territorial and state designations were embedded in the escalating tensions over state sovereignty. Illinois Senator Stephen A. Douglas, chairman of the US Senate Committee on Territories, introduced the Minnesota Territorial bill on December 20, 1848, the same day he introduced the Nebraska Territorial bill. Though these two bills took different courses—Minnesota became a territory on the last day of that session, March 3, 1849, and Nebraska would become a territory with the Kansas–Nebraska Act of 1854—they shared a particular ideal of Douglas's.

Douglas, a state maker and a Minnesota booster, believed in the Jacksonian ideal that people (as opposed to politicians) were able to decide all aspects regarding their government. A key feature of the Kansas-Nebraska Act of 1854, which Douglas also authored, gave each state the right to decide the legality of slavery. He applied the concept to the capital of Minnesota as well. With the creation of Minnesota Territory, St. Paul was designated the capital, though it was not permanent. Douglas ensured the capital could be moved if the people chose through a popular vote or through the action of their representatives.

With statehood, St. Paul remained the capital, and the popular vote clause stayed on the books. Dozens of states have moved their capital city for a variety of reasons, such as population shifts, economic stimulus, and so on. These reasons applied to Minnesota's debates too.[28]

But for Minnesota this flexibility of locating the capital by popular decree became an ongoing squabble that featured an array of political antics over the years. The unending battle of the capital city location, and consequently the Capitol building's location, fueled the rivalry between the twins. The arguments over the capital's location demonstrated the hazards of democratic decision-making. "If democratic excess implied indecision and self-seeking," commented historian Neil B. Thompson, "then the pioneers of the North Star State would prove the point."[29]

From territorial status of 1849 until 1893 the government was under a constant barrage of proposals for relocating the capital. Rumors circulated—and were stirred up constantly—claiming the legislature would decide on a new location for the capital at the next session. Talk about moving the capital became a sort of backdrop to the routine of life, a fishing expedition, always looking for the right mix of political will, popular support, and money.

In a comic picture that is now lost to history, an illustrator captured the onset of the capital-removal effort by sketching an image of the Capitol building on wheels. At the front, a legislator is tugging on a rope, pulling the building toward his preferred town, St. Anthony. On the other end were a number of St. Paul legislators pulling back on the ropes attached to the Capitol and blocking the wheels to stop its movement. Over the years, the people at the front pulling the Capitol to new destinations changed, but St. Paul was always in the same position, fighting to keep it. And "the Capitol on wheels," which symbolized the capital removal efforts, became an enduring and truthful phrase.[30]

The capital location was on the move from the first draft. Douglas initially proposed Mendota as the capital and placed the capitol building on Pilot Knob, the highest point for miles around and a sacred site for the Dakota people. St. Paul, being the largest town, was chosen instead. In the first legislative session, 1850, the St. Paul delegation tried to fix the capital there permanently. But that was upset by others who wanted St. Anthony to be the seat of government. That battle came to a draw. The legislature was hesitant to make St. Paul the permanent seat because members knew they couldn't predict where the future center would be. The capital location remained open to a future vote.[31]

As Minnesota's economy was baptized in land speculation, it would have been a surprise if the capital didn't get in on the play. In 1857, at the height of the speculative paper towns, a group of men, including Territorial Governor Willis A. Gorman, organized the St. Peter Company. They laid claim to land near the bend in the Minnesota River's southern apex and built temporary buildings to accommodate the territorial government. They recruited support from legislators with kickbacks of town lots

The first Capitol opened for the fifth session of the legislature on January 4, 1854. It was a simple building two stories tall and topped by a dome, with the long side facing southeast on Exchange Street and fronted by a Greek portico with four columns.

The second Capitol stood in the same location as the first. Built quickly on a small budget, it was cramped, had structural problems in the roof, and had poor air circulation. Everyone complained about it from the first day. It was condemned within a few years, prompting the battles for the capital city and the Capitol building to continue.

and stock. The legislature passed the capital move and Gorman signed it into law. In a crime–comedy, State Representative Joseph Rolette Jr., a longtime resident of the area with interests along the northwestern border and close ties to St. Paul politicians, absconded with the bill and holed up in a hotel. He stalled the process and contributed to the effort's failure. St. Paul remained the capital city.[32]

People made efforts to move the capital to Nicollet Island, the mouth of the Crow River, Crookston, and more. As the state population grew, a tug-of-war developed between rural and urban representatives. The state owned ten sections of land, donated from the US government for public buildings, near Big Kandiyohi Lake in the west-central region. Repeatedly the rural caucus introduced legislation to move the seat of government there. This happened so often yet it was hardly considered realistic until, in 1869, the bill surprisingly passed both houses. The governor vetoed the measure and an attempt to pass the act over his veto failed.[33]

The capital relocation served other purposes such as a sort of political gesture. In February 1873 Frederick Douglass, the African American statesman, visited St. Paul and gave a lecture. Afterward, he went to check into a room at the Merchants Hotel, St. Paul's premier lodging. There, the hotel's owner refused him "on account of his color." In response to this insult, a legislator introduced a resolution to remove the capital from St. Paul. The politician offered no destination, and the resolution didn't pass. The act of proposing to move the capital was a way to snub St. Paul.[34]

Since St. Paul and Ramsey County politicians needed to routinely defend the location of the capital, they held a political bargaining chip with other legislators in other affairs. If someone else needed backing for a legislative agenda item, St. Paul legislators could offer their support in exchange for that party's alliance on the capital location question.[35]

Capitol in the Midway

While relocating the capital city was a state matter requiring legislative action, a number of people argued that St. Paul could situate the Capitol building within its limits as it pleased. Members of the Minneapolis Board of Trade were amenable to this idea as an alternative plan. If they couldn't capture the capital city, their next priority was to bring the Capitol building closer to them. Minneapolis civic and business leaders began as early as 1873 to promote a location for the Capitol building between the two city centers.[36]

The Midway area between the two cities was initially a broad, rolling prairie, notable for its wildflowers and prairie chickens, interspersed with clusters of oak trees. Much larger than today's St. Paul Midway neighborhood, it included the expanse from Fort Snelling at the confluence up to the State Fairgrounds, from St. Paul's Snelling Avenue west to the Seward neighborhood in Minneapolis. It featured Como Park, Hamline University, the State Fairgrounds, the agricultural college (also known as the Experimental Farm), the Minnesota Transfer (a train transfer and switching zone), Minnehaha Falls, St. Anthony Park, and many other "interurban" developments. Several of these locations, such as the State Fairgrounds, were close to equal distance from each of the city centers. The Midway stood apart from either city and held its own gravitas. It contained enough unique developments to play a part aside from being a residential suburb.[37]

Minnehaha Falls became an early favorite location for a new Capitol building. Minnehaha was in the country, allowing an escape from the noise and confusion of the city, but moving it there guaranteed that the typical institutions associated with the legislature—whiskey saloons and gambling houses—were sure to follow. The thought of the Capitol building at Minnehaha revived the ideas of Franklin Steele, the principal owner of the property, for a new city at the confluence.[38]

The *Tribune* joked at this proposal in an operatic spoof. To add a third city to unite the other two would result in a metropolis stretching ten miles in each direction. A gigantic city, it would be world-class just because of its size. "[T]he world would stand in awe of Minnesota. Where then would be your Jedda, your London, Paris, New York and Mendota? They, sir, would be dubbed but hamlets, villages and cross roads beside our mammoth, colossal, gigantic city." The humor touches on a theme of how people, especially boosters, forecast the future growth of the Twin Cities. The populations were growing rapidly. People saw the grand cities of the Old World, and they noticed how New York City and Chicago were becoming world-class cities. They easily projected the Twin Cities as next in that lineage.[39]

But a Capitol site between the cities was attractive, and supporters of the idea focused along the river gorge. A new Capitol built on the elevated plateau midway between the cities would overlook them both. The idea of arranging the layout to facilitate uniting the cities gained traction. No longer would people passively wait for the cities to grow together. From the mid-1870s through the 1880s, the Midway would get more attention and gain in popularity as the idea of uniting the two cities became more popular.[40]

Meanwhile, after the fire, the legislature built a second Capitol. It was built quickly for about $275,000 in the same location as the first one, fronting on Exchange Street, facing southeast (where the History Theatre stands today). Within a few years, inspectors declared the new Capitol hazardous because some of the roof supports were broken and about to fail. In 1888 one building inspector said he would not enter the Capitol with a crowd, as he had condemned the building two years prior. He had advised the governor and recommended the repairs that were finally being funded. One person concurred it was "a rat trap" and of use only as "an insane asylum," with the architect of the current Capitol to be the first man admitted. The architect argued the problem was the legislature's planning process. As the building's construction on a small budget neared completion, more money was approved for a fireproof roof—a slate that was heavier than the structure was designed to support.[41]

The situation raised the age-old questions of what to do when you have a lemon: Do you spend money on repairs, or do you cut your losses and build from scratch? This crisis of the poor structural integrity, along with overcrowding and poor air circulation, meant the Capitol location was up for grabs again.

The legislature created a commission to study the Capitol's location, and members were not without their biases. Minneapolis commissioners argued the current St. Paul spot did not have enough land to be the permanent home of the Capitol; it needed more room. Rumors circulated that Hennepin County was lobbying to move the capital to Minneapolis and build a new Capitol building there. St. Paul leaders were accustomed to defending their city's claim to the capital, but this latest effort by Minneapolis seemed to have better chances. "St. Paul will have to do some good work to thwart their scheme," said one editor. From early on, St. Paul sensed something amiss and suspected some ulterior motive.[42]

Minneapolis commissioners argued that the original compact of 1848 that had dispersed the essential facilities—the penitentiary in Stillwater, the university in St. Anthony/Minneapolis, and St. Paul as the capital—was not binding. It was difficult to believe, they argued, that a small group of men in St. Paul would restrict millions of people of succeeding generations to a particular location. Were people today bound by the founders' decisions? If the legislature would open the process for relocation of the capital, Minneapolis leaders planned to offer $2 million and ten acres of land for the Capitol building.[43]

Naturally, St. Paul commissioners defended the original compact. For forty years, St. Paul had stood as the capital. The government had doled out public institutions to Rochester, St. Peter, Stillwater, Minneapolis, and Faribault. The commissioners conceded that if there were problems with St. Paul's location and it was difficult to reach that would be cause to move the capital to a more convenient site. That point implicitly highlighted St. Paul's centrality in the railroad network and its convenient access.[44]

The Capitol crisis led to a broader discussion about the Capitol location between St. Paul and Minneapolis leaders. The Minneapolis Board of Trade and the St. Paul Chamber of Commerce played similar roles in each city. On this question, these business leaders were at the forefront of the conversation. The business and development organizations advised the municipal governments on these matters. They formed a committee consisting of members from each organization to discuss a new Capitol site.

At the February 1887 meeting of this collaborative group, the Minneapolis representatives came bearing flowers with Bill King in the lead. King realized his reputation preceded him, noting that the people of St. Paul viewed him as "Saul of Tarsus," but he declared a conversion to Paul's enlightenment. He was there to preach the gospel of saving and of benefit "for the ultimate good of St. Paul." Nothing could make St. Paul representatives more uneasy than a Minneapolis promoter telling them he was acting benevolently in St. Paul's best interests. The Minneapolis contingent's proposal would unite the two cities' interest, but the location would benefit St. Paul. "Place [the Capitol] anywhere on your border lines—for you have carried them clear to our city limits," King said. Two years earlier, St. Paul had annexed the Midway, expanding the city limits to the river. It was a preemptive move as the area was sparsely populated, but city leaders wanted to control it. The maneuver frustrated the various efforts of Minneapolis men. In this way, the second half of King's quote, "you have carried [the St. Paul border] clear to our city limits," may have come in a tone of agitation. Locating the Capitol in the Midway, in St. Paul, would appear to be to that city's benefit.[45]

Though building the Capitol was a state expense, if some city offered the land and money to build the Capitol the state wouldn't turn it away. Minneapolis offered to pay up to twenty-five percent of the building costs for a Capitol building located in the Midway. Plus, anywhere a new Capitol was built, people generally forecast rapid development and increasing values, which would help offset any expenses St. Paul incurred for construction. This offer, as well as the earlier proposal of $2 million and ten acres, suggested the Minneapolis group was serious. More than anything, these proposals put pressure on St. Paul to make a decision, one that might accommodate Minneapolis's wishes.[46]

The St. Paul committee members listened and said they would take the ideas back to the Chamber of Commerce and Jobbers' Union, the two organizations that would clear any decision. In Minneapolis the Board of Trade made these decisions, and King along with several other committee members served there as well.

St. Paul members suspected the Minneapolis proposal was a bluff, "but if it is, it is the kind of bluff the state would take to," said one senator. People wanted to see the Capitol built free of charge. The next day the *St. Paul Daily Globe* publicly accused the Minneapolis contingent of playing "a game of bluff." By introducing legislation to move the Capitol and offering land and money to build there, they were trying to "force" St. Paul into appropriating funds for a new Capitol building. "Why would our friends do this?" they asked.[47]

The St. Paul Chamber of Commerce met to discuss the issue. The meeting's importance was evidenced by the presence of one of the few surviving state founders, Henry H. Sibley, who attended only his second meeting that season. The chamber strongly believed the Capitol building should be "at the Heart of St. Paul." Its members were accustomed to the furtive efforts of opportunists to remove the capital, and in the case of the Capitol building they felt the same. The best option, they decided, was to rebuild on the same site a permanent and fireproof structure that would meet future needs. To achieve "equal justice towards all the people of the state" the new Capitol should be located so it is "most convenient for the larger number to reach it," along with adequate accommodations, most likely in proximity to a significant business center. They were highlighting the shortfalls of the Midway.[48]

Some people at the chamber meeting believed those in favor of moving the Capitol building were real estate boomers. Landowners would benefit from the Capitol being relocated nearer their land. These suspicious people went so far as to accuse a handful of men of generating a "little real estate scheme" for self-enrichment. With regards to the Minneapolis Board of Trade proposal to build the Capitol at the agricultural school location west of the State Fairgrounds, people objected because they didn't trust Minneapolis. However, the city representatives were not in perfect harmony. The agricultural school land, along with land to the west of it, sat on a ridge that had views of both downtowns.[49]

Manly B. Curry rebutted this accusation of a real estate scheme even while he was heavily invested in St. Paul real estate. The real estate firm McClung, McMurran and Curry owned hundreds of acres in that area, from Como Lake west to St. Anthony Park. He felt the downtown St. Paul site was "unsightly" and believed the state had outgrown that location. More importantly, he pointed to regional competitors, such as Duluth and Chicago, who were actively angling to be the business gateway of the Northwest. The competition was pressing the St. Paul Chamber to act. The Midway location would consolidate the two cities and create a large commercial center. "If we join hands with Minneapolis," Curry said, "we can build up an immense city here." A Midway location was an offer to recalibrate and reorient a combined metropolis and respond to the larger challenges in the region.[50]

The meeting began to drift. A few directors who were amiable to relocating the Capitol building tried to table the resolutions for keeping the status quo. The meeting fell into disarray and much "wrangling" followed. The chair lost control of the meeting, but in the end the resolution to keep the Capitol in downtown St. Paul carried: 31–5. They had rejected the Minneapolis proposal.

The Midway Wants the Capitol

At the same time that the Minneapolis Board of Trade and the St. Paul Chamber of Commerce were meeting, the people of Merriam Park gathered and considered the idea of having the Capitol built in their suburb. This neighborhood lay most directly between the two downtowns and perhaps had the most residents anywhere in the Midway. "Midwayites wanted the capitol, and wanted it badly," noted the *St. Paul Daily Globe*.

D. A. J. Baker called the meeting to order. He was a schoolteacher and a land speculator and had become a judge. He sold his farm to William R. Merriam, who then laid out Merriam Park. He held three parcels north of Desnoyer's land just west of Lyman M. Ford's Groveland Nursery. Real estate values were obviously important to him.

The Midway was being "ground between two great millstones," said one person. St. Paul residents expressed concern that if they didn't seize this opportunity to work with Minneapolis, they might lose the Capitol. That urgency is likely the precise response King and other Minneapolis representatives were hoping to prompt. The Midway residents wrote two resolutions in twenty minutes. First, they offered five to twenty acres to the state for a building site, emphasizing that the site lay between the business centers and enjoyed easy access to the railroads. The second resolution put them at odds with the Chamber of Commerce; they would lobby their legislators to compel the legislature to remove the Capitol, contrary to the chamber's resolution. As a final item before adjournment, Baker offered the state a ten-acre parcel of his land that overlooked the two cities. This gain in the value of the Midway was exactly what Desnoyer had anticipated fifteen years earlier.[51]

The next day, February 22, 1887, the Chamber of Commerce held another meeting to consider moving the Capitol building to the Midway. A raucous crowd of 300 people attended, mostly suburbanites from Merriam Park and the Midway district, who were newcomers to the chamber's meetings. "Carpet baggers, every one of them," complained the city attorney, "I don't know a dozen men in the house." It could have been viewed as an uprising. The resolutions from the neighborhood meeting the night before were read, and the crowd asked that the chamber cooperate with them.

Though unacquainted with the ways of public meetings, the crowd made up for procedural ignorance with "plenty of enthusiasm and cheering and hissing," according to one report. Spectators supported with loud applause any purely patriotic sentiment to St. Paul, regardless of the Capitol scheme. If someone expressed being in favor of locating the Capitol building at the railroad transfer or beyond, they applauded still louder. But when someone spoke against their project, they hissed for up to five minutes. The meeting dragged on over two and a half hours. "Old battles were fought over and old sores probed," reported the newspaper.

In front of the raucous crowd the chamber backpedaled from its previous resolutions to keep the Capitol downtown and reconsidered those that supported the Midway. Its members resolved that "it was time that small jealousies and animosities should be dropped," and they selected a committee to work with Minneapolis.

Yet one voice of caution stood up to the single-minded crowd. He focused the attention of the Midway residents on the long game Minneapolis was playing. Having been in the meeting with Minneapolis, he warned them that this idea of a Capitol in the Midway originated in the sister city. Minneapolis claimed it was solely in St. Paul's interest, but that assessment was inconsistent with their history of thirty years. Yes, with a Capitol in the Midway the property would gain in value and business opportunities would emerge. But moving the Capitol would take a devastating $40 million of government business away from the heart of St. Paul.[52]

The speaker got to the heart of the Minneapolis proposal—it would diminish St. Paul's downtown. Therein was the motive for the Midway offer. Minneapolis lacked one thing: the capital. It could claim to be the metropolis of the Northwest in wealth, manufactures, and population, but it lacked the prestige of being the capital city. With the Capitol in the Midway, Minneapolis would quickly dominate. And as King suggested regarding land along the gorge, Minneapolis could later expand the city limits to absorb the Capitol building and become the capital. The warning was unheeded.

Henry H. Sibley said he was in favor of finding a location for a new Capitol that "will harmonize all conflicting interests and best accommodate the people of the state." The capital's location, he suggested, is not set in stone. Sibley's words held weight. A resolution largely reflecting his view was passed. Whereas "the two chief cities of Minnesota are nearly equal in population and wealth . . . [and] their corporate limits are now continuous, the location of a new and permanent Capitol building, when selected, should be in St. Paul, in the so-called Midway or interurban district, mutually satisfactory to the people of both cities."[53]

Notably, the most agreeable resolution lacked any specific location or funding. Participants could agree in general but not on a specific site. Everyone pushed for their preferred option, and they had too many choices. Gridlock ensued and inertia set in. The legislature threw money at the rickety Capitol building that threatened to fall down around them.[54]

Two years later, in early 1889, people of the Midway area had formed the Central Union of the Midway district. They lobbied for legislation that ordered the state to select, buy, and preserve a site for the future Minnesota Capitol in the Midway district. The legislature passed this resolution, and a commission was created to examine and report sites. The commissioners had a two-year appointment, no compensation, and the charge to prepare plans, select a site, and estimate the cost. They began their work June 1, 1889, to find a site "somewhere midway between the Twin Cities."[55]

A skeptic at the *Minneapolis Tribune* pierced through the land speculation and the calls to unite the cities. The skeptic wondered how it was that Minneapolis would benefit from building the Capitol "out on the prairie" even if it were somewhat closer. Previously, more than once, the author noted, Minneapolis has "favored some such move in retaliation for impositions practiced by St. Paul," such as St. Paul's annexation of the "vast expanse of prairie" to keep Minneapolis at bay. But neither city would gain from the move, the skeptic declared, nor would the state at large. After spending an exorbitant amount to buy the land and build the Capitol, the "state officials and legislators would find themselves plumped down in the country with poor hotel facilities and all the other embarrassments incidental to their out-of-the-way position." The Capitol needed the conveniences of a large city. Let's face it, the skeptic continued, "St. Paul is likely to remain the capital of this state for many years to come."[56]

The Midway proponents persevered into the 1890s. They focused on a piece of land just north of Marshall Avenue that would become as grand as Pennsylvania Avenue in Washington, DC. The new Capitol would overlook the river gorge with a view of both cities. Railroads would provide access to everybody in the state. The Midway district would be the center of population and the most convenient location for the lawyers and other people who have business at the Capitol, such as supreme court, law library, railroad, and dairy representatives.[57]

From the time the legislature adjourned in April 1891 until the meeting of the committee in November, the people of St. Paul discussed the best site for a new Capitol building in the event of favorable action by the legislature in 1893. They made a determined effort to locate it on Desnoyer's land.[58]

CHAPTER 9

The Heart of the New Metropolis

The Easter celebrations of 1891 proved to the leaders and members of St. Paul's Catholic community that they needed a larger cathedral. Every Sunday was a reminder, but on Good Friday the evening mass was so full that conducting the service became nearly impossible.[1]

The growth of the Catholic population in St. Paul had routinely outpaced the size of the cathedral. The church built a second cathedral, completed in 1851, but it was immediately insufficient for the growing diocese. Immigrating German and Irish Catholics streamed into the state and replaced the earlier population of French voyageurs. The church built a third cathedral in 1858 at Sixth and St. Peter Streets. John Ireland, the third bishop to serve St. Paul, was promoted as its first archbishop in 1888. And Archbishop Ireland had big plans.

For several years, overcrowding had spurred proposals to build a new cathedral. In 1888 Ireland had dedicated a chapel, St. Luke's (the nineteenth chapel of the city) at Summit Avenue and Victoria Street. Many viewed it as fait accompli for that location to give rise to a new "Grand Cathedral," one that would fit the city's growing needs into the future. They called the new property the "old Wann Estate" and projected that in a few years the church would build an ambitious building.[2]

The move west out of St. Paul's downtown and up what was called St. Anthony Hill was in line with the population changes. People were moving out of the city and into residential neighborhoods on the hill. The small African American community established itself at this time in the Rondo neighborhood a few blocks to the north of Summit Avenue. The neighborhood still had large areas of open space in the late 1880s, but development in general had a westerly direction. Real estate agents boomed the properties, predicting a wild rush primarily near the cathedral.[3]

For the cathedral, Ireland imagined a legacy building. Just after Easter 1891, he and Thomas Cochran Jr., a friend with financial and real estate ties, were in New York City to raise money for the new monumental cathedral. Newspapers reported a construction budget of $1 million and

Archbishop John Ireland in 1887

touted a highly regarded architectural design, though the details were unknown. The intention was to build a cathedral that would be "at once a credit to the state and the city." The newspapers projected construction as imminent.[4]

Ireland had even greater ambitions than just a legacy building. Location was as important. He wanted the new building to serve the congregations in Minneapolis as well as St. Paul. For that purpose, St. Anthony Hill missed the mark. Ireland was looking for a site that fulfilled three conditions: visibly prominent, in a nonbusiness neighborhood, in a centralized location between the two cities.

Ireland had his eyes on the unique Midway district. The archbishop had already made heavy investments in the Midway. He opened a seminary at the west end of Summit Avenue. He underwrote a bond to extend the electric streetcars west into the district. And he had acquired a large amount of land in the area south of Stephen Desnoyer's property by the river. He subscribed, along with others, to a particular vision of the future and was taking part in shaping it. He viewed the Midway as offering the location to accomplish that vision.[5]

At the dedication for the electric trolley opening on Grand Avenue, Ireland expressed his awe and intentions for the Midway. "Tread reverently upon this ground. It is the Midway, the very heart of the coming great city. Look at it! Admire it! Has not Providence been generous to it?" he said. "No wonder that friends of mine across the river covet it. It is the precious gift by which St. Paul will woo and win fair Minneapolis."[6]

The Midway

"It is the center," said the *St. Paul Daily Globe*, a newspaper that promoted the Midway continuously. "Most great commercial centers grow from a common center. Here it is reversed, and the Twin Cities—always original—are growing from outward points to the common center." The rapid growth of the two cities (their populations tripled between 1880 and 1890) gave the sense of momentum and from that came the projection that they would grow together.[7]

That mood changed as the industrial self-realization of Minneapolis gave the burgeoning city confidence. At the same time, the two cities were learning the hazards of being equals so close together. The railroads remained stretched between the two. After an attempt to consolidate in St. Paul, the railroads realized the layout required terminal facilities in both cities. St. Paul operated the lion's share of wholesale and warehouse interests, and Minneapolis had more of the manufacturing and milling. The rivalry began to ease with the emergence of a shared sense of identity as the Twin Cities. After thirty years battling for supremacy, both cities began to see that when viewed as one they were polar ends of a magnetic dynamo. They were separate municipalities that, in combination, could serve as a regional center for business, finance, and manufacturing.[8]

Change was in the air as collaboration replaced defensiveness. Joint committees worked to find solutions on the electric street and cable railway systems. The two cities had collaborative interests that brought them together physically. The change was seen most obviously in the Midway.[9]

Ireland's vision for the area was not new. In 1872, just seven months after Minneapolis absorbed St. Anthony, the *St. Paul Press* published "a wise foreshadowing of manifest destiny" for the Twin Cities. The anonymous author (he signed off as B. F. S.) warned of the coming conflict as the cities grew together. He believed they would fight for their independent identities. To counter that impulse he recommended they develop connecting ties. He proposed a road between the two cities, and not just an ordinary one. He suggested it be 100 feet wide with 50-foot boulevards for landscaping with trees, shrubbery, and fountains, not unlike the wide boulevards of Paris. At the midpoint on 2,000 acres stretching across each side of the road, he imagined a new Capitol and governor's mansion.

Further, he proposed adding land for a state medical college, normal college, law college, and other state institutions as needed, as well as land for each religious denomination's theological seminaries or other educational institutions. Such a cluster of institutions between the two cities, he said, "would add largely to the wealth and population of both."[10]

This idea of the Midway as a political and cultural center had floated locally for some time. That same year of 1872 Desnoyer claimed that his land would be the new Bridge Square of the united St. Paul and Minneapolis. And a real estate developer proposed that St. Paul and Minneapolis should follow the example of St. Anthony and Minneapolis. They agreed, generally, with the idea that transportation was the means of connecting the two cities. A few years later, John S. Pillsbury, then a state senator, proposed a state road between the university and the Capitol. In fact, University Avenue was laid out much in the way proposed by the anonymous B. F. S. The Chicago, Milwaukee, and St. Paul Railroad opened in 1880 and had significant impacts on the Midway. Known as the Short Line or the Milwaukee Road, it became the main travel conduit between St. Paul and Minneapolis. It was the catalyst that attracted residents and industry to the Midway. It made Merriam Park a viable proposition too.[11]

John L. Merriam bought 100 acres of D. A. J. Baker's farm in 1872 with anticipation of future developments. He platted Merriam Park in 1882, originally extending from the Short Line tracks south to Marshall Avenue and from Cleveland Avenue to Fairview Avenue with a three-acre park near the center. This suburb's growth exceeded the rate of building record in both cities. Residential demand was surging. Within two years of its platting Merriam Park was thriving with a brick school building, a small church, a row of brick stores, a good hotel, and a depot. The city widened Marshall Avenue to 100 feet with plans for a motor line or streetcars. Several more enlargements to Merriam Park extended it south of Marshall Avenue and west toward the Mississippi River.[12]

The Short Line became a commuter line, and several neighborhoods developed along it: Union Park, Prospect Park, St. Anthony Park, Desnoyer Park, Macalester Park, and Groveland Park. Merriam Park platted several more additions. The train made a thirty-five-minute run between the cities about every hour from 7:00 A.M. to 7:00 P.M. every day except on Sundays, when it ran four trains. Over the years fares ranged from seven to twenty-five cents. The service was so punctual that people grew impatient if they had to wait more than five minutes.[13]

Ireland enlisted Thomas Cochran Jr., a lawyer and real estate broker from New York and St. Paul, to help with the development of the Midway, including the Macalester addition. Ireland and Cochran propelled the Midway into more rapid settlement by financing the conversion of the Grand Avenue and the Randolph Avenue streetcars from horse-drawn to electric. They also extended the lines west to Cretin Avenue. These were the first electric streetcars in St. Paul, and they had a direct impact on the development of the Midway, propagating it as a residential area.[14]

Overall, the railroads of Minneapolis and St. Paul had so much success that they were crippled by their busy, overly congested rail lines. To move freight to local, regional, and national destinations, the railroads needed a more efficient means of transferring freight. Organized by J. J. Hill in 1880, a group of nine railroads created the Minnesota Transfer, a switching and transfer facility located in the Midway district. They leveled 200 acres of hills in the area of Prior and University Avenues and put in eight miles of railroad tracks, largely in a parallel configuration, that unknotted the system. Trains could drop off and pick up cars much more easily. Adjacent to the transfer station were the Union Stockyards, where traveling livestock could be watered. The transfer station became an important shipping hub, reflecting the projections of earlier railroad promoters based on their geographic position.

The business of the transfer station spawned a wide variety of light

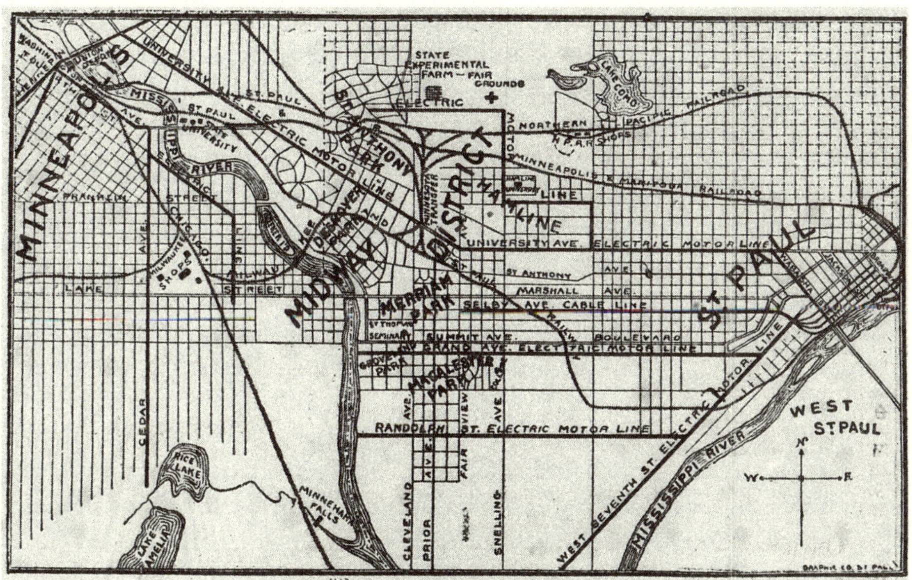

This map emphasizes the early 1880s transportation network and how it connected Minneapolis and St. Paul through the Midway district.

industrial and affiliated businesses, such as manufacturers of wagons, tractors, and motors. Interestingly, the geographic center of the Twin Cities was filling in *after* the cities were established, yet the Midway was a legitimate industrial center not unlike what might have been at a city's original center. Having so many railroads at the center of the Twin Cities improved transportation as well, which increased the population. Those trying to unite the two cities planned a singular Union Depot in that area that would serve both cities.

In January 1885, when the state established the permanent home of the State Fairgrounds, St. Paul incorporated the Midway district. The city limits jumped from Lexington Avenue, established in 1874, to the county line over three miles to the west. The cities now shared a border, much of it along the river. People in the Midway area were nearly unanimously opposed to the expansion. Previously, the Midway was a neutral ground, but now, they believed, the new city limit would hinder incoming investments from Minneapolis. People and businesses from Merriam Park, the Minnesota Transfer, and the Harvester Works also opposed St. Paul's annexation of the Midway.[15]

The majority of the Midway was in Ramsey County, allowing St. Paul easier expansion into it. The people of that time had a flexible outlook on political lines. For example, the county line had been adjusted in 1855, transplanting St. Anthony from Ramsey to Hennepin. Others imagined the entire region would become one county. St. Paul, however, expanded earlier than the area's population warranted. "They want to know why we took in this Midway district," recalled one St. Paul man, who felt the answer was obvious. "We took it in because we had to, or Minneapolis would gobble it."[16]

As with the State Fair, the head of navigation, and the Capitol, the people in the two cities would spare nothing in their efforts to gain supremacy. Jealousy and animus compelled them "into acts of positive hostility," according to one newspaper, which was a detriment to the two cities, if not the entire region. Representatives from both cities were scheming to undermine each other, brewing bad blood that stirred bickering in newspaper columns and on street corners. Observers watching from the outside thought it looked exhausting. The two cities spent an excessive amount of energy unproductively, and the friction chased away talent and money to the benefit of their true competition, such as Milwaukee and Chicago.[17]

If only they could shift their attitudes toward mutual development and a shared future.

Horace W. S. Cleveland

It's odd that an outsider would be able to step into the family feud—the still "contorted, twisted-up kind of politics" of the Twin Cities—and turn the focus from antagonism to collaboration. But Horace W. S. Cleveland succeeded through his vision of parks.

Cleveland is best remembered for his inspiration to create the Grand Rounds in both cities, bike and pedestrian routes designed to connect people with the natural settings. He also focused on preserving the river gorge from development, including Minnehaha Falls and the river boulevards. A park was nothing without access, so he designed multimodal transportation corridors, including trolley lines and pedestrian ways.

Cleveland learned his craft as a landscape architect with Frederick Law Olmsted, the father of landscape architecture and designer of New York City's Central Park. After Cleveland got his start in Boston, he relocated to Chicago in 1869. He came to the profession later in life, at age forty, and based his work in opposition to endless grid plats perpetuated by homesteading and railroad design. He brought that experience to Minnesota in 1872. On an invitation from William W. Folwell, the first president of the University of Minnesota, he presented his ideas of how to design a livable city. The St. Paul Chamber of Commerce asked him to give the same talk

Horace W. S. Cleveland as a young man, date unknown

in St Paul the next day. Within a month, the state legislature authorized the purchase of up to 650 acres near the capital city for a public park. The city of St. Paul purchased Como Park a few months later. Cleveland began working with various entities, including cemeteries, towns, schools, and the University of Minnesota.

Cleveland arrived at a critical moment in the development of the Twin Cities. St. Paul and Minneapolis were expanding beyond their immediate commercial districts and stretching out into the Midway. He was an evangelist for uniting the two cities. His conceptual framework gave residents a common purpose that distracted them from the title chase for bigger, better, or superior. To that end, he used their own tactics, played them against one another, and channeled their competitive relationship so they worked toward a common vision. Year after year he picked new projects for them to focus on and then compared each to their rival. He had a rock-bottom faith that the cities would unite, but he and others didn't have to try to unite them, he argued: Build the infrastructure, let the growth follow the parkways—and unification would happen organically as they grew. His designs were meant to facilitate that inevitable day.

In designing a city, Cleveland said, keep the natural features, create many parks, and then connect the parks with parkways. As a firsthand witness to America's urban development in New York City, Boston, and Chicago, he knew how cities evolved. Too often he saw developments sprawl out in a carpet of same-sized rectangles with no variation, obliterating any natural features along the way. He often criticized the rectangular grid, though he must have had words for some of the skew-angled settlements of St. Paul and Minneapolis. His work was a direct response to and rejection of the settlement land rush.

Cities grow along lines of transportation, he said. If those boulevards are laid out in advance of development, they determine the arrangement of suburban additions. If the Midway were filled in with suburban villages, or platted in lots and streets, it would be too late to create the continuous lines of boulevards. He advised that the city planners should, like the railroads, plan their routes before preemption claims interfered and made it more complex and expensive to change the urban design.[18]

A boulevard, in Cleveland's design book, was a grand avenue wide enough for two or three different purposes. One was for the heavy traffic of business wagons, one for pleasure and driving, and one for equestrians, along with paths for pedestrians. The various modes were separated by rows of trees and grass plots. These boulevards and parkways were ultimately a connective infrastructure, a way of bringing the two cities together. His work had that purpose in mind, and he no doubt recruited many business and civic leaders. The period of the late 1880s was unique in that peaceful relations had taken hold between the cities. Cleveland was in the middle of the conversation about growth, and he gave the leaders of the Twin Cities a different vision of their future.[19]

By 1885 Minneapolis had projected at least twenty-five miles of the wide, multipurpose boulevards. The *St. Paul Daily Globe* urged St. Paul to match that effort and create a similar system of boulevards to serve the needs of the millions of people it predicted would eventually live there. Cleveland also pushed St. Paul to keep pace with Minneapolis. The planners in Minneapolis have already begun to build, he said, adding that their parkways extended toward St. Paul. If the two cities united the boulevards, it would be a premier design for the country. Specifically, Cleveland identified two corridors to connect the cities: Marshall Avenue–Lake Street and Summit Avenue–Thirty-Fourth Street. St. Paul and Minneapolis would eventually, and sooner rather than later, "become virtually one city," he predicted, and their future success will be so intertwined that they would both benefit equally if they united in designing and arranging the Midway.[20]

Cleveland asked the residents of both cities to look into the future. They had open space, exactly what New York had only a little of and what Chicago had lost and couldn't get back. He was living in Chicago when the great fire of 1871 incinerated a large area of the city. He advised Chicago city planners to rebuild by adding a series of connective parkways. They did not heed his advice then and, he noted, it later cost millions of dollars to insert parks and parkways. To lay out the parks and parkways at the outset would save the twins a lot of money later.

Imagine what the city would look like when it was ten times larger, Cleveland said. He had seen the same growth in Boston and New York City. By pointing to the great cities of the time—both as disasters and successes—he incited the competitive zeal in Minnesota, suggesting the Twin Cities might even replace Chicago as the gateway to the Northwest. Visions abounded of becoming like Paris or London. He enticed and directed their views and ignited their pride in building for the future. And that future was a united city. Undoubtedly and inevitably.

Cleveland believed so much in the work that was unfolding in the Twin Cities that he left Chicago in March 1886 and moved to Minneapolis. In over thirty years in the profession, he exclaimed, he had not seen a city take such decisive action at such a young stage in building parks and parkways.

With that, he prodded the cities to plan for Minnehaha Falls. He asked if they had neglected or perhaps just overlooked the dramatic waterfall. He viewed the area as already complete with little need for "artificial decoration." The park only needed better accessibility. Let the falls be "the crowning charm" of the park, he advised. The picturesque, world-renowned feature contributed more to "the two cities than they can attain by any possible display of wealth in their own streets." Minnehaha Falls was "the center of gravity" for the entire metro area in his mind. The parkways of the future, he predicted, would radiate out from the falls and Fort Snelling via the river and lakes. "A glance at the map at once shows Minnehaha to be the key to the whole situation," he said. He visited Minnehaha with state park commissioners and sold them on the idea of purchasing the land.[21]

Next he proposed expanding the park across the river to save the gorge in its natural state. Do it, he insisted, before the trees are cut down and people begin to quarry the stone. Those resources will be easy picking for building residences. Let the natural setting stand as it is found as much as possible. The bluffs that border the river should remain untouched. He even resisted the idea of building a bridge to connect the two sides at this prime location. The parks would be united by the beauty of the river gorge.[22]

Cleveland seemed unaware of the role this area played in the early years of Fort Snelling. His focus here was the Entry, the place above the confluence where the first settlers had envisioned the original city. Joseph R. Brown had begun laying out his city "Simonenee" in the same location as Hidden Falls, though it never rose above the sobriquet of Rumtown. A couple early Selkirk refugees had developed the best steamboat landings just below where Minnehaha Creek flows into the river. Joseph Plympton had expanded the Reserve to block these landings for his personal gain, yet inadvertently he had preserved the area from development. Now, in the late 1880s, with the industrial economy spreading across the land, a visionary was pushing to preserve natural sites for the sake of future generations. Hindering the settlement of the confluence preserved the area's natural beauty. Cleveland prophesized its lasting value.

Summit Avenue provided a case for preserving the gorge. On its eastern end, the parkway was bounded by stylish mansions that blocked the view from the bluff to the south over St. Paul. The city preserved one open space on Cleveland's recommendation. The way to preserve the gorge for the public was a parkway along the rim. St. Paul had preserved the fifty acres across from the mouth of Minnehaha (now Hidden Falls Regional

Park) and completed a survey for a road along the river gorge from the confluence to Marshall Avenue (today's Mississippi River Boulevard). With that, those planners preserved the gorge in its "native grandeur and beauty." But Minneapolis had yet to preserve the west side of the gorge.[23]

Just as Cleveland had prodded St. Paul earlier about replicating Minneapolis's efforts, he now used the same art of persuasion to move Minneapolis. He painted a picture and narrated a scene from the future. A parkway along the rim "will be the favorite drive of the citizens of St. Paul," he said, "but it will be shorn of half its attractions if Minneapolis fails to make a similar improvement on her side of the river." The view from St. Paul's road would be "a dreary scene of desolation," the slopes denuded and marred with quarries. In St. Paul people would take their friends for a drive to see "the natural features which have been preserved like a jewel in a costly setting," only to be disturbed by a "dismal scene across the river." They will tell their friends, "That is Minneapolis."

Then he offered feedback from the future: Think of "the muttered curses

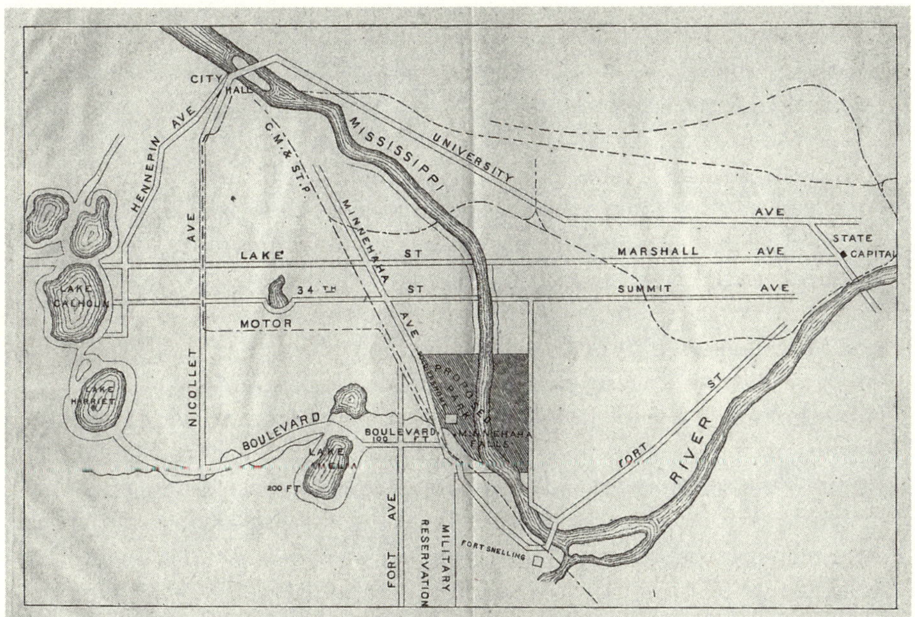

Cleveland's map of Minnehaha Falls as a central park with proposed parkways to connect the two cities. Today's Cleveland Avenue in St. Paul, visible here on the east side of the proposed park, was originally named Union Avenue. The map has an anonymous character with no city names. Instead, Cleveland identified only the State Capital in place of St. Paul and the City Hall in the location of Minneapolis. We can view this map as a united city plan.

that will be heaped upon us by future generations," he said, when later arrivals imagine what might have been. It would darken the reputation of Minneapolis forever, and St. Paul could claim superiority with its development.

In his grand finale, Cleveland reminded his audience that they were accustomed to the wild, uncultivated aspect of the landscape. They were the generation that was reshaping it. In its wild state, it was uninteresting to people bent on cultivating the place. But someday this uncultivated landscape would be a diamond in the rough, and if not preserved it would be unretrievable.

By creating a network of connected parkways the two cities would determine the future shape of development. The responsibility was this generation's burden, made easier by the fact that they were creating "one of the great capitals of the world." Either the future historian would celebrate them and exult their wisdom or the future critics would "mourn over the narrow minded policy of those who cast the horoscope of the city in its infancy."

Cleveland was persuasive. He had buy-in from city leaders and most especially the real estate developers. John W. McClung, for example, a Kentucky lawyer who came to St. Paul in 1855 and became a real estate broker, subscribed to Cleveland's ideas. He owned hundreds of acres with Frederick D. Hager, J. Royall McMurran, and Manly B. Curry in the Como area and was developing the boulevard corridor there. On February 16, 1888, McClung led a meeting of representatives of the top leaders from both cities. The meeting appears to have had some delicate politics involved. They were discussing, he said, "the common interests and the common dangers of these two cities."

To be clear, the meeting was not about uniting them in any way. These representatives would leave that to the natural "logic of events and by evolution." McClung focused their attention on the need "to shape that future." The past decades had been difficult and the rivalry "simply served to harden our muscles and develop our energies." For now, he said, they would be conciliatory and send a message "to the world that these two cities are to be one—not married now, but betrothed," he said. One of the most popular op-ed cartoons from this era features McClung and this idea. In the cartoon, a young man in a tuxedo kneels before a lady in a formal dress with a fan. They are St. Paul and Minneapolis. Behind the young couple stand "Father McClung" and "Mother Pillsbury," the former governor John S. Pillsbury, who represented Minneapolis in the meetings. The picture is titled "The Betrothal," the engagement or promise to marry. Someday.

THE BETROTHAL.

Father McClung and Mother Pillsbury—Chorus: "Bless ye, my children." Wedding cards later.

"The Betrothal": Father McClung and Mother Pillsbury, representing two of the guiding figures of their respective cities, St. Paul and Minneapolis, oversee the promise of a future union. "Wedding cards later," reads the caption.

Behind the promise of a future union lay concern about an encroaching danger from outside interests, such as Duluth and Chicago. These cities might try to usurp the Twin Cities' regional supremacy, and a united front would stave them off. "St. Paul can no longer think to oppose Minneapolis to its own interests," said Henry M. Rice. "The time has come when the two cities should unite." Duluth also might surpass the two cities. "United we need not fear," said Isaac Atwater, former newspaper editor and judge. "We should act as one individual in protecting our railroad and navigation interests," said Orlando C. Merriman, the former mayor of St. Anthony and Minneapolis. In other words, the two cities should get married.[24]

Voices from the Street

By the end of the 1880s an atmosphere of distinct congeniality had developed between the two cities. City leaders were uneasy about outside competition and were looking for the right means to bring the cities together. But what did the people think about combining the two cities into one? In 1888 the *Globe* went about town and asked people: Are you in favor of an actual union of the Twin Cities? Its reporters discovered that, indeed, the bitterness was gone. The people spoke of the other "in a friendly, kindly, even sisterly spirit." The agitating "envy, malice and jealousy" from only a few years ago had dissipated.[25]

While the responses ranged widely, the upshot was a widespread feeling that Minneapolis and St. Paul shared the same destiny as one city. Tradition held that "the generous rivalry" was the lifeblood of the two cities, but now they benefited from a "united effort of aggression and defense." Some called openly for an end to "petty jealousies and rivalries" in the face of shared business interests.

When people talked about a union, they focused on two areas: commercial and municipal. People believed the first was naturally underway. So let that happen first, people said, and then municipal union can come later. The newspaper felt that most people believed it will happen someday, the cities "will become *de jure* what they are *de facto*."

In the bigger regional picture, the two cities were the gateway to the Northwest. Tethered to the world by the Mississippi River, the Twin Cities were the last stop before the great Northwest. "We are favorably situated at the head of the Mississippi river," said one man, "in the center of a vast empire of the great Northwest and in the belt of the grain-producing center of the world."

Picking a new name for a combined city proved challenging: St. Paulopolis or Minneapaulous came to mind. But finding a name would be much easier than the work to actually unite the cities, which required "vast legislation" to reconcile the differences in their municipal and county systems, the courts, the recording and tax levying and collecting systems, even the sewer systems.

Some people were rather flip: "Yes, of course, do it." But when asked how, they demurred. Let the Chamber of Commerce take care of it, they said. Or have the press educate readers about the idea so they can vote on the issue. Once approved by popular vote the legislature would have to legalize it. But the public had "to become more alive to its necessity," said John Ireland. He felt the idea was not widely enough known in either city. "We have nothing to do at present but to talk and write," he said.

The city leaders were serious enough about the idea of a union to ponder the details, the "thousand points of difference to be adjusted only by pain-staking finesse." Could anyone reconcile the conflicting laws and methods, taxation, and scattered minutia? Former newspaper editor and state supreme court justice Atwater thought not: "The question involves many things and is not practical," he said. "I do not wish to talk on the subject." Others agreed; it was impossible and not worth discussing.[26]

Like any major bureaucratic transition, any benefits would come after serious reconstruction expense. However, some felt the long-term gain in shared municipal expenses would be worth the effort. The benefit from the union would lessen municipal expenses for infrastructure such as waterworks.

The St. Paul mayor was "emphatically in favor" of a commercial union followed by consolidation under one municipal government. The financial advantage would be incalculable: Real estate would boom along with the population. A larger city would concentrate power and bring greater regional influence, especially to the West. More influence in federal legislation would bring more resources to the state. In the end, one large city of 500,000 would wield more commercial and political power than two cities of 250,000. The view from outside was certainly more impressive.

At this time, the great cities of America could be counted on one hand. "Unite the two," said one businessman, "and we stand at once with only New York, Brooklyn, Philadelphia and Chicago ahead of us." Merging was part of the growth process. Philadelphia had swallowed up a dozen municipalities. The oncoming developments, such as the Sault Ste. Marie railway, would help create a united city beyond the size of Brooklyn and Chicago.

The project loomed large. The city centers lay ten miles apart. Much of that area was open land in the Midway. If the cities were within a mile of each other, said one man, perhaps any operational redundancies could be reduced. But the project lacked any necessity. Each had a functioning city government and an independent business center.

The two cities were in different phases of their development. "St. Paul has now grown up to be an old bachelor," said one man, "while the frisky 'Minnie' is still young and ambitious." Some respondents likened the difference in the character and ideas of the people as repellant as oil and water, New York and San Francisco, London and Paris—the Twin Cities were even worse than the English and the French.

St. Paul was viewed as "cosmopolitan," which meant it had a large foreign immigrant population. Minneapolis had more American emigrants and seemed like a "genuine Yankee town." The customs in St. Paul were entirely different from those in Minneapolis. Some saw the difference as unbridgeable, like that between "the North and the South." In 1885 the cities were political opposites. St. Paul remained solidly Democratic and Minneapolis was stridently Republican. Just seven years earlier President Rutherford Hayes had highlighted this cultural divide within one locale that was akin to that of the country at large. The two cities, within the size of one larger city, had embedded in them cultural differences so insoluble that they exceeded the worst known in the nation.

Some found it was impossible to overcome the different interests of the two cities given the gulf in their forms of municipal government, their independent manner of doing business, and the ambitions of their leading men. They had recently achieved a plateau of mutual acceptance and could tolerate each other as neighbors; but each was in pursuit of life distinct from the other. To put these strong-willed separate identities under one city government would raise a destructive friction. Combining them under one city name could never rectify the reality of two cities that had so much jealousy between their business centers. Such a situation would invite eternal infighting over the direction of the city and improvements.

Others were fatalistic. They felt the cities shared nothing in common except for their "generous, wholesome rivalry." If you unite them, more than one person said, you would take away a primary stimulus of both cities—their "life blood." Without their rivalry, what would there be? "The rivalry between these two cities was the life of each," said one newspaper. "Minneapolis would not have been what it is but for St. Paul," said one believer, "nor would St. Paul have been what it is without Minneapolis." Uniting them would take away their purpose and cause self-destructive infighting.[27]

In order to get past the rivalry, one man proposed a zero-sum solution. The smaller city must submit or surrender to the larger city, as St. Anthony did when Minneapolis absorbed it. Since Minneapolis was larger, St. Paul should "give up all her city institutions," even the capital status. For others, this capitulation was out of the question. Any type of conciliatory behavior was detrimental to Minneapolis because, from their perspective, it elevated St. Paul to an equal footing.

At the heart of such hard feelings lay matters of fair taxation. St. Paul was having trouble satisfying different neighborhoods with tax responsibilities. This issue was at the heart of the early rivalry when St. Anthony didn't want to pay Ramsey County taxes. But issues such as fair taxation take on a different scale when combining two cities.

Instead of a complete merger all at once, supporters proposed practical intermediate steps toward the union. For example, start with the infrastructure such as a common water supply. St. Paul now had plentiful good water while Minneapolis did not. Both were in the process of developing parks and parkways, per the advice of Horace W. S. Cleveland, who believed his design would unite them. Improved rapid transit lines would also help move them together. If these things went well, they might venture into the realm of shared bureaucratic structure to provide other services, such as police and fire departments. A gradual development of specific, targeted municipal services could lead to eventual unification.

In some ways, the two cities already enjoyed the benefits of a united city, especially in transportation matters. The railroads looked on the cities as one market. The businesses already saw a common ground against outside markets and continually developed their general interests and protections. The commercial interests of both cities shared benefits and disadvantages and acted to protect their combined commercial interests by, for example, securing favorable freight rates.

The overall attitude in this informal survey was that immediate consolidation wasn't practicable or desirable. People felt things were trending in that direction and it was best to wait for the natural course of events to bring the cities together. Unity depends on good feelings, and the longstanding rivalry was real and would continue to exist. But let the merger happen organically, over time, and the people would find it better to be together under one municipal government than apart, for economic and other reasons. But "that time has not yet arrived."

Indeed, there was a paradox in these views. On the one hand, people said the cities would unite organically, so it was best to leave well enough alone and the time will come when they grow together. On the other hand, every day that they grew closer in space, they grew more independent and further apart from each other in identity.

The Census War of 1890

The harmony of the 1880s ended abruptly on Tuesday, June 17, 1890, at 9:00 P.M. A US marshal along with police officers forced entry into a Minneapolis building, arrested seven Minneapolis citizens, and took them to St. Paul, where they faced the judge and were put in the St. Paul jail. The charge: falsely inflating the population of Minneapolis.

The citizens were census enumerators finishing their respective counts for that year's census. The census had become a point of heated contention. "Population is the true test of a city's greatness," wrote the author of an analysis of the so-called census war. As of 1880, with 46,887 people, Minneapolis had moved ahead of St. Paul by about 5,000 people. The census of 1890 was a highly anticipated event. Minneapolis could taste the victory, and St. Paul was on the defensive.[28]

Then, as Minneapolis saw it, St. Paul came over and arrested the census workers. Because the judge and the census official, who was the former city attorney and longtime Minneapolis antagonist, were St. Paul residents, Minneapolis viewed the arrests as an attempt of archrivals to use federal law to undermine its superior numbers. The incident sparked an intense and bitter reaction in Minneapolis. A group of Minneapolitans went to the St. Paul courthouse and, in trying to get information, offended an officer. He whirled on them and, they later claimed, cussed at them for being from Minneapolis. Soon several officers arrived to usher them out of the courthouse.

Newspaper reports in both cities sensationalized the events and inflamed public opinion. St. Paul newspapers claimed that Minneapolis was caught red-handed trying to skew the census numbers. In Minneapolis fantasies of retribution abounded, along with the claim that the arrests had been made, many believed, to discredit the Minneapolis census and feed St. Paul's hatred for its sister city.

Meetings were held to address the concerns, and the largest filled the Armory with 10,000 people. Speeches rallied the audience. St. Paul had acted without authority of law or pretense of right, the aggrieved Minneapolitans said, taking census materials without cause. "The clear and unmistakable purpose of all said acts is maliciously and wantonly to destroy the records of the census of the city of Minneapolis," read one of their resolutions, and "enviously to attack her business growth and prosperity . . . is an assault upon the honor of her every citizen."[29]

Whenever the speakers mentioned the names of the St. Paul judge who issued the warrant, the census official who filed the charges, or the US marshal who made the arrests, the crowd hissed and booed. They brought a retired judge on the stage to read the warrant, and he concluded that he had never seen such "a thin complaint." The seven arrested census workers (out on bail almost immediately) were brought to the stage, and the crowd cheered them as heroes. Resolutions were read to thundering ovations.[30]

Minneapolis seethed that St. Paul's "acts of insolence and violation of every principle of common decency and law" were "direct attacks upon the spirit of harmony" that Minneapolis had "publicly and earnestly encouraged" between the two cities. People who had recently subscribed to uniting the two cities retracted their commitments. This malicious act to undermine Minneapolis's census count had reversed all the work of the past decade. The "slowly-closing chasm" between them was ripped open and could now "never be bridged." St. Paul's underhanded maneuver revealed it was no longer a worthy rival, said one man. Minneapolis "should hoist the black flag," said another, and called for a boycott of the downriver town.[31]

John De Laittre, a former Minneapolis mayor and one of the more prominent persons involved in the retaliation, read another resolution. Obviously, the insulting actions of St. Paul's leaders and the attacks by their press reveal that the people of St. Paul "have no sympathy for us, and have no desire for our friendship." He pulled out the old standard. He vowed to remove the state capital from St. Paul—and the governor too! The speakers promised, further, to cooperate with anyone who shared their sentiment from anywhere and any party to make the removal of the capital a reality. The crowd accepted the resolution with such a loud roar they nearly raised the roof.[32]

Meanwhile, the St. Paul election official was optimistic. He knew Minneapolis was calling it a bluff, but he had evidence that the city had padded its census reports. He was confident of a conviction. Most everyone felt that if fraud was committed, those guilty should be punished.

Generally, St. Paul was caught flat-footed by the extreme Minneapolis response. The city had nothing to do with the arrests and did not know of them in advance. Few businessmen cared to comment, at least on the record. Those who did gave a mixed message. Yes, it appears there was illegal activity, but should it have been handled in that way? It was a new federal law, so it was a federal matter. Yes, it would have been better if federal authorities had handled it. And, certainly, better if it had been carried out in Minneapolis and not at such a late hour. Since the rivalry between the two cities for supremacy had been the incentive for any padding of the census, the raid of one of the twins on the other set off a perfect storm.

The judge went on record and explained the process. He had ordered the former city attorney to do exceptional work to necessitate the warrant, then at the end of a long day of regular business the judge issued the warrant. As a new law it required background reading. He claimed there was nothing unusual in bringing a Minneapolis case to his court. A former US marshal backed up the judge, saying the conduct was in accord with practices he knew.

The local US district attorney was elusive. He had been away at the time, had not known anything about it until he returned, and expected to hear explanations from people. If the law was to be attended to, it seemed to rest on St. Paul. The scandal rose to the solicitor general of the Department of Justice in Washington, DC—an unknown from Ohio, William Howard Taft. The future president became officially involved in the Minnesota "census war," pushing the local census administrators to act. The scandal, Taft determined, was real. There was a concerted and preplanned conspiracy to pad Minneapolis numbers. The census enumerators made up names by the dozen. But the first trial found the defendant not guilty and so prosecutors, as is typical, dropped the other cases.

St. Paul was also investigated, and it was discovered that individual enumerators had also padded the count there. The difference between the two was that one was viewed as conspiratorial and the other was an individual action.

A recount was ordered. Minneapolis had a population of 182,967 by the first count and 164,738 by the second count, a difference of 18,229. St. Paul had 142,581 by the first count and 133,156 by the second count, a difference of 9,425.

Minneapolis had reacted before knowing the truth. One St. Paul resident had an interesting insight on the character this reaction displayed. The Minneapolis people took a deep interest in the affairs of their own city. "They are, as a people, protuberant optimists. They fancy there is no such other city and no such other people," he said, declaring also that he was a loyal St. Paul citizen. In comparison, St. Paul's attention to city matters was indecisive and apathetic. "We have a lot of old fossils" who don't care much beyond their own interests. They were "patriotic over there" in Minneapolis, always trying to make a city out of their place. What they did with the census was wrong, but "it is an indication of public spirit."[33]

An editorial in the *St. Paul Daily Globe* acknowledged that the excitement had led to things being said and done that might well have been omitted. But once passions had cooled, reason would surely return. Regretfully, the event had reawakened "the old-time hostility between the people of these two cities" when instead "amity and harmony should prevail."[34]

The event was "evidence of the folly" that allows for two cities, said Thomas Cochran, Archbishop Ireland's ally and real estate developer. "St. Paul and Minneapolis are one city," he said, "one in interest and one in the sentiment of the best citizens of each." He rejected the movement among Minneapolis men to withdraw from Twin City clubs and institutions of all kinds.

At the Department of Justice, Solicitor General William H. Taft oversaw the case of the Twin Cities' census war. The future president strongly advised an early consolidation into one municipality and suggested the name "Twin City." Newspapers picked up on this use of the singular form as it implied oneness, as opposed to the plural terms "twin cities," "dual cities," "twins," etc., which had been the standard for thirty years. This idea maintained that if residents adopted a name in the singular form, the name itself would convey the fact that the two cities were undeniably one.[35]

CHAPTER 10

Utopian Vision Meets Contentious Reality

In a field of rolling hills above the Mississippi River, the two men had their choice of lots. On the east side of the Mississippi, with a view to the west, the terrain offered a variety of options. If they bought their lots on top of the hill, they could see downtown St. Paul to the east and downtown Minneapolis to the northwest. Or, if they bought lots at the base of the hills on the bluff overlooking the river, they would have a view up the river to downtown Minneapolis. Ambrose Tighe and William Peet were shopping for land, so the story goes, for their club. The club wanted a house in the country where they could gather and enjoy a variety of sports throughout the year.[1]

Peet and Tighe chose an area near the recently completed Marshall Avenue bridge, on a bench above the gorge, on the south side of Rum Pitch, where Donald McDonald's old groggery had stood. In October 1889 they bought several lots in Desnoyer Park from the Union Land Company and transferred them to the Town & Country Club. They deliberately situated their clubhouse between the two cities. They hoped the new location would help grow membership from both sides of the river. Peet would later say that the game of golf saved the club and gave it a purpose. But in 1889 that story had not yet begun. When they moved to the river on Desnoyer's land, these men had something more in mind.[2]

Desnoyer had called his property the future Bridge Square of the united Minneapolis and St. Paul. Over the years, multiple efforts to join the cities had focused on his property. In October 1885 a St. Paul newspaper printed a hand-drawn map that labeled the Desnoyer property as the "Proposed Site for Future State Capitol." People had made other proposals for a new city center of a united Twin Cities in other areas of the Midway, from Minnehaha Falls to near the State Fairgrounds. In 1889, when Tighe and Peet bought the lots in Desnoyer Park, they were acting in concert with others in the community. They appear to have been part of a combined focus to bring the Capitol to this area and unite the Twin Cities.

The Town & Country Club was three years old when it built the clubhouse by the river, yet, as Peet told the story, the club was already well on its way through a cat's nine lives. It was organized on December 8, 1887, in time to participate in St. Paul's second Winter Carnival. In those days social clubs were very popular and typically oriented around the Winter Carnival. People formed clubs for the carnival parades and sport competitions in snowshoeing, tobogganing, and ice-skating races. Businesses, such as Northern Pacific Railroad, Ryan Hotel, and *Pioneer Press*, and social organizations, such as Nushkas, Windsor, and Town & Country, sponsored teams. The teams wore colorful, uniform costumes with toques, sashes, and stockings.

The Nushkas was a club of "the Best Society People," according to the *Daily Globe*, that embraced the Winter Carnival and sporting events. Based in the Carpenter's Lookout (near the University Club) at the top of the toboggan slide on Ramsey Hill, they attended parades in two old Concord stagecoaches that were retired from the St. Paul–St. Anthony stagecoach line.[3]

The Town & Country Club was born from a cast of exiles from the Nushkas. Peet had been a member of the Nushkas (along with other future Town & Country members Maurice Auerbach, George R. Finch, William A. Van Slyke, Cass Gilbert, Lucius P. Ordway, and likely more), but, as he remembered, the Nushka group was too rowdy. He helped form the Town & Country Club as a more genteel alternative. William Henry Patterson instigated the club, and Manly B. Curry helped organize it, with the intention of having a year-round sport club. The club was described as "an auxiliary of the Minnesota Club" because the membership overlapped so closely with that prestigious club. The Minnesota Club also offered some sports, such as tennis and rowing, but its members were more formal in their social gatherings.[4]

Town & Country soon became the elite club of the city with its exclusive membership capped initially at sixty. Members competed in some events, like toboggan slides, but they did not participate in the parades. That first winter of 1887–88, they leased a three-story brick house at the end of Lake Como, a block north of the Northern Pacific Como station. The house had parlors with space for dances and a large dining room on the first floor, cards and billiards rooms on the second. They hired a chef and waitstaff. In the winter, they built a toboggan slide that ran out on the lake. They cleared snow for ice skating, went snowshoeing, and took sleigh rides. In the summer, they enjoyed tennis, boat or canoe rides, bathhouses, music, and other entertainment. "A great object of the club is to induce people to take advantage of the pleasant Como drive during the summer," said the *Daily Globe*. Members envisioned a resort atmosphere like New York's renowned Saratoga Springs.[5]

Just as Town & Country realized its success, Peet recalled, members felt their country clubhouse was being crowded by the railroad. Too many people were coming to the area. It was "not quite far enough away to make it a good drive," Peet said. They were unable to attract new members, and the club languished, saved only by the talented French chef Adolf Montant.[6]

Then Emerson Peet, William's father, who sold mortgages and had his finger on the pulse of real estate markets in the Twin Cities, suggested the club buy land on Desnoyer's property, which had only recently opened up for sale after much delay. The idea led to building a clubhouse midway between the cities and expanding the membership to 200 so the club could include people from Minneapolis. Club leaders were looking to improve the relationship between the two cities, which was "rather frigid," according to Peet. They thought, "we might even be the 'tie that binds.'" That idea was a part of the climax in the effort to unite the Twin Cities and gets to the real reason the club moved there.[7]

Peet and Tighe bought the lots near the rim of the gorge, overlooking the river, in 1889. They transferred the lots to the Town & Country Club, and the club built a clubhouse for about $25,000. It was designed by one of its members, the architect Cass Gilbert. The housewarming party took place in December. The clubhouse featured skeet shooting, bowling, and billiards, and it became a hot spot for bike lunches (thanks to Chef Montant). Bike trails were built along the gorge connecting the property to Summit Avenue and along the river to the north. The club sponsored bike races along Lake Street to Bde Maka Ska.[8]

Peet describes the club's early history as one of uncertainty, featuring a series of flops, until golf came at just the right time and gave the club a defined purpose. The club acquired the empty acreage adjacent to its property, and the rest, as they say, is history.

Peet omitted one item from his story, however, and it isn't a small thing. When Peet and Tighe bought the lots at Marshall Avenue and the river, the talk about uniting the Twin Cities in the Midway area was filling editorial pages in the newspapers. The newspapers printed maps that featured the Capitol building on the large fields to the east of Town & Country's new clubhouse. Club members had every intention of being near the new Capitol.[9]

Club members surely participated in the conversations about moving the Capitol to the Midway. Architect Cass Gilbert, for example, was on the St. Paul Chamber of Commerce, one of the organizations engaged in the discussion of uniting the cities and at the heart of deciding the new Capitol's location. Other members were involved in similar capacities. Land speculation had matured to include city planning. They knew Horace W. S. Cleveland and were acting on his ideas. In that broader perspective, there was more to the idea of being a part of "the tie that binds."

Cleveland's Influence

Peet said the club was looking for a place in the country and Como Park had too many visitors, yet it wanted to be a part of what tied the cities together. Club members' ambitions seemed wrapped around an irony: wanting to be both in the country and in the middle of the cities. And that is a clue to their intentions. It fits their times and Cleveland's prescription. His method of uniting the Twin Cities through parkways and accessibility fit the needs of the club. In fact, its first clubhouse at Como served a similar purpose.

Cleveland had identified St. Paul's Summit Avenue as a conduit to be extended across the river to Thirty-Fourth Street in Minneapolis, a ten-mile boulevard tying Bde Maka Ska to St. Paul (going along the south side of Powderhorn Lake) as a main thruway to tie the cities together. That connection never materialized, which may have influenced Town & Country's decision to relocate to Marshall Avenue later. (See map of Cleveland's Minnehaha Park proposal from 1888, page 179). Cleveland also envisioned an early version of the Grand Round, a route from St. Paul along Como Avenue to Como Park, the State Fairgrounds, and then on to Minneapolis. Como stood midway between the two downtowns. He laid out St. Anthony Park in 1873 with his trademark arching meander for Como Avenue, the "Grand Interurban Boulevard" connecting the "United Cities," as he called it.[10]

Cleveland's ideas had captured the attention of some Town & Country members. Manly B. Curry, one of the original instigators of the club, and J. Royall McMurran were real estate developers, in partnership with John W. McClung. In 1885, when Cleveland was designing Como Park, Curry's firm (along with Frederick D. Hager) bought the 300 acres north of Como Avenue in St. Anthony Park. As interested parties, Curry and McMurran were on the association a few years later that arranged the location of the boulevard along the shore of Lake Como, which Cleveland had encouraged be preserved in the public domain. The developers would have known Cleveland through meetings, if not personal consulting. Their neighborhoods were designed on principles he introduced and emphasized, such as nonlinear streets that followed the natural topographic features.[11]

The developers also owned the sixty acres between Como Park and the State Fairgrounds. They subscribed to Cleveland's vision and planned to develop Como Avenue as one of the intercity boulevards. Como Avenue came up from St. Paul downtown as it does today. They initiated its extension through Como Park, across to the State Fairgrounds on a northern route, through the Experimental Farm (University of Minnesota, St. Paul campus), and then along a high ridge overlooking both cities, which the same partners owned. At that point, it reached the Hennepin County line and met up with Minneapolis.[12]

The Minneapolis city council, at about the same time, approved a boulevard in alignment with Como Avenue. Minneapolis had secured $10,000 from the legislature to develop this broad avenue to the fairgrounds. Meanwhile, the developers sought to widen St. Paul's Como Avenue to 120 feet. St. Paul and Ramsey County authorities were in agreement with this route beyond Como, though a few other property owners needed to buy into the plan.[13]

Curry, McMurran, and Hager were all early members of Town & Country. Whether McClung joined the club later is unknown, but he was on the St. Paul committee for streets, roads, and parks. These men stood at the forefront of the efforts to put the new city center in Desnoyer Park. Curry had spoken up to defend his work at a Capitol building meeting, denying that as a real estate developer he was only trying to move the Capitol to boost his real estate values. He was actively incorporating Cleveland's vision of parkways into efforts to unite the two cities. The club's first clubhouse at Lake Como was likely associated by convenience with this connection between Curry and his real estate partners and their interests. Hager and McMurran visited Como Park to participate in these club activities. Cleveland designed the park for this precise purpose. Curry and his Town & Country friends were realizing Cleveland's vision in real time.[14]

Cleveland had sold his vision to city leaders but also to developers by downplaying any special effort in the development of the real estate. The business of building for a better future "requires neither the eye of the visionary or the enthusiast, but simply the shrewd intelligence of the business man," he said. He incited the developers as businessmen to engage in his idea of enhanced living. He successfully recruited Curry and his associates in his effort to unite the Twin Cities through parkways and boulevards.[15]

Cleveland's earlier plan for extending Summit Avenue across Minneapolis on Thirty-Fourth Street did not materialize. That connection, which he called "Union Parkway," had an alternative route along Marshall Avenue and Lake Street. Town & Country Club's move to Desnoyer Park can be viewed as a response to Cleveland's plan. If club leaders waited for the developers to lay out neighborhoods and sell lots to individual owners, the moment would be lost. When Peet, who was on the Chamber of Commerce Transportation Committee, said that the club might be the tie that binds, this is what its members were thinking. Their time at Como Park was of the same nature. When the club moved to the river it wasn't just real estate speculation. They had a grander plan.

Desnoyer's Dream

When Tighe and Peet bought property for the Town & Country Club on the Desnoyer estate in late 1889, they did not buy it from Desnoyer himself. He was on record in 1872, seventeen years earlier, asserting that his property would become the Bridge Square of the united cities. But he had died before his big brag could be confirmed.[16]

There was no reason to believe him. He couldn't see the future. And he was a braggart of the old frontier, renowned for claiming his land was worth more than it was. He sued and was sued for various reasons, often based on distortions of the truth but also for slander. If he lost, he appealed to the Minnesota Territorial Supreme Court. He hired the best appellate lawyer in the territory, William Hollinshead of Rice, Hollinshead and Becker.[17]

Desnoyer's notoriety often worked against his credibility, but in the case of his land being the center of the future united city, other people agreed with him. Since the territorial days, people believed the villages would eventually morph into one city. Henry M. Rice believed from an early date that the cities would unite. Newspapers backed up this idea with comments about the future. The Midway was at the heart of the metropolis.[18]

A halfway house was a common term of the day for a tavern, possibly with sleeping facilities. Desnoyer's Halfway House was almost exactly halfway on the St. Anthony Road between St. Paul and Minneapolis. Desnoyer also ran a farm of several hundred acres that sat along the river between Marshall and what is now I-94 (the eastern property line was Cretin Avenue). He routinely exhibited his livestock at the St. Paul fair and raced his horses, which he named in honor of his new hometown, such as Paul Kirkwood and Flying Paul. He and his drinking establishment were known to most everyone, yet he did not engage in public activities like his neighbors Lyman M. Ford (Groveland Nursery across the St. Anthony Road), William R. Merriam, Auguste Larpenteur, Isaac Rose (of Rose Township and later Roseville), D. A. J. Baker, and Archbishop John Ireland.[19]

Perhaps Desnoyer's isolation was because his English was poor. He spoke mostly his native Québécois French with his family and friends. He couldn't read or write. He had people read his papers to him, and he dictated his letters. He was unable to tell people how to spell his name. The silent "s" and "r" in his name threw people off, and they spelled his name many different ways, from "Danoye" to "Desnoyer." At his home in St. John, the family spelled it Desnoyers, which means walnut trees.

Father Augustin Ravoux, a French immigrant who had been a missionary to the Dakota people, became Desnoyer's confidant. They would have known each other since their days in Dubuque in the early 1840s. Ravoux had performed Desnoyer's last two (of four) weddings. Shortly after arriving in St. Paul, Ravoux conducted the wedding of Desnoyer and Matilda Donnolly. She apparently went by Letitia, as she is referred to in the newspapers, in their aborted divorce proceedings, and on their shared tombstone. His fourth wife, Sarah Johnson (she went by Sally), worked for him at his Halfway House.[20]

Ravoux knew Desnoyer's quixotic nature. Desnoyer believed if he made a will, it would invite death. He had nearly died at St. Anthony Falls in 1866 when he was thrown from his carriage and hit his head. Ravoux encouraged him repeatedly to dictate a will. It was coincidence that Desnoyer died in a similar accident, eleven years later, when his carriage overturned on a late-night return from St. Anthony. He never did dictate his will.[21]

Desnoyer died a rich man. It was rumored that he had buried gold on the property, a normal savings plan in those days. He had survived the crash of 1857 better than most, as hoarding coins of precious metal in the earth was good insurance for hard times. He had played the land speculation game well and owned various properties in St. Paul as well as another farm some fifty miles away.[22]

Desnoyer died on December 3, 1877, when the fight over the State Fair was at its most intense. Now the fight for his property, the center of the Twin Cities, could begin.

At that time, he had no known surviving children. In each of his first two marriages, he had a child. One child died young, though the other may have lived. He had two sisters and a brother who had followed him west, and they, and their children, were in line to receive his assets. His wife Sally was to receive the homestead and an annuity of $500 for the rest of her life.[23]

After the probate was settled, Sally sued her in-laws for a larger share, claiming Desnoyer had promised her more money. She lost and appealed the decision to the Minnesota Supreme Court. When she lost, she sued again, only to lose a second time. The family sold the land to Dennis Ryan, and he bought Sally out of her annuity, the farm, and the Halfway House.[24]

All of this took time and delayed the development of the land. Just as the inheritance issues were settled, a man claiming to be Desnoyer's lost son appeared in 1884 and took Ryan to federal court to claim his alleged inheritance. A sensational case that would not have a chance today, it required a good deal of research, much of it by an attorney who was also (and perhaps not coincidentally) a member of Town & Country, William H. Lightner. The case dragged into 1885, and the "lost son" lost and was denied an appeal.[25]

Ryan, who owned one of St. Paul's finest and largest hotels, bought the property for a real estate firm, the Union Land Company (ULC). The president of Union Land Company was Frederick D. Hager, a Town & Country member who owned acreage around Como with Curry. In 1887 ULC laid out the Desnoyer property with roads and lots and called the neighborhood Desnoyer Park. Cleveland was now living in the Twin Cities and ad-

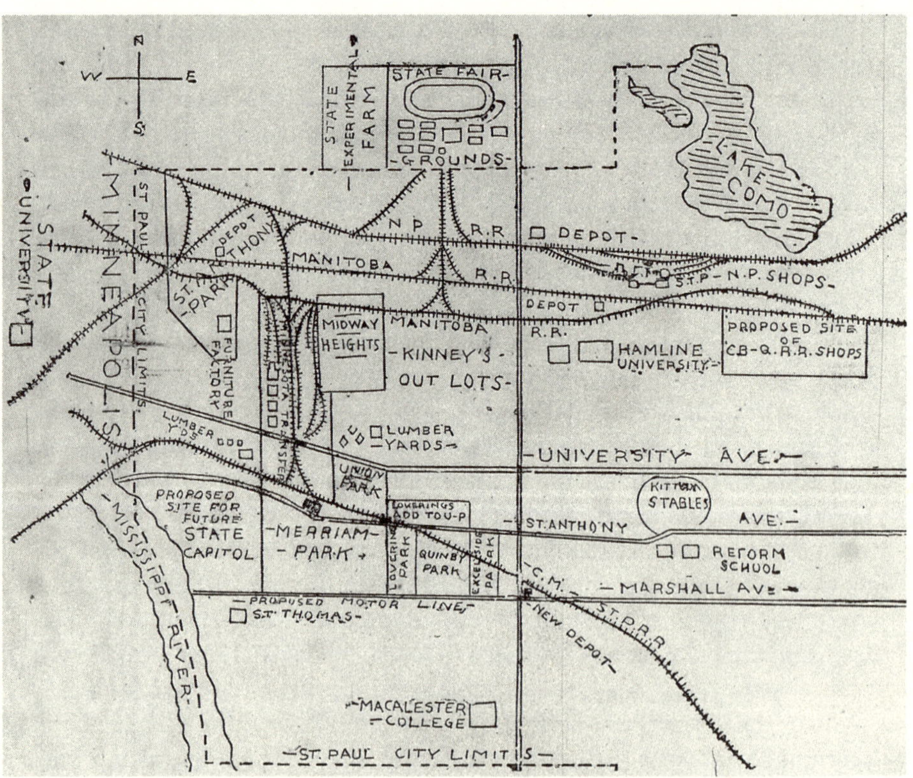

In the mid-1880s the Midway featured Lake Como, the State Fairgrounds, the Minnesota Transfer, and the proposed location of the University of St. Thomas on Marshall Avenue. Adjacent to the river, just north of Marshall Avenue, Desnoyer's property is labeled "Proposed Site for Future State Capitol."

vocating for preserving the gorge with boulevards along the rim and for a park that straddled the river.

A decade after Desnoyer's death, his property was ready for sale. If Desnoyer had prepared a will, his land could have gone on the market much sooner, possibly by 1880. Instead it was tied up in various legal challenges that kept it off the market. That next decade was a conciliatory time for the Twin Cities. At this point Desnoyer's property was a gem because it was unencumbered by any development, and it sat on Marshall Avenue. It was exactly what Cleveland was talking about developing. The land alongside the river was the perfect place for a new city center to unite the Twin Cities. Desnoyer and Cleveland were such different people, yet they had the same idea about this land. Both had envisioned a city center in the place now known as Desnoyer Park.

Twincite

On Christmas morning 1889 the *St. Paul Daily Globe* sent its readers a Christmas gift in the form of a utopian fantasy. On the front page was a sketch of two boys sliding on an icy sidewalk beneath a banner, "A Merry Christmas to All." Next to that was the headline "Twincite," and top center was a sketched map of the Twin Cities. People had suggested that the cities unite and go by the singular Twin City. Perhaps Twincite was pronounced that way.

The headline feature was the farthest thing from journalism, by the standards of that day and ours. The author told the story in a utopian science fiction format with the narrator in the not-too-distant future sharing details in a flashback. The year was 1900, eleven years into the future, and the cities had united three years prior. The story portrays a harmonious world where social, cultural, and economic issues are ideal and stable. Like Cleveland imploring townspeople to think of how future generations would judge them, this story evoked a vision of what was possible if the cities united.[26]

In the Christmas story, Paul and Minnie are married and celebrating their second anniversary. They are waiting for a report on their new municipal machinery, the latest development. At the center of the new city was Triangle Park, with three buildings from the three levels of government: city hall, the courthouse, and the capitol. Triangle Park was on the east side of the river, between Marshall Avenue and the Short Line. This was, in fact, the recently established Desnoyer Park, where Tighe and Emerson bought the land for the Town & Country Club. The park was laid out in triangular form with its base along the river and its apex on top of the hill in Merriam Park. The buildings were in the corners and oriented toward the common center.

The three buildings were similar in design and all constructed of native Minnesota stone, such as limestone and granite. The construction of the buildings was a test of the new labor laws. Residents had built the courthouse by contract (the old way) and the city hall with day labor under the new eight-hour law. They were interested in comparing the relative cost of each method and whether the eight-hour and anti-contract systems were cheaper.

Near the triangle was the transportation hub: Union Station and the terminal facilities of Twincite Belt Line Company. Five electric train lines branched out from this center, and an elevated electric train ran from Lake Phalen to Lake Harriet. Senator Lowry was raising funding for another elevated train line from Pig's Eye Lake to north of Minneapolis. A steamboat service on the river departed to Pig's Eye or St. Anthony Falls every half hour. Whether by steam, electric train, or elevated rail, a person could buy a round-trip ticket to anywhere for ten cents.

Of great promise was the intracity pneumatic tube line. Just the day before, an employee volunteered to take a test run through the tube. He was put in the mail car and sent from St. Paul's Ryan Hotel to Minneapolis's West Hotel. The trip took less than four minutes.

The article almost seems to be the dream of Horace W. S. Cleveland himself. It mentions him as enjoying "the crowning glory of his life." He had designed Triangle Park, and true to his style it was not only "the most novel, but the most beautiful park of its character in the world." The landscaping added lawns, shrubbery, flower beds, promenades, and statuary. The emphasis on fountains of various designs lent Twincite the popular nickname Fountain City.

The lines of the new park system followed the river boulevards and parks, and featured Hiawatha (Hidden Falls) and Minnehaha Parks on opposite sides of the river—beyond question the two most magnificent spots in the country.

The upcoming census excited the folks of Twincite. No longer a contest between embattled siblings, the census was a source of shared pride. At nearly one million people, Twincite was the fifth largest city in the United States, behind only Chicago, New York, Brooklyn, and Philadelphia. The amalgamation of the two cities had produced a growth spurt; the population had doubled in the past five years. The growth attracted new businesses, and two large packing plants had left Chicago and relocated to Twincite.

Triangle Park naturally brought new development around it. Private buildings included the Tremont Temple of Amusement, the Masonic Temple, the Academy of Science, the Auditorium, and the Metropolitan Museum. Palatial residences facing Triangle Park were in the works. "Beyond a doubt," the people boasted, "Twincite will again lead New York and Chicago in building for the year."

A tower at Marshall Avenue Heights provided a view from nearly 700 feet. The Midway district was now the heart of Twincite, and all the neighborhoods—Merriam Park, Hamline, and St. Anthony Park—blended into one. The growth had crowded out the gun club and now threatened the Twincite baseball team's stadium. The land was too valuable as residential property even though the team had been successful. Last year, the Twincite and New York teams had vied for the league pennant. It came down to the final game, and Twincite won the pennant by a score of 3–2 in nineteen innings.

Not a bad Christmas story.

The idea of merging the two cities with a governmental center in the Midway was popular enough to be presented as an alternate reality on Christmas morning. The story might have been written as a new form of land boosterism. Numerous people were invested in this scenario; many, such as Merriam and Ireland, owned large parcels of land. Perhaps the story would prompt the reader to wonder how they might obtain this idyllic world that was being presented as destiny.

The answer came in 1891.

Federal City

Short, small ads of one line of text began appearing in the newspapers in late March 1891. They looked like editorial comments, and they prompted the reader with questions:

> "Have you heard of Federal City?"
> "Where is Federal City, Main?"
> "What do you know about Federal City?"

The ads changed over the next week to statements:

> "Federal City, Minn. has 900,000 inhabitants."
> "Earth's loveliest women live in Federal City."
> "Look on the map for Federal City."

> "Chamber of Commerce: Every member must read 'Federal City.'"
> "Every man owning a lot must read 'Federal City.'"[27]

The ads effectively generated interest for the forthcoming thirty-six-page booklet of the same name, *Federal City: Being a Reminiscence of the Time Before St. Paul and Minneapolis Were United*. The author was anonymous, listed as "An Optimist." This detail amplified the buzz even more.

In the end, Harry P. Robinson was revealed as the author. A publisher, editor, and writer, he started and successfully developed the *Northwestern Railroader*, an industry news periodical that became the regional standard. He also wrote fiction and had success with several short stories published in the East Coast literary magazines. *Federal City* was his first, and only, foray into science fiction.

A dedicated member of the Town & Country Club, Robinson lived in Minneapolis and led one of the top tobogganing teams there. At the club he was the head of membership. His friend Thomas Lowry, a Town & Country member, appears to have underwritten Robinson's periodical. (Shortly after Robinson published *Federal City*, he announced his engagement to Lowry's daughter.)[28]

Federal City used the same narrative style as its predecessor, "Twincite," that is, the utopian flashback. The narrator in *Federal City* looked back from 1916 on the epic union of the Twin Cities as Federal City, which occurred after the embarrassing fallout of the 1890 census. The story showed the reader an alternative path for the two cities and explained what the future might be if that path were followed.

Robinson typed out his manuscript in the incandescent glow of an early electric light bulb. The first interurban electric line opened the previous December, giving residents easy transportation between St. Paul and Minneapolis via University Avenue. Electricity was transforming the world, bringing changes in communications and power. It was playing a significant role in the growth of cities. Robinson's readers would understand that electricity was "more potent than anything else in welding St. Paul and Minneapolis together."

But now, writing from the future, it was difficult, he conceded, to describe life with the "electric line." Unless a person had their own memories, it was so different from what they had in 1916 that the past was unimaginable. "Almost instantaneous transportation" now allows us to "breakfast in Minneapolis or St. Paul and dine in New York." Look at what we called "rapid transit," he wrote. "We talked pompously of having 'annihilated space.'" True, it was all much faster than the stagecoaches and steam locomotives. But at the time Robinson was writing the electric line between the cities took seventy minutes. And now in 1916 they could travel from Federal City to London in the time it took to travel from Chicago to Duluth.

Yet "we were proud of it and of ourselves—very proud of our advanced and enlightened selves," he said. It had been twenty-five years since the cities united, and in another twenty-five years they would look back and consider the "slow-going old days of 1916 with precisely the same pitying and curious amusement that we look back with now to 1891." Consider the telephones, "though they were as annoying as they were convenient," and electric light, which was so unrefined, and the telegraph that remained so vulnerable. The typewriter had been passed and forgotten. He described how advances in medicine and chemistry made it hard to recognize nineteenth-century life. In 1891 "the secret of life was still a secret." Now everybody is "taught the chemical formula of the life principle."

The transition into the twentieth century was a time "of utter social confusion," and despite the wealth of the nation they were unable "to seize the peace and prosperity that seemed so near." Such times made it difficult for people to see clearly, and that was true for the people of St. Paul and Minneapolis. To understand the quality of life today, Robinson said, it was best to return to the past in order to understand the conditions from which they had come.

Of greatest importance, the business organizations opened up their membership to individuals from the other city. Instead of seeking advantage over their neighbor, "the two cities could divide the spoils amicably and, by each assisting the other in the acquisition of her share." It was better than competing, he claimed. Soon the cities were interested in each other's business as it would impact them both. He envisioned a socialist-tinged capitalism perhaps. The businessmen and the daily papers joined the effort, and the press became "the chief agent in promoting union."[29]

In Robinson's fictious version of the future the new city's government was set up so that neither could take absolute control. The cities formed one common government with one mayor and one council meeting in the center. But the cities remained deeply suspicious of each other. They were unwilling to entrust any system that might allow "the treachery of one member" to control the interests of the other. The "long-standing traditions of enmity" had handicapped people's ability to think beyond their rivalry and understand "the meaning of union in all its bearings," he wrote.[30]

As the Midway district was transformed into an urban area, Robinson described the undeniable influence of Horace W. S. Cleveland. City leaders set aside land for public parks and public buildings, leading to a city without precedent. Once they established a center with public buildings, such as city hall, the capitol, and the central depot, more would follow, for example, the library, the museum, and the art institute. Broad avenues lined with trees had "an effect of stateliness and grandeur which is not to be seen in any part of the world," he wrote. And they were able to complete Cleveland's proposed boulevard that tied the communities together from the east end of Summit Avenue, through the Midway, to Bde Mka Ska. It was almost too long to take in one continuous drive.[31]

Surprisingly, the cities found that union brought them an increase in power in state and national affairs. Conflict and hostility had impaired their political clout. Now, together, they drew more attention and respect in Washington. "The voice of a million people must be listened to," he surmised. And most improbable of all, a Federal City citizen served in the White House as president of the United States.[32]

The name Federal City came about "only after long controversy." Other names "strongly urged" were:

Dual City
Twin City
Union City
United City
Junction City
Peace City
Mississippi City
Metropolis
Double City
Central City

And "even Minnepaul and Paulopolis were seriously entertained," he said.

Probably the greatest advantage the Midway offered was an open space between two established cities. Unlike older cities that need to raze blocks of buildings, dismantle churches, and move cemeteries to make room, "we had all the advantages of space and freedom of a new city," he wrote. Residents had the strength and operating industries in two full-grown cities along with open land. "There was nothing to undo." They viewed it as essentially a new city with a developed infrastructure. The centralization of the transportation system was a big advantage over cities that grew organically. The same applied to the distribution of an electric power network.[33]

Robinson's idea resurrected the old dream from Franklin Steele and Henry Rice of Minnesota's central location in the continent. By taking "fullest advantage of the new condition," the united cities opened even more possibilities, he wrote. The greatest of these was the recent "accession of Canada to the United States." A "commercial union" enlarged the area of trade, and the results were not yet in on how the State of Mantoba would impact Federal City. But it was easy to project that Federal City retained and regained all of its manufacturing distribution powers for the whole of the Northwest.[34]

The dream of connecting the Great Lakes with the Mississippi River still lingered in front of them. A "stupendous engineering work" in progress would make them "almost a maritime city," with a waterway for Great Lakes vessels to travel downriver to Federal City. With this connector, forecast to be operable in three years, Federal City would become the central hub between the Great Lakes and the Gulf of Mexico, creating a circular route with the Atlantic. "Federal City will have an industrial empire," Robinson claimed, "greater than has ever been subject to one city since the days of Imperial Rome."[35]

Robinson felt, like the generations before them, that "before a city is built or a people grows, its destiny is written on the face of its land." For so many years people had known that a great city would rise here between the Great Lakes and the Mississippi River. Once they solved this nineteenth-century problem of their rivalry, the ebullience of Manifest Destiny resurfaced as strong as ever. He recalled the cynics, when the people of St. Paul and Minneapolis "railed at one another as children do," when small-minded people were jealous of the other and thought that prosperity came with quarreling and not with peace, and when the oblivious said that union held no future better than what they had achieved in rivalry. "It all seems ridiculous to us now and very far away from our present life," he wrote.[36]

Twincite and Federal City are the only known fictional accounts of the Twin Cities uniting. They have many similarities, but they had different ambitions. "Twincite" was a frolic, a play on the ideas at hand, while *Federal City* had a sense of pragmatism. After all, real people were talking about making this blessed union happen. We can read Robinson's work as a transcription of conversations he had with proponents of the idea. He talked with others at the Lowry home and at the Town & Country clubhouse. He had conversations with Lowry, Curry, McClung, Hager, and Merriam, among others. Robinson wrote about the ideas discussed by the major players, such as Merriam and Ireland, large landowners who also had the political capital to develop these ideas.

Federal City, as we know, didn't come true. But Robinson had laid out in detail what many foresaw as possible—the vision of a Federal City they were trying to develop. His book may be the crowning moment of this idea.

One Last Try

Shortly after *Federal City* was published, an anonymous Minneapolis resident submitted a request to his legislative representative. The request echoed the premise of *Federal City*: It was time to unite the cities. The request was referred to the committee of statistics and correspondence, and the committee replied two weeks later. Despite "sharp collisions" that were "a standing menace" to the efforts, no such collusions can "paralyze the forces of mutual interest and reciprocal intercourse, which inexorably draw these communities together." Adding to that, the committee said, the infamous animosities for which the Twin Cities were known were "to a great extent imaginary," misconstrued by the newspapers.[37]

The committee felt that technology was driving the union forward. They were talking about the interurban electric line with its web of transfers and termini that had brought an economic boom to the Midway district. The new line "has done infinitely more to unite these cities than all combined adverse influences have done to separate them." With that, the committee said the union of St. Paul and Minneapolis was practicable and would be mutually advantageous. "The time has come to seriously consider the means and methods of bringing about this result," read their report, "and people of both cities are better prepared for their proper consideration than at any epoch in the past."

Of course the committee wouldn't do any of the hard work of planning a way or means to accomplish this union. Its members passed the idea on to the full legislature and recommended it go on record with affirmative support of the proposition. How and when to engage the solution to the problem was to be decided later.

With that proposition in process, the St. Paul Chamber of Commerce adopted related resolutions in July 1891. First, its members directed their president to appoint a committee on the union of the Twin Cities. The committee should work out the best way for a "speedy union of St. Paul and Minneapolis." And second, they asked Minneapolis to do the same.

The Minneapolis Board of Trade followed up in September with a surprising rejection of the idea because it offered Minneapolis "no advantage." Its representatives considered the idea to be an effort by people who owned land in the Midway. Besides, they had previously organized similar committees but those committees "accomplished nothing whatever toward the solution of the question." In stern though political language, the Minneapolis representatives called for an end to the pursuit of a united city. They referred to "these anxious unionists" who had absorbed the entire Midway district into the St. Paul city limits. The 1885 expansion of St. Paul to the river remained a contentious sore point.

The open space of the Midway had shrunk some, yet it was still "practically impossible to merge the two city governments into one over this extended area." The issue of union stalled again, and the Board of Trade declined to take action. Gone were the efforts by Minneapolis to draw the Capitol nearer. Despite the excitement represented by "Twincite" and *Federal City*, the new configuration of representatives on the Minneapolis committee was done. That rejection of the idea might have killed any chance at union. But it was only the beginning of the fall.[38]

Archbishop Ireland was a proponent and supporter of *Federal City*. "These two cities were made to be one," he said. The Midway held in its hands "the fortunes of St. Paul and Minneapolis." If the city leaders wanted to unite the two cities in the future, he said, they might as well go forward with it now. The vital link, in Ireland's mind, was the Minnesota Transfer Board of Trade. Transportation routes would tie together the cities. A Midway passenger depot would be well suited to the place where the eleven converging railway systems met and the traveling public could quickly transfer to other lines. Convenient transportation was, in his mind, the priority. The Midway had 82 miles of track and saw 1,500 cars daily. With the infrastructure already present and with room in which to expand, it was an inexpensive solution to uniting the transportation hub.[39]

Ireland worked to coordinate the assemblage of buildings in the central area. He owned most of the land south of Marshall Avenue and west of Cleveland Avenue and had built the St. Thomas Aquinas Seminary on Summit Avenue, west of Cretin Avenue. He had received $500,000 from James J. Hill, a Town & Country member, to finance a new seminary and a college, the latter he planned to build on Marshall Avenue, adjacent to Desnoyer Park. Here was the place for the legacy cathedral. The area met his criteria of a prominent locality, away from a business district, and closer to Minneapolis. All of these plans made the recently laid-out

Desnoyer Park lots valuable, and many of them were held by Town & Country members.[40]

Then the plan took some fatal blows.

The first occurred when some Town & Country members unintentionally revealed their plans. The best lots in the development were closer to the best access, which was near the Milwaukee Short Line depot that ran adjacent to the Desnoyer property on the northern border, just before the railroad crossed the gorge. When Ireland announced the plans for the Hill College, as it was known then, the property on the southern end of Desnoyer Park became more valuable.

In response to this shift, Daniel R. Noyes, a warehouse jobber in downtown St. Paul and a Town & Country member, along with other large property owners, transferred holdings with Union Land Company from the northern to the southern end of the Desnoyer Park property. They "rubbed their hands with glee over their good luck," reported the *Daily Globe*. The overlap in membership of the club and the land company was so great that the newspaper treated them as one entity.

In the summer of 1891 Ireland approached the Union Land Company and met with the president, Frederick D. Hager, and asked for a deal. Since Hill College would increase property values in the area, he asked for "several lots" as compensation or a "bonus" for that increased value. The Town & Country members delayed responding to the idea. They believed Ireland was already committed to the location on Marshall Avenue, so there was nothing to negotiate. They felt "they had Ireland in a tight spot," reported the *St. Paul Daily Globe*. "They did not feel they needed to compensate him in any way." Hager informed Ireland that the company lawyers said the company "could not legally donate land as a bonus."[41]

Ireland became irritated. In a flash he pulled the school plan and moved it a half mile south to Summit Avenue, near the St. Paul Seminary. (It is today the University of St. Thomas.) The cathedral fell from view as well. The legacy building he wanted was built overlooking St. Paul and opened in 1915.[42]

"It's a horse on us," said one man of ULC, "and we deserved it." Indeed, he admitted, though the company couldn't legally give the land, any of the individual owners could have. The club forfeited what would have been "a great stroke," and instead they were left "in the cold." He blamed those who had opposed donating, claiming the college would not benefit them, and yet they "rushed off and selected lots on that side of our tract. It was a keen retort by the archbishop, and served us all right."

Noyes responded immediately in a letter to the editor and asked for a correction as the statements reflected on him "very unjustly." He said, as a director of ULC, he had always advocated for giving lots to Ireland to support his college projects, and he did so before owning the lots. He denied being a large landholder there, and he denied transferring ownership of lots. (Land purchases in the newspaper show that ULC had transferred ten lots to him in early April 1891.)[43]

The second blow to the idea of uniting the Twin Cities in the Midway was the loss of the Capitol. John L. Merriam, a member of Town & Country, was working on locating it in the capitol addition of Merriam Park, which was laid out to accommodate it. Merriam's son, William (the governor and a member of Town & Country), offered twenty acres on the height of land between Cleveland and Cretin Avenues. The site overlooked the river gorge and the downtowns of both cities were visible from it.[44]

While *Federal City* was at the top of its sales, on April 3, 1891, the Minnesota Senate appointed a committee of five senators to answer the question if a new Capitol was necessary and, if so, where it should be built. Their answer came in the next legislative session, two years later, on February 3, 1893. Unanimously they agreed, yes, the state needed a new Capitol building. On the second question they split 4–1. The majority decided that Capitol Square in downtown St. Paul was the best site (bounded by Wabasha–Cedar and Exchange–Tenth Street). They prioritized "public convenience," which included such needs as being near the center of downtown St. Paul, the capital, and its convenient transportation. If more space was needed, the state could acquire adjacent lands or find a better site. Any new site had to be within three-quarters of a mile from the present Capitol. The prescribed distance "squelched agitation" for other areas, be it Kandiyohi County, Minneapolis, or the Midway district.

The senate Capitol search team consisted of one senator from each of Ramsey and Hennepin Counties and three nonmetro politicians. The only one in support of the Midway was the senator from Hennepin County. In the end, the effort to move the Capitol to the Midway escaped the advocates. In the story of "Twincite," the author mentioned that the idea of a central city faced opposition in "the Granger element in the legislature." The fantasy allowed the bill to pass through without a struggle. In reality the senate committee, being sixty percent from rural counties, determined to leave the Capitol downtown and build a fireproof building (that is, one of stone construction). The majority report prevailed, and the senate adopted the recommended site. And so ended a second major project for the Midway. With the collapse of the Capitol plan, hopes for a united depot also waned.[45]

Thus marked the end of building a new center, an idea driven by the antebellum ideal of Jacksonian diplomacy that gave people direct power over state business, including where the Capitol would stand. Another economic depression hit in 1893, and Ireland was badly pressed for cash due to the debt he carried on his speculative lands. The Town & Country members found opportunity in the depressed prices. Peet recalled buying properties in Desnoyer Park for low prices. The final curtain fell when Town & Country vacated the streets and alleys on its land in 1905. That move signaled golf was here to stay.[46]

EPILOGUE

How the Twin Cities Might Merge

The effort to create a new political and cultural center for the Twin Cities died in 1893. The Minnesota Legislature restricted a new site for the Capitol building, requiring it to be within St. Paul's downtown area. Architect Cass Gilbert, a member of the St. Paul Chamber of Commerce and the Town & Country Club, designed the new Capitol, which opened in 1905. Archbishop John Ireland built the University of St. Thomas on Summit Avenue. A new site for the cathedral, his legacy building, was found in 1904, and the building overlooking St. Paul opened in 1915. The idea of a central Union Depot dissipated, and each city retained a depot, reflecting the parallel feature of the rail service in the two cities.

Minneapolis and St. Paul would remain twins, even while they grew more independent. St. Paul developed manufacturing to balance its commercial strengths, and Minneapolis filled in its commercial businesses alongside its manufacturing prowess. Minneapolis outpaced St. Paul in growth and became the financial center when the Federal Reserve chose it in 1914 as a regional bank for the Ninth District, which included Montana, North and South Dakota, Wisconsin, the Upper Peninsula of Michigan, and Minnesota. As combined economies, the two cities were able to take over from Chicago the business of the Northwest.

Despite the assumptions and the efforts of many people, the Twin Cities never merged into one city. They remained obdurate in their independence for decades. Yet they have evolved, and it would be wrong to say they remain entirely separate. The question this book tried to answer was "Why have they never merged?" And people often follow up with "Will they merge?" As the story shows, the answers are complex and filled with "what if" scenarios. Yet the Twin Cities today have evolved in a special way worth noting. There is more here than initially meets the eye.

As American cities grew in the early twentieth century, city planners removed factories from the congested downtown districts and established industrial zones at their perimeter. The Twin Cities were different because they had the Midway district. Since 1883 the Minnesota Transfer railroad yard, a transfer and switching zone, had concentrated the railroad traffic and industrial development in the Midway. "This double-centered tract is unique in the industrial world," wrote Harold F. Chapin, an industrial statistician for the St. Paul Association of Commerce in 1917. The Transfer had originally solved the existing problem of complicated and inefficient railroad routes. But now the cities could lighten their centers of the industrial burden with the bonus of distribution across the railroad network at very low prices. With the Transfer, the Midway district's 175 miles of track in 1917 had direct connections with nearly 40,000 miles of railway across the continent. This far-ranging transportation network, along with the Midway's cheaper land and room for expansion, lured factories to relocate outside the cities.[1]

The cultural identity of Minneapolis and St. Paul continued to be distinct and separate from each other, according to Richard Hartshorne, a prominent geographer at the University of Minnesota. He described the type of "twinning" found in the Twin Cities as two cities almost completely separated, politically and geographically, despite their shared border and interest in the Midway district. Hartshorne even described them in 1932 as "radically different." They operated with a "functional independence," in that they did not specialize in complementary ways or integrate their services.[2]

While they developed into independent cities, each was unable to replicate some elements that flourished in their sibling city. Packing plants were located in South St. Paul, an industrial suburb of St. Paul, while Minneapolis failed to develop an independent stockyard. Grain elevators and flour mills became a dominant feature of Minneapolis, while St. Paul had only a few. The same specialization can be seen from the early days of lumber mills and the processing of furs. The cities' economic profiles were unique from each other.[3]

Aside from these select industries, each city featured its own independent business district. The most active railroads built terminal yards and stations in both cities, as well as "car shops" for train car maintenance and repair. The two cities had a similar variety of factories, warehouses, and wholesale houses. They each had a commercial core that was common to American cities of their size, containing all the "nuclear features," such as large department stores, tall office and newspaper buildings, large hotels, theaters, and auditoriums.[4]

Hartshorne noted that the "functional independence" resulted in very little intercity street traffic. In the 1920s one streetcar company served both cities, yet it had only four car lines that crossed their boundary. The majority of the people who traveled between the cities were students and factory workers. At that time, some shoppers would cross the river, he said, but there was little need to shop in both cities. Even the various theater performances were "nearly always duplicated" in both cities, "as though they were a hundred miles apart."[5]

The separate character of each city was seen "to a marked degree" in the psychology of the citizens. "The early violent animosity" during the "struggle for supremacy" dissipated as Minneapolis became the larger city. In the 1930 census Minneapolis had a population of 464,350 and St. Paul's was 271,600. But a "very keen rivalry" remained, and Hartshorne found it "by no means always friendly." The newspapers served their home city and were reporters on and perpetrators of the rivalry. The result was a political separation at the municipal and county levels that prevented nearly all types of cooperative development. Each city blamed their problems, such as crime, on the other. Even in major health crises, such as epidemics, the health authorities acted as independently "as would those of Philadelphia and New York." Unlike the 1880s, the two city planning boards no longer had mutual correspondence or a guiding visionary like Horace W. S. Cleveland. Except for two bridges, the residents enjoyed no joint facilities in public buildings or parks of any kind. The only exception Hartshorne could see was "the pressing problem of sewage disposal" in the river, which needed to be addressed by "a common system." But even with such a mutual problem the cities could not get beyond themselves to find a solution. In the 1930s their rivalry was locked in.[6]

While the railroads and the Transfer railroad yard tied the Twin Cities together, this transportation system also made the development rigid and seemingly permanent. The layout of the cities had been established during the steamboat era and solidified in the current configuration during the early conversion to railroads. The Midway, which was a "zone of contact," was a unifying feature. The cities should not be "considered as completely separate" because of the concentration of all routes through the Transfer in the Midway, which connected the two centers into "a unit—though double—rail center." Any effort to unite them in the 1930s had to look at "the structure of the all-important city-building factor of the region—the railroads," Hartshorne said. Indeed, the railroads were very much a dominant economic force. Hartshorne noted that, by 1919 numbers, half of the male workforce had either occupations with the railroads or jobs associated with regional rail centers, such as flour mills and grain elevators, stockyards and packing plants, warehouses and jobbing houses, foundries, and so on.[7]

How to unite the double-center metropolitan area with its dependence on two rail centers? The one possibility, he suggested, was to "create a new center" for passenger and freight rail traffic in the Midway district as a priority over the city centers. A precedent of this type of change existed in Neenah and Menasha, Wisconsin. But in the Twin Cities such a layout would put the new passenger station five miles from the city centers. Any change in the transportation structure would be prohibitively expensive. The twins had developed ten miles apart, which was "too far from the other to be in any serious danger of submergence or even subordination," he said. Another alternative would be to select one city as the primary transportation center. In some similar situations the railroads had discriminated in their passenger service in favor of one city. For example, the railroads eliminated express train stops at Kansas City, Kansas, giving Kansas City, Missouri, a primary position. Had the railroads done the same in the Twin Cities in the 1880s, there might have been a similar focus on one city over the other.[8]

As long as the railroads served the two commercial cores equally, Hartshorne believed the situation would continue. The cities had grown together, which in the 1880s had been a stipulation for uniting them, but now they were too big to adapt. He imagined that only another mode of transportation that greatly increased the speed of urban transportation could threaten the situation. "To a minor extent," he said in the early 1930s, "the automobile has done that."[9]

The remaining possibility that could unite the cities, in Hartshorne's assessment, was "only phenomenal and totally unexpected growth." Perhaps, he suggested, if travel became faster and independent of the railroads, such as with subways or elevated lines, it might disintegrate the "present marked separation in the local business." He could not foresee the growth in the automobile and the rise of the interstate highway network still over thirty years in the future, but in the 1930s Minneapolis was growing west, away from St. Paul, not toward it. The problem remained the same as in the 1880s. Any relocation of the city center to the Midway district "would involve such enormous loss in invested property as to appear totally impracticable." The situation was likely unchangeable, he thought. The railroad was dominant and its structure "a strong factor of inertia," along with the two commercial cores with their vast fixed investment, strengthened by psychological factors—all tended to make permanent this unique geographical form: a double center of separated cores.[10]

Meanwhile, the growing population was beginning to stress the system. People were noticing the limits of the infrastructure on a broader scale. They saw an "increasing need for coordination" on various elements of infrastructure, from transportation such as streetcars, to communications (telephone), public health and safety, water supply, and, the most often mentioned issue, sewage disposal. Hartshorne held out these basic functions for a standard of urban life that "might conceivably lead to some sort of combined political organization." He was aware that this possibility had been discussed since the early days, and yet it remained unrealized. The Twin Cities' problem seemed unchanged since Zebulon Pike, Joseph Plympton, and Stephen Desnoyer had encountered the area and bet on the future. "Cities are controlled from their centers," Hartshorne wrote, and the commercial cores will continue to give their identity to each respective city. He believed that any merger would have to be different from any ordinary unified city. In order for it to happen, he said, "a new form of political organization would be needed."[11]

A New Type of Government

At the end of World War II, nearly ninety percent of the metro population lived in St. Paul and Minneapolis. The era of the suburbs began, and the new communities became financially and psychologically independent of the two cities. The postwar suburban boom introduced a "geographical polarization," according to Ted Kolderie, executive director of the Citizens League in the 1960s. The economic conditions were imbalanced. For example, home sizes in the western and southern areas were larger than those in the northern and eastern areas. Along with this dynamic was a tax burden that tended to be the inverse of the home valuation. To address any issues that spanned the region the administrators had to consider this imbalance.[12]

While most US cities faced a polarization between their core and the suburbs, in Minnesota the idea of "metropolitan unification" was complicated by the rivalry between the two cities. Instead of simply "a demand for city/suburban cooperation" planners had to develop the same between Minneapolis and St. Paul. A person's alliance and identity depended on where they lived. They were "ambivalent," Kolderie wrote in 1973. "A Minneapolis citizen might feel suburbanite in relation to Minneapolis, yet a Minneapolitan vis-a-vis St. Paul."[13]

Neither city moved quickly to extend services to the new suburban communities. These so-called "recessive policies" in the initial phases of growth manifested regional issues. "St. Paul used its water and sewer systems to restrict the rate of suburban expansion," according to Kolderie, and "Minneapolis was fiscally conservative." On top of that, Minnesota had a strong legislative influence over municipal governance. As suburbs developed, the legislature was passive and waited for problems to come to them.[14]

A number of crises accumulated simultaneously as those "recessive policies" were exposed through development. The suburbs expanded using individual water wells and septic tanks, and the nitrates from the septic tanks began leaching into the home water wells. In 1959 about half of the new homes (300,000 people) had high nitrates in their water. Those nitrates ended up in the rivers, lakes, and underwater reserves. The legislature was not able to address a problem spread across so many jurisdictions. Several years passed with only talk and no solution. By 1965, after a third legislative session was unable to address the sewage issues, frustrations grew. At the same time the legislature failed to pass a plan for metropolitan transit. Other rising concerns included air pollution, road expansion, parks, and a new airport. It was clear that a representative agency, such as the Metropolitan Planning Commission, was ineffective in solving multiagency issues.[15]

A unique approach to addressing these growth-related crises came about from a number of coincidences. First, by the mid-1960s the region was evenly split between the cities and the suburbs, both in population and in property values. "Neither could clearly dominate the other," reported Kolderie. Second, on the state level, the influence of the metropolitan population grew to match the rural population. Previously, the Minnesota Legislature had been driven largely by the rural interests. In 1964 the US Supreme Court ruled in *Reynolds v. Sims* that state legislative districts had to contain similar numbers of people. This redistricting tilted the legislature in favor of metropolitan interests.[16]

This tipping point in the legislature allowed for the design of a new type of government structure that would better address the growing conflicts between the two cities and between them and their suburbs. Across the country a number of municipalities (Jacksonville, Nashville, Indianapolis, and Miami) addressed such growth with city–county mergers. The percentage of successful city–county consolidations was low. At the time these were accomplished by referendum with a majority vote of the electorate. The consolidations eliminated the old government structure and replaced it with a new, larger government. While a reorganization promised alignment, efficiency, and cost saving, they were limited in policy adjustments made to address the existing problems. The typical city–county merger left power structures in place, and complications arose because of overlapping agency responsibilities. Because of the Twin Cities' complex scenario with intra-urban and urban–suburban issues, such a merger was out of the question. Also, such restructuring was inflexible to the larger-scale problems beyond its jurisdiction, and it left those who set policy in charge of administration, which limited accountability.[17]

So when in the mid-1960s members of the cities' governments "first seriously considered" the "creation of a metropolitan government for Minneapolis–St. Paul," they rejected the framework of city–county consolidation. Merging St. Paul and Minneapolis was inadequate because the development was in the outer rings of suburbs. The problems they were addressing were not limited to the two cities or even their counties. The metropolitan area involved seven counties (Hennepin, Ramsey, Anoka, Dakota, Washington, Scott, and Carver) and 1.8 million people, about half of the state's population.[18]

Fostered by the accumulating crises of the 1960s, people talked of a new type of government. Through time their conversations developed into the idea of the Metropolitan Council, designed to help the legislature manage the complex multi-district metropolitan area. The Council would take input from volunteer advisory committees and members, develop proposals that address particular issues spanning the metro area, inform the legislature, and develop solutions the legislature would then pass. The Council operated with seventeen members appointed by the governor and confirmed by the senate. Sixteen of those members represent districts of equal population that do not replicate the political boundaries of cities or counties and serve on a part-time basis for four-year terms. The seventeenth member is the full-time chairperson, who serves at the pleasure of the governor. Over time the Council had a staff of more than 150 people who conducted ongoing research, planning, and coordinating. Several hundred volunteers served on advisory committees to supply some measure of citizen input to decisions. As of 2025 the Council partners with 181 cities and townships, seven counties, other government entities, businesses, nonprofit organizations, and others. Elected officials, local government staff, and residents share their expertise with the Metropolitan Council by serving on key advisory committees.

Focused only on issues that span the metro area, the Council's design involves a crucial and distinguishing feature: separation of policy and administration. That is, the developers of the Council didn't try to create another administrative apparatus at the regional level, as seen in the city–county merger option. Instead, they left in place all the local managers. They separated the entities that plan and establish policies, and left it to the local agencies to implement the policies, as well as to deliver public services and governmental operations. "Clearly evident from the Twin Cities experience," wrote Kolderie, one of the key actors in the Council's creation and evolution, "is a willingness by the public and political officials to move much more rapidly toward regional arrangements in the area of policy making than in the area of program operations."[19]

The Council has no direct contact with the municipal and county governments. Yet in matters of regionwide impact, such as public transit, wastewater treatment, water supply and monitoring, planning for future growth, regional parks and trails development, and affordable housing for low-income households, the Council can either compel or prevent local governments from specific actions. This status was both a part of its success and what gave rise to people's antagonism to it: The design gave the Council teeth in order to direct the course of policy. The state attorney general determined that the Metropolitan Council was neither an agency of local government nor a part of the state government. Answerable to the legislature and having its own source of funding, it was described as a hybrid of a metropolitan government and a state agency, endowed with various powers to plan, coordinate, control, and direct the region's growth.[20]

One analysis described the Council's design as "analogous to Alfred Sloan's model of organization of General Motors," which featured centralized planning and coordination separate from the decentralized management operations. Another viewed the Council as fitting the state's political tendencies to put power in the control of legislative bodies and local councils rather than strong executives. "This is an inheritance from the Populist period of the late nineteenth and early twentieth centuries when strong executives in government were suspect," wrote Stanley Baldinger in 1971. Council membership was designed to be part-time, which also matched that ideal: "Politics and government should be an avocation for the public spirited rather than the province of the full-time, professional politician who is subject to financial and partisan influences." Another description, by John Fisher in *Harper's Magazine*, cited locals calling it "the state's unique political tradition." He described Minnesotans as "intensely ambitious, not only for themselves but for their society," a characteristic that seemed born of being "almost obsessively anxious to prove that they belong in the big leagues." At that time, the ethos in Minnesota circles was that "more prestige comes from conspicuous public service." But the advantage the Minnesota culture had over others burdened with hierarchy and territorialism was that it was a "young people's country. The whole power structure—in government, politics, and business—is run predominantly by men in their thirties and forties." Minnesota had come up with a custom-made regional government, the first of its kind in the nation. They had responded in full to Hartshorne's call in 1932 for "a new form of political organization." Another metro area might use its framework, but the Metropolitan Council could not be replicated. It was as unique as the Twin Cities themselves.[21]

In 2025 the Chambers of Commerce for each city discussed merging into one Chamber of Commerce, and some people naturally wondered, why not merge the cities too? The answer, of course, depends on how you parse the details. The postwar growth and the development of a metropolitan organization to solve mutual problems is in significant ways a merger of the communities. The two cities stand at the heart of the metropolitan area, and they are interrelated with the region. Different political entities can work together without merging in name through joint powers agreements, which are contracts between government entities. St. Paul and Ramsey County, for example, have consolidated a number of their operations, from 911 calls to building maintenance, through joint powers agreements. These agreements are flexible and can be designed for a broad range of operations. In fact, there are existing joint powers agreements among all four entities: Minneapolis, Hennepin County, Ramsey County, and St. Paul. In a few circumstances they are working as what could be called a united city.

But obviously not for the most part. The commercial centers remain separate, and residents routinely see their differences in municipal issues from police operations and taxes to alley plowing and garbage collection.

As for bringing the twins together, as Hartshorne wrote in 1932, something must compel them. He thought a new mode of transportation or rapid growth might break the mold of the past. Since 1872, when St. Anthony merged with Minneapolis, the siblings have needed a bridge that brings them together. For a while in the 1880s external competition seemed to move them toward each other. While they have tried, and many times the idea seemed possible or favorable, the right conditions have not yet come about.

The change may come when we see them as united and find a name that fits. Best, perhaps for now, to call them the Twin Cities.

Acknowledgments

This book began ten years ago when in an old newspaper I came across a strange claim. I was looking for information on my neighborhood's namesake, Stephen Desnoyer. He ran a renowned tavern halfway between Minneapolis and St. Paul. In the newspaper clipping, he proudly claimed in 1872 that he had declined an offer of $100,000 for his property because of its importance to the Twin Cities. He believed his land would someday be the Bridge Square of the united St. Paul and Minneapolis.

I had no idea what Bridge Square meant, and I had never heard of the idea of a united Twin Cities. With that my project was launched, a puzzle of undefined proportions with one piece leading to another. It wasn't until I began writing this book that I understood I was working on an urban history of the Twin Cities and their abiding rivalry. And, here at the end, I look back at that first piece of the puzzle and see that Desnoyer had good reason to make what initially sounded like outlandish claims.

In finding my path through the rich history of Minneapolis and St. Paul, I received much help along the way. Thank you to the kind and capable staff of the Minnesota Historical Society's Gale Family Library and its microfilm room. They patiently guided me through the finding aids, made requests on my behalf to see old manuscripts and maps, and retrieved some especially dusty records.

Part of my research appeared in Ramsey County Historical Society's *Ramsey County History*. Thanks to editor Meredith Cummings for her work on my article, and to the anonymous reviewers for their helpful comments.

At the Minnesota Historical Society Press, I extend my deepest thanks to Ann Regan for putting my research on the path to publication. Thank you to editor Ryan Hemmer for our exploratory conversations, some good laughs, and his confident patience. I appreciate the thorough, professional work of Shannon Pennefeather, along with the rest of the team at MNHS Press.

I am indebted to several people who read parts of the book. James W. Oberly, professor emeritus of history at University of Wisconsin–Eau Claire, read chapters in Parts I and II. He shared his extensive knowledge of the development of early Minnesota and the history of land claims. Donald L. Empson read the entire manuscript and gave insights on early

St. Paul. John O. Anfinson read two chapters on the geology and history of the gorge. Of course, the book is my attempt to get it right, and any mistakes are my own.

One of the pleasures of archival research is finding people who are doing deep dives into specific subjects. I enjoyed conversations with John Vanek and learning from his expertise on early settlers, particularly the Gervaises. Charlie Evans at St. Paul Public Works shared his research on early trails and his collection of early maps of the area. Thanks also to local historians, such as Josh Biber and Greg Brick, who published their work on the internet.

Projects like this take time. The accumulation of information leads to more questions, followed by more research. My family has been a bedrock of support. Kirsten Fischer, my partner and friend, gave me immeasurable support in all aspects of the writing journey. She cheered my discoveries and encouraged me through each round of drafts. A writer herself, she read every chapter and raised the quality of this book. Our daughter, Ava Fischer-Ross, shines her light on our lives in positive and inspiring ways. Thank you both.

Notes

Abbreviation

MNHS Minnesota Historical Society

Notes to Introduction

1. *Minneapolis Star Tribune*, March 31, 2023.
2. *Minnesota Weekly Times*, December 6, 1856, p2; *Weekly Minnesotian*, April 17, 1858, p1.
3. Hartshorne, "The Twin City District," 431–42.
4. Hartsough, "The Development of the Twin Cities (Minneapolis and St. Paul) as a Metropolitan Market," 48; Hartshorne, "The Twin City District," 431–42.

Notes to Chapter 1: Solving Nature's Puzzle

1. The melting of the glaciers and the fluctuations in Lake Agassiz took place over a few thousand years. For the purposes of this story, I'm using a general reference to the time period.
2. The Platteville Limestone has four layers: the Magnolia, Hidden Falls, Mifflin, and Pecatonica. There is also a layer of Glenwood shale between the Pecatonica layer and the St. Peter Sandstone.
3. This would have been ideal in the confluence area but there was a waterfall at St. Paul at that time: see Sardeson, "Description of the Minneapolis and St. Paul District."
4. Except where noted, the following account of Pike's travels is sourced from "Pike's Explorations in Minnesota, 1805–6"; see also Coues, *Expeditions of Zebulon Montgomery Pike*.
5. Orsi, *Citizen Explorer*: see ch. 3, "A Barrier to Their Trade," for Pike's Mississippi River exploration and engagement with the Dakota. Pike was using the Doctrine of Discovery, a legitimized authority to colonize the Indigenous lands: see DeCarlo, *Fort Snelling at Bdote*, 16.
6. Pike's authority to negotiate a treaty is challenged because the president of the United States had not authorized his expedition, and, according to Peter DeCarlo, Pike had no legal authority to negotiate treaties with Indigenous people. In addition, the two Dakota men who agreed to the treaty that day lacked authority to represent their people. DeCarlo, *Fort Snelling at Bdote*, 27.
7. The St. Croix reserve would have been half the size of the larger reserve. The Mdewakanton ceded approximately 155,000 acres of land to the United States at the two confluences according to the Shakopee Mdewakanton Sioux Community website, shakopeedakota.org.

8. Castle, *History of St. Paul and Vicinity*, 636.
9. The Indian gun or Indian trade gun was a flintlock, muzzle-loading, smoothbore gun that was imported and used in the fur trade for many years. Williams, "History of the City of St. Paul," 63; Ross, "Plympton's Reserve, St. Paul's Founding, and Desnoyer's New Bridge Square."
10. "Our Oldest Settler Gone," *Northern Pacific Farmer*, May 26, 1881, p4. McDonald died at White Earth on January 14, 1884, and was survived by two sons and five daughters according to the *St. Charles (MN) Union*, January 16, 1884, p2. Williams, "History of the City of St. Paul," 63; Hennessy, *Past and Present of St. Paul*, 19. Williams and Hennessy locate McDonald at Rumtown, but the army's 1837 census conducted by Lieutenant E. K. Smith does not mention McDonald among the others there (see page 29). Joseph Brown built his groggery after Smith made the map. If McDonald also built after that survey, his wasn't the third house to be built. Perhaps he was located beyond the survey's scope.
11. Hennessy, *Past and Present of St. Paul*, 22; Williams, "History of the City of St. Paul," 82. The ravine was later called Kavanagh. The Town & Country Club filled in the ravine in 1970. See Ross, "Reclaiming Mississippi River Boulevard." The ravine carries the name Rum Pitch for the first time on Lieutenant John Thompson's October 1839 topographic map (see page 38).
12. "Communicated: A Trip 6 Miles Down from Saint Paul, to Little Crow Village, (Kaposia)," *Minnesota Pioneer*, March 20, 1850, p2; *Iowa News* (Dubuque, Upper Lead Mines, Wisconsin Territory), October 14, 1837, p2, reprinted from the Burlington (WI) *Gazette*.
13. "Early Days at Fort Snelling," 421.
14. One obituary reports his birth as May 15, 1805: see "Obituaries," Minnesota Historical Society Scrapbooks, 1, 52. See also "Forgotten Pioneers VI," 19; the source of this information is not noted. However, his tombstone at Calvary Cemetery in St. Paul convincingly says April 22, 1805. Ross, "Plympton's Reserve, St. Paul's Founding, and Desnoyer's New Bridge Square."
15. Ross, "Plympton's Reserve, St. Paul's Founding, and Desnoyer's New Bridge Square."
16. "Etienne Desnoyer's Estate," *St. Paul Daily Globe*, May 8, 1884, p1. Mary died shortly after giving birth apparently from complications of childbirth. One witness stated they were married in Plattsburg, New York, in 1835, which is where Desnoyer had two brothers. Young and Lightner (St. Paul) papers, folder 1, MNHS.

    As his father was Etienne, his son was Etienne III, but Desnoyer never appears to have presented himself as junior.

    See Young and Lightner papers, folder 3–4; Ross, "Plympton's Reserve, St. Paul's Founding, and Desnoyer's New Bridge Square"; US Circuit Court, Minnesota, Petition and Affidavits for Rehearing, *Geo. I. Denoyer vs. Dennis Ryan*, Exhibit "A." "Forgotten Pioneers" says that he was in St. Louis for four years, again, without noting a source. In a letter to lawyers on May 7, 1884, Zepherin Doiron, his ex-brother-in-law, says Desnoyer arrived in Prairie du Rocher in 1839. It seems that he was based near St. Louis but not living there. Doiron worked with Desnoyer and mentions they would go into St. Louis for trading. He also mentions that Desnoyer sold some equipment at auction in St. Louis. Young and Lightner papers, folder 3; letter from Dubuque Catholic Church, February 1, 1884.

17. Larpenteur, "Recollections of the City and People of St. Paul," 370.
18. Larpenteur, "Recollections of the City and People of St. Paul," 370.
19. Wingerd, *North Country*, 161; Fairchild, "Sketches of the Early History of Real Estate in St. Paul," 423; Larpenteur, "Recollections of the City and People of St. Paul," 378.
20. Bogue, "The Iowa Claim Clubs," 242.
21. *Minneapolis Morning Tribune*, April 1, 1912, p6.
22. *Minnesota Weekly Times*, July 3, 1855, p1; *Minnesota Weekly Times*, September 13, 1856, p2.

Notes to Chapter 2: Plympton's Original Sin

1. *Sale of Fort Snelling Reservation*, 40th Congress, 3rd session, House Executive Documents, no. 9–serial 1372, 16; Folwell, *History of Minnesota*, 1:217–118n12.
2. Stambaugh memorial, September 1837, *Sale of Fort Snelling Reservation*, 14–16.
3. Holcombe and Bingham, eds., *Compendium of History and Biography of Minneapolis*, 60.
4. Neill, "Fort Snelling, Minnesota," 8; "Early Days at Fort Snelling," 429.
5. Flandrau, "St. Paul: The Personality of a City," 3; Plympton letter, October 19, 1837, *Sale of Fort Snelling Reservation*, 16. Ann Adams recalls Colonel Snelling had given the settlers permission to settle there, but it is unknown if the permission was for permanent settlement. Also, Plympton would have known some of these settlers from his first time stationed there. Adams, "Early Days at Red River Settlement," 95.
6. Brown letter to Representative Tweedy, *Sale of Fort Snelling Reservation*, 19–20.
7. Plympton, *The Life and Services of Colonel Joseph Plympton*, 7; Holcombe and Bingham, eds., *Compendium of History and Biography of Minneapolis*, 57.
8. Plympton made first lieutenant by July 1, 1813: Gordon, *Compilation of Registers of the Army*, 20; enlistment date and active duty in Plympton, *The Life and Services of Colonel Joseph Plympton*, 4. Hall, *Fort Snelling: Colossus of the Wilderness*, 9; Forsyth, "Fort Snelling: Col. Leavenworth's Expedition," 159; Sibley, "Reminiscences of the Early Days of Minnesota," 473. The 1838 Smith "Proposed Reservation" map notes "only good landing" on the west side of the river. White, "Frontier Feud," 106.

   Hampton Smith questions whether the soldiers were ill due to scurvy, food poisoning, or malaria. Scurvy is due to a lack of vitamin C. The soldiers did collect evergreen needles, which contain the vitamin and could have relieved their symptoms. But the symptoms as reported, Smith points out, are not typically associated with scurvy and they recurred: Smith, *Confluence*, 31.

9. Folwell, *History of Minnesota*, 1:217–18n12; Forsyth, "Fort Snelling: Col. Leavenworth's Expedition," 140; Neill, "Fort Snelling, Minnesota," 7; Holmes, *Minnesota in Three Centuries*, 2:48.
10. Neill, "Fort Snelling, Minnesota," 16, 18. Plympton's son gives a return date of 1822, but that source has several incorrect dates.
11. "The Enlisted Men," 2, box 10, folder 21, Fort Snelling Papers, MNHS; Adams, "Early Days at Red River Settlement," 99.
12. Adams, "Early Days at Red River Settlement," 99; "The Enlisted Men," 1–2, box 10, folder 21, Fort Snelling Papers, MNHS.
13. Flandrau, "St. Paul: The Personality of a City," 4; Hall, *Fort Snelling: Colossus of the Wilderness*, 12; Stevens, "The Early History of Hennepin County," 2.
14. Holcombe and Bingham, eds., *Compendium of History and Biography of Minneapolis*, 57; Green, *A Peculiar Imbalance*, 9–11; DeCarlo, *Fort Snelling at Bdote*, 31–35.
15. Hall, *Fort Snelling: Colossus of the Wilderness*, 12.
16. Rodenbough and Haskin, eds., *Army of the United States*, 467; Ziebarth and Alan, *Fort Snelling: Anchor Post of the Northwest*, 5. Other forts, such as Ripley and Ridgely, would be built as settlement pushed west but were not part of Calhoun's plan.
17. Hall, *Fort Snelling: Colossus of the Wilderness*, 11–12. This may be why Leavenworth chose a building site back from the edge of the bluff featuring the location's strategic practicality as opposed to the grandiosity of the precipice.
18. Andreas, *History of Chicago*, 84, 163; Rodenbough and Haskin, eds., *Army of the United States*, 467. Fort Armstrong (IA/IL), Fort Howard (Green Bay, WI), Fort Winnebago (Winnebago, WI), Fort Dearborn (Chicago, IL), and Fort Snelling (MN): Plympton, *The Life and Services of Colonel Joseph Plympton*, 11.
19. Holcombe and Bingham, eds., *Compendium of History and Biography of Minneapolis*, 84. Her Swiss-French name of Perret was often misspelled.
20. Lieutenant Smith letter, *Sale of Fort Snelling Reservation*, 16; Snyder, "John Emerson, Owner of Dred Scott," 448; Plympton letter, *Sale of Fort Snelling Reservation*, 16.
21. See Smith's proposed map, 1838, MNHS: http://www2.mnhs.org/library/findaids/00844/images/msf05066.jpg.
22. Folwell, *History of Minnesota*, 1:139; Bliss, *Reminiscences of Fort Snelling*, 340–41.
23. Blegen, "The 'Fashionable Tour' on the Upper Mississippi," 379, 383.
24. Atwater and Stevens, eds., *History of Minneapolis and Hennepin County*, 1249.

Brown was able to live there on the reservation "by tolerance of the commanding officer, at Fort Snelling."

25. Goodman and Goodman, *Joseph R. Brown*, 152–53; *Minnesota Weekly Times*, May 23, 1854, p1. The online dictionary translates siŋtomni as "universal."
26. Goodman and Goodman, *Joseph R. Brown*, 156.
27. Adjutant General letter, November 17, 1837, *Sale of Fort Snelling Reservation*, 17.
28. Goodman and Goodman, *Joseph R. Brown*, 166.
29. Stambaugh letter, *Sale of Fort Snelling Reservation*, 25.
30. Millikan, "The Great Treasure of the Fort Snelling Prison Camp," 15n3: Millikan called out this story as a legend, and his article discusses the various accounts and sources around it. Folwell, *History of Minnesota*, 1:225, 452–54: Folwell discusses the different accounts thoroughly, pointing out the various people connected to Steele, but those accounts contradict. More reliable, in my opinion, is Stambaugh's description—the only firsthand account we have—in his letter to the War Department of February 11, 1839. Folsom also contributes important information: see Folsom, *Fifty Years in the Northwest*, 499. Finally, with the new biographical information on Plympton's previous time at Fort Snelling and his location at Fort Dearborn in 1836, we can see that if he did stake a claim and build a cabin in 1836, it would have been during travels from that point, which is completely possible.

    Johnson, "Fort Snelling from Its Foundation to the Present Time," 433. Plympton's cabin comes from John H. Stevens's *Personal Recollections of Minnesota*, possibly the earliest source. William H. Folsom says Plympton staked his claim by a special use permit issued by an army officer: Folsom, *Fifty Years in the Northwest*, 499. At odds with this tale is that the parcel was not on the Reserve and was not yet ceded, so the permit was not applicable, which Stevens notes. That contradiction raises the question of why Plympton didn't stake a claim by permit on the west side of the falls, an area that was inside his jurisdiction though it was also unceded land. Stevens wrote that later "several of the army officers became interested in choice lands on the west bank of the river, which were included in the military reservation. They held the winning cards, from the fact that claims could only be held by their permission." Stevens also mentions that the following year Sargeant Carpenter of Company A staked a claim to the north of Plympton. This name does not occur in any other accounts. Stevens seems to suggest Steele got the premier claim and Plympton took a neighboring claim with Emerson.

    Holcombe and Bingham, eds., *Compendium of History and Biography of Minneapolis*, 60. Folsom writes, "Steele bought out the interests of the officers associated with him and in 1848 secured a title from the United States." That coheres to Stambaugh and agrees with Stevens. Folsom, *Fifty Years in the Northwest*, 499.
31. Stambaugh letter, *Sale of Fort Snelling Reservation*, 24.

32. Goodman and Goodman, *Joseph R. Brown*, 167; Holcombe and Bingham, eds., *Compendium of History and Biography of Minneapolis*, 58. Emerson letter, April 23, 1839, *Sale of Fort Snelling Reservation*, 24; Brown letter, 1840, *Sale of Fort Snelling Reservation*, 20. The settlers hung their hopes on a life at the confluence based on correspondence from Washington, DC, and St. Louis that the fort's Reserve would not expand across the river. Washington and St. Louis suggest the correspondence came via military channels, as the army had a post called the St. Louis Barracks. If they heard from military sources, that would suggest Plympton had others at odds with his expansion of the Reserve.
33. Goodman and Goodman, *Joseph R. Brown*, 156.
34. "Topographic Plan of the Military Reserve Embracing Fort Snelling," 1839, National Archives and Records Administration, Wikimedia Commons, https://tinyurl.com/3z9zw9h2.
35. Emerson letter, April 23, 1839, *Sale of Fort Snelling Reservation*, 23.
36. Goodman and Goodman, *Joseph R. Brown*, 161, 167; Wool letter, June 27, 1839, *Sale of Fort Snelling Reservation*, 26; Adams, "Early Days at Red River Settlement," 99. Adams describes the pageantry put on for General Scott's arrival in 1826.
37. Goodman and Goodman, *Joseph R. Brown*, 167; Folwell, *History of Minnesota*, 1:428.
38. Goodman and Goodman, *Joseph R. Brown*, 167; "The Enlisted Men," 1, 4–5, box 10, folder 21, Fort Snelling Papers, MNHS; Adams, "Early Days at Red River Settlement," 95.
39. Stambaugh letter, *Sale of Fort Snelling Reservation*, 24–26.
40. Williams, "History of the City of Saint Paul," 93; Brown letter, *Sale of Fort Snelling Reservation*; Goodman and Goodman, *Joseph R. Brown*, 167; Stambaugh letter, *Sale of Fort Snelling Reservation*, 24–26.
41. Folwell, *History of Minnesota*, 1:222; Brown to Representative Tweedy, December 30, 1847, *Sale of Fort Snelling Reservation*, 19–20; *Reservation at Fort Snelling; Resolutions of the Assembly of Wiskonsin*, 1–5, 26th Congress, 1st session, House Documents, no. 144–serial 365.
42. Folwell, *History of Minnesota*, 1:422; Stambaugh letter, *Sale of Fort Snelling Reservation*, 24–26.
43. Stambaugh letter, *Sale of Fort Snelling Reservation*, 24–26; Folwell, *History of Minnesota*, 1:222; Brown to Representative Tweedy, December 30, 1847, *Sale of Fort Snelling Reservation*, 19–20; *Reservation at Fort Snelling; Resolutions of the Assembly of Wiskonsin*, 1–5, 26th Congress, 1st session, House Documents, no. 144–serial 365.
44. Emerson letter, April 23, 1839, *Sale of Fort Snelling Reservation*, 23; Neill, *History of Minnesota*, 917; Smith, *Confluence*, 96; Taliaferro journal, July 21, 1838; Brown to Doty, December 10, 1839, in *Reservation at Fort Snelling; Resolutions of the Assembly of Wiskonsin*, 1–5, 26th Congress, 1st Session, House Documents, no. 144–serial 365; Goodman and Goodman, *Joseph R. Brown*, 165.

45. Snyder, "John Emerson, Owner of Dred Scott," 441–43, 448; Holmes, *Minnesota in Three Centuries*, 66; Green, *A Peculiar Imbalance*, 6; see also Adams, "Early Days at Red River Settlement," 140.
46. Plympton, *Life and Services of Colonel Joseph Plympton*, 10–11.
47. Plympton, *Life and Services of Colonel Joseph Plympton*, 10–11.
48. Folsom, *Fifty Years in the Northwest*, 499.
49. *New York Herald*, February 6, 1842, p2; *Camden (SC) Journal*, February 9, 1842, p2; *Richmond Enquirer*, March 15, 1842, p4: *North-Carolina Standard*, March 23, 1842, p3, Plympton, *Life and Services of Colonel Joseph Plympton*, 5; Neill, "Fort Snelling, Minnesota," 9.
50. Holmes, *Minnesota in Three Centuries*, 89.
51. Holcombe and Bingham, eds., *Compendium of History and Biography of Minneapolis*, 58.

Notes to Chapter 3: Finding St. Paul

1. Ireland, "Memoir of Rev. Lucian Galtier," 225.
2. Folsom, *Fifty Years in the Northwest*, 499. The settlers were removed under the act of March 3, 1807, which aimed to prevent settlement on ceded lands until authorized by law. The removal was initiated by Plympton and the land to be cleared was in the new Reserve. He could have cleared the Reserve, as the army would do later many times. Yet Secretary of War Joel R. Poinsett sent a letter dated October 21, 1839, to US Marshal Edward James requesting him to clear the Reserve. The War Department could apparently use the federal territorial court in certain situations, though the relationship is unclear. When Brunson arrived as a deputy US marshal of the federal territorial court, he mobilized soldiers at the fort to carry out the law's enforcement. The War Department and the federal territorial court were intermingled in an interesting way. Yet it was Plympton who initiated it and soldiers who cleared it.

   Newson, *Pen Pictures of St. Paul*, 110; Holmes, *Minnesota in Three Centuries*, 2:87–88; Williams, "History of the City of Saint Paul," 100.
3. Williams, "History of the City of Saint Paul," 66.
4. Williams, "History of the City of Saint Paul," 63, 83; A number of people left their homes near the fort in 1838 after Plympton put out this order.

   McDonald may have used trails established by the Dakota who crossed the river in the vicinity of Raspberry Island and used several routes across the prairie toward St. Anthony Falls. Thompson's Embracing map was produced in November 1839; however, we only have a copy of that map, produced in 1853. Several details were added to the copy that did not exist in 1839, such as Desnoyer's place, the claims across the road from him, and the road itself.

   Proceedings of the County Board of Supervisors, November 29, 1821–November 19, 1850, Madison, WI, Wisconsin Territorial Papers, Crawford County, WI, Wisconsin Historical Records Survey, 1941, 81. We know the location of McDonald's groggery at Rum Pitch from the Thompson maps and Desnoyer's location.

5. Hennessy, *Past and Present of St. Paul*, 22. The soldiers would "*go up* to that groggery" of Donald McDonald's, according to Mrs. James Patten, whose father was a soldier. They "lost their lives *by falling down on their way back* to the fort . . . while intoxicated" (emphasis added). See Williams, *History of the City of St. Paul*, 82. The directions the soldiers traveled according to her account point to Rum Pitch, which was a legal establishment off the Reserve: Ross, "Plympton's Reserve, St. Paul's Founding, and Desnoyer's New Bridge Square," 13–22. Mrs. Patten's father, Richard W. Mortimer, was enlisted until 1842, and she remained in the Twin Cities after that.
6. People began settling in St. Anthony in 1847 and Minneapolis in 1851.
7. Williams, "History of the City of Saint Paul," 111; McNulty, "The Chapel of St. Paul," 238.
8. McNulty, "The Chapel of St. Paul," 238.
9. *Minnesota Pioneer*, June 7, 1849, p2; Moss, "Biographic Notes of Old Settlers," 144; Elfelt, "Early Trade and Traders in St. Paul," 164; McNulty, "The Chapel of St. Paul," 239. Galtier takes credit for proposing St. Paul as a name to counter Pig's Eye.
10. Moss, "Biographic Notes of Old Settlers," 144; Newson, *Pen Pictures of St. Paul*, 38; Fairchild, "Sketches of the Early History of Real Estate in St. Paul," 428; Chaney, "Early Bridges and Changes of the Land and Water Surface in the City of St. Paul," 136.
11. Chaney, "Early Bridges and Changes of the Land and Water Surface in the City of St. Paul," 139; Larpenteur, "Recollections of the City and People of St. Paul," 377–78; Smith, *Confluence*, 106.
12. "Speeches at the Capitol," *Daily Minnesota Pioneer*, August 2, 1854, p2.
13. Lass, "Minnesota's Separation from Wisconsin," 309.
14. Gilman, "Territorial Imperative," 5.
15. Moss, "Biographic Notes of Old Settlers," 144.
16. Larpenteur, "Reminiscences of the City and People of St. Paul," 378.
17. McNulty, "The Chapel of St. Paul," 240.
18. Larpenteur, "Reminiscences of the City and People of St. Paul," 378; Castle, *History of St. Paul and Vicinity*, 84; Fairchild, "Sketches of the Early History of Real Estate in St. Paul," 423. The plat map was not adapted to the US Surveyor General surveys by state legislation until 1866. Technically, the people in St. Paul Proper did not have ownership of their land until that late date.
19. "Organization of Minnesota Territory," 59–60; Lass, "The Birth of Minnesota," 267–79; Wills, *Boosters, Hustlers, and Speculators*, 37.
20. "Organization of Minnesota Territory," 54, 57; Sibley, "Reminiscences of the Early Days of Minnesota," 484.
21. "Organization of Minnesota Territory," 58, 60.

22. "Organization of Minnesota Territory," 54. The official was John Catlin, former secretary of treasury for the Wisconsin Territory.
23. Lass, "The Birth of Minnesota," 267, 277; Proceedings of the Board of Commissioners of County of St. Croix, Wisconsin Territory, October 5, 1840–May 12, 1849, 135–36, in Washington County Historic Courthouse, Stillwater, MN.
24. "Organization of Minnesota Territory," 61, 62, 63; Sibley, "Reminiscences of the Early Days of Minnesota," 271.
25. Brown letter, December 30, 1847, *Sale of Fort Snelling Reservation*, 19–20, emphasis in the original.
26. Brown letter, December 30, 1847, *Sale of Fort Snelling Reservation*, 19–20.
27. Brown letter, December 30, 1847, *Sale of Fort Snelling Reservation*, 19–20.
28. Jesup letter, February 28, 1848, *Sale of Fort Snelling Reservation*, 21.
29. Folwell, *History of Minnesota*, 1:425.
30. Newson, *Pen Pictures of St. Paul*, 33–34; Williams, "History of the City of Saint Paul," 128.
31. Hennessy, *Past and Present of St. Paul*, 143; Folsom, *Fifty Years in the Northwest*, 579; Bond, *Minnesota and Its Resources*, 119; Williams, "History of the City of Saint Paul," 128.
32. Lass, "Minnesota's Separation from Wisconsin," 310; "Organization of Minnesota Territory," 63; Sibley, "Reminiscences of the Early Days of Minnesota," 271; US House Journal, March 3, 1849. Earlier, on March 1, 1848, Daniel P. King had presented a memorial request from the citizens of the territory of Minnesota to Congress asking them to organize a Minnesota territory and remove it from the limits of the territory of Wisconsin. The language they used highlights their uncomfortable status. Neither the territory of Minnesota nor the territory of Wisconsin existed at that time.
33. "The Breaking Up of a Hard Winter," *Minnesota Pioneer*, April 28, 1849, p3.
34. Folwell calls the story of claiming a Wisconsin Territory still existed a "benign fiction": Folwell, *History of Minnesota*, 1:238.
35. Folwell, *History of Minnesota*, 1:394; Johnson, "Fort Snelling from Its Foundation to the Present Time," 433; Kane, *The Falls of St. Anthony*, 35.
36. Minnesota Territory, *Laws* 1849, 161, https://www.revisor.mn.gov/laws/1849/0/General+Laws/Resolution/2/pdf/; Kane, *The Falls of St. Anthony*, 35; Folwell, *History of Minnesota*, 1:394.
37. Holmes, *Minnesota in Three Centuries*, 2:123; Newson, *Pen Pictures of St. Paul*, 307.
38. *Minnesota Pioneer*, July 19, 1849, p1; Folwell, *History of Minnesota*, 1:352; Folsom, *Fifty Years in the Northwest*, 542, 551; *National Era* (Washington, DC), February 24, 1853, p1; "Letter of Inquiry Respecting Minnesota," *Minnesota Pioneer*, August 16, 1849, p2.
39. Bond, *Minnesota and Its Resources*, 119–20; Folsom, *Fifty Years in the Northwest*, 537; "Letter of Inquiry Respecting Minnesota," *Minnesota Pioneer*,

August 16, 1849, p2; Fairchild, "Sketches of the Early History of Real Estate in St. Paul," 427.

40. "The Plan of Saint Paul," *Minnesota Pioneer*, April 15, 1852, p1; Duprey, "Territorial Daguerreotypes," 208; *Graham's Magazine* (Philadelphia), 46 (January 1855): 3–17.
41. *National Era* (Washington, DC), February 24, 1853, p1; "The Plan of Saint Paul," *Minnesota Pioneer*, April 15, 1852, p1.
42. "The Plan of Saint Paul," *Minnesota Pioneer*, April 15, 1852, p1.
43. *Minnesota Pioneer*, January 23, 1850, p2.
44. Hennessy, *Past and Present of St. Paul*, 143; Ravoux, *Reminiscences, Memoirs and Lectures*, 59; Folsom, *Fifty Years in the Northwest*, 542, 551.
45. *National Era* (Washington, DC), February 24, 1853, p1; *Minnesota Pioneer*, April 1, 1852, p2.

Notes to Chapter 4: The Reserve Conspiracy

1. *New York Herald*, June 14, 1854, morning edition, p2.
2. Williams, "History of the City of Saint Paul," 353.
3. Andrews, *History of St. Paul*, 68; Newson, *Pen Pictures of St. Paul*, 464; Schmid, *Social Saga of Two Cities*, 5; letter from Lt. Col. Francis Lee, August 21, 1851, *Sale of Fort Snelling Reservation*, 44.
4. The Reserve also included a slice of land south of the rivers known as Mendota. This section was put aside during the first sale in 1854.
5. *St. Paul Daily Globe*, May 19, 1890, p8; "The One-Idea of a New Country—A Correspondent of the *Pittsburg Token*," *Weekly Minnesotian*, November 20, 1852, p2.
6. Chatelain, "The Federal Land Policy and Minnesota Politics," 227; Fairchild, "Sketches of the Early History of Real Estate in St. Paul," 427.
7. Chatelain, "The Federal Land Policy and Minnesota Politics," 241.
8. Folwell, *History of Minnesota*, 1:426; Ritchey, "Claim Associations and Pioneer Democracy in Early Minnesota," 85. *Daily Minnesota Pioneer*, July 24, 1854, p3, has a reprint of proclamation 514.
9. *Perrysburg (OH) Journal*, June 10, 1854, p2, authored June 1, 1854, in Galena, Illinois.
10. *The American* (Washington, DC), October 3, 1857, p2.
11. "The Many vs. The Few," *Minnesota Pioneer*, March 13, 1850, p2.
12. *The American* (Washington, DC), October 3, 1857, p2.
13. Holmes, *Minnesota in Three Centuries*, 123. The US Surveyor General surveyed the area in October 1847 and published the map in 1848. That map is the only one we have of that early survey of the townsite: see Moss, "Biographic Notes of Old Settlers," 161.
14. Larpenteur, "Recollections of the City and People of St. Paul," 378–79; Williams, "History of the City of Saint Paul," 184–85; Folwell, *History of Minnesota*, 1:428; Sibley, "Reminiscences of the Early Days of Minnesota," 244.

15. Sibley, "Reminiscences of the Early Days of Minnesota," 244; Flandrau, *The History of Minnesota and Tales of the Frontier*, 69.
16. Ritchey, "Claim Associations and Pioneer Democracy in Early Minnesota," 87; Bogue, "The Iowa Claim Clubs," 231–53.
17. *Daily Minnesota Pioneer*, July 7, 1854, p2; *The American* (Washington, DC), October 3, 1857, p2.
18. *Minnesota Pioneer*, August 12, 1852, p2; see also Swierenga, *Pioneers and Profits*; "Browne Report," *Weekly Minnesotian*, April 28, 1855, p1; *Weekly Minnesotian*, January 28, 1854, p2.
19. *The American* (Washington, DC), October 3, 1857, p2.
20. *Minnesota Pioneer*, August 12, 1852, p2; Ritchey, "Claim Associations and Pioneer Democracy in Early Minnesota," 85.
21. *Weekly Minnesotian*, January 28, 1854, p2.
22. Military Reserve Claim Association record book, 1853–54, 3–4, MNHS.
23. Letter dated December 7, 1854, Register's Letters Sent, Stillwater Land District, US General Land Office, MNHS; *Daily Minnesota Pioneer*, September 11, 1854, p2. The number of 300 from Hennepin County was reported by the newspaper and is probably inflated. The Military Reserve Claim Association had passed a resolution that allowed claim holders west of the river to join their group: see Military Reserve Claim Association Papers, MNHS. Also, the Stillwater Land Office estimated 200 people were present at the auction, although, as this report was in the context of them downplaying their previous claim of a combination, they had reason to underestimate attendees.
24. "The Reserve Lands—Report of the Spy," *Weekly Minnesotian*, April 28, 1855, p1; *The American* (Washington, DC), October 3, 1857, p2.
25. Letter dated December 7, 1854, Register's Letters Sent, Stillwater Land District, US General Land Office, MNHS; Larpenteur, "Recollections of the City and People of St. Paul"; Warner and Foote, *History of Ramsey County*, 195; *The American* (Washington, DC), October 3, 1857, p2; *Daily Minnesota Pioneer*, July 7, 1854, p2.
26. *Weekly Minnesotian*, April 28, 1855, p1; Letter of September 18, 1854, Correspondence: Letters Received from General Land Office, 1854–89, Receiver's Letters Sent (2 vols.) and Recorder's Letters Sent, Stillwater Land District Papers, US General Land Office, MNHS; Section 4, Act of March 31, 1830, regulating sales of public lands: https://tile.loc.gov/storage-services/service/ll/llsl//llsl-c21/llsl-c21.pdf.
27. *Weekly Minnesotian*, April 28, 1855, p1; letter of September 18, 1854, Correspondence: Letters Received from General Land Office, 1854–89, Receiver's Letters Sent (2 vols.) and Recorder's Letters Sent, Stillwater Land District Papers, US General Land Office, MNHS.
28. *The American* (Washington, DC), October 3, 1857, p2, emphasis in the original.
29. *Weekly Minnesotian*, December 23, 1854, p2; *The American* (Washington, DC), October 3, 1857, p2.
30. *Weekly Minnesotian*, December 23, 1854, p2.

31. *Weekly Minnesotian*, April 28, 1855, p1.
32. *Weekly Minnesotian*, February 24, 1855, p4, November 26, 1853, p2; *Minnesota Weekly Times*, May 23, 1854, p1; *Alexandria (VA) Gazette*, January 4, 1855, p2. The Winslow House in St. Paul preceded the one in St. Anthony.
33. *Alexandria (VA) Gazette*, June 3, 1854, p2; *Daily Evening Star* (Washington, DC), May 8, 1854, p2. The book had various titles, including *A Crusade in the East* and *Yusef or the Journey of the Frangi*. Browne's writings are credited with influencing Herman Melville in the writing of *Moby Dick* and Mark Twain in his *Far West*.
34. *Weekly Minnesotian*, February 18, 1854, p2; *Minnesota Weekly Times*, February 20, 1855, p2.
35. *Empire County Argus* (Coloma, El Dorado County, CA), August 5, 1854, p2; *Evening Star* (Washington, DC), October 28, 1854, p2. Another source says he fired twenty customs workers.
36. *Alexandria (VA) Gazette*, June 3, 1854, image 2; *Georgetown Weekly News* (Riverside, CA), March 8, 1855, p1, reprint from San Francisco *Herald*; Nichols, *Franklin Pierce*, 405.
37. White, "The Power of Whiteness," 187.
38. "Report in Relation to the Official Transactions of Willis A. Gorman," April 6, 1855, 5, MNHS.
39. "Life and Public Services of Hon. Willis A. Gorman," 316; Folwell, *History of Minnesota*, 1:340.
40. Newson, *Pen Pictures of St. Paul*, 381; "Report in Relation to the Official Transactions of Willis A. Gorman," April 6, 1855, 5, 13, MNHS; "Life and Public Services of Hon. Willis A. Gorman," 317–18.
41. "Report in Relation to the Official Transactions of Willis A. Gorman," April 6, 1855, 15, MNHS; Nichols, *Franklin Pierce*, 405.
42. *The American* (Washington DC), October 3, 1857, p2; Fairchild, "Sketches of the Early History of Real Estate in St. Paul," 427.
43. "Browne Report," *Weekly Minnesotian*, April 28, 1855, p1; "The Reserve Lands—Report of the Spy," *Weekly Minnesotian*, April 28, 1855, p1.
44. "The Reserve Lands—Report of the Spy," *Weekly Minnesotian*, April 28, 1855, p1.
45. "Browne Report," *Weekly Minnesotian*, April 28, 1855, p1.
46. Kane, *The Falls of St. Anthony*, 35; *Minnesota Pioneer*, August 12, 1852, p2 (Dakota); Ritchey, "Claim Associations and Pioneer Democracy in Early Minnesota," 86, 88.
47. "Browne Report," *Weekly Minnesotian*, April 28, 1855, p1.
48. "Browne Report," *Weekly Minnesotian*, April 28, 1855, p1.
49. "Browne Report," *Weekly Minnesotian*, April 28, 1855, p1.
50. *Minnesotian*, April 24, 1855. The *Minnesotian* was a daily paper; it published an anthology of articles on the weekend as the *Weekly Minnesotian*.
51. *Weekly Minnesotian*, May 5, 1855, p3.

52. *Weekly Minnesotian*, April 28, 1855, p3.
53. "The Secret Spy," *Weekly Minnesotian*, April 28, 1855, p3, reporting on Thursday morning, April 26, 1855; *Weekly Minnesotian,* May 5 (4), 1855, p3, emphasis in the original.
54. "The Reserve Lands—Report of the Spy," *Weekly Minnesotian*, April 28, 1855, p1.
55. *Weekly Minnesotian*, April 28, 1855, p3.
56. "Henry M. Rice's Reply to the Spy, Washington, April 9th, 1855," *Weekly Minnesotian*, April 28, 1855, p3.
57. "Henry M. Rice's Reply to the Spy, Washington, April 9th, 1855," *Weekly Minnesotian*, April 28, 1855, p3; *Weekly Minnesotian*, April 28, 1855, p2.

Notes to Chapter 5: The Birth of a Rivalry

1. "By the President of the United States—No. 514," *Daily Minnesota Pioneer*, July 24, 1854, p3.
2. "Land Sales at Minneapolis," *Weekly Minnesotian*, September 23, 1854, p1.
3. Atwater and Stevens, eds., *History of Minneapolis and Hennepin County*, 1145; Lehman, *Slavery's Reach*, 70–73; see also Lehman, *Slavery in the Upper Mississippi Valley*; Newson, *Pen Pictures of St. Paul*, 707. Newson mentions William Cahoone, who arrived in 1854 and was in real estate. Others who came north during those years were John W. McClung and Girart Hewitt. They were all in real estate, and may well have attended this auction.
4. Atwater and Stevens, eds., *History of Minneapolis and Hennepin County*, 1145–46.
5. Oliphant, *Minnesota and the Far West*, 272; Newson, *Pen Pictures of St. Paul*, 282, 378, 384; Lehman, *Slavery's Reach*, 32–34.
6. Holcombe and Bingham, eds., *Compendium of History and Biography of Minneapolis*, 99.
7. "Land Sales at Minneapolis," *Weekly Minnesotian*, September 23, 1854, p1; Chatelain, "The Federal Land Policy and Minnesota Politics," 238.
8. *Minnesota Weekly Times*, August 1, 1854, p2.
9. Williams, "History of the City of Saint Paul," 188–89; Oliphant, *Minnesota and the Far West*, 252; Gilman, *Henry Hastings Sibley*, 110.
10. Newson, *Pen Pictures of St. Paul*, 502.
11. "Saint Paul," *Weekly Minnesotian*, April 2, 1853, p2; *Minnesota Pioneer*, January 23, 1850, p2.
12. Newson, *Pen Pictures of St. Paul*, 500, 502; Williams, "History of the City of Saint Paul," 357.
13. "Saint Paul," *Weekly Minnesotian*, April 2, 1853, p2; *Minnesota Pioneer*, April 28, 1849, p2; "Speeches at the Capitol," *Daily Minnesota Pioneer*, August 2, 1854, image 2c2–36; Williams, "History of the City of Saint Paul," 307.
14. *Minnesota Pioneer*, May 19, 1849, p2.
15. *Minnesota Pioneer*, October 4, 1849, p3, August 12, 1852, p2, April 15, 1852,

p1; Journal of the Council during the . . . Session of the Legislative Assembly of the Territory of Minnesota 1849, 102; *Minnesota Weekly Times*, July 25, 1854, p2.

16. *Perrysburg (OH) Journal*, June 3, 1854, p100, p4; *New York Herald*, June 14, 1854, morning edition, p2; Kane, "Governing a Frontier City," 117–29; *Minnesota Pioneer*, April 15, 1852, p1.
17. *Minnesota Pioneer*, April 15, 1852, p1; Stevens, *Personal Recollections of Minnesota*, 184–85.
18. *Daily Minnesota Pioneer*, November 21, 1854, p2; *Perrysburg (OH) Journal*, June 3, 1854, p100, p4; *Weekly Minnesotian*, January 28, 1854, p2; Folwell, *History of Minnesota*, 1:430.
19. *Minnesota Pioneer*, November 24, 1853, p2; Kane, "Governing a Frontier City," 117–29.
20. Holcombe and Bingham, eds., *Compendium of History and Biography of Minneapolis*, 99; Stevens, "Recollections of James M. Goodhue," 499.
21. Lehman, *Slavery's Reach*, 71; *Minnesota Weekly Times*, September 11, 1855, p1; Holcombe and Bingham, eds., *Compendium of History and Biography of Minneapolis*, 122; Green, *A Peculiar Imbalance*, 77–79.
22. Holcombe and Bingham, eds., *Compendium of History and Biography of Minneapolis*, 125; Green, *A Peculiar Imbalance*, 77–79.
23. "That Hokus Pokus Bill," *Minnesota Weekly Times*, March 13, 1855, p1; *Minnesota Weekly Times*, March 13, 1855, p2; *Minnesota Weekly Times*, March 13, 1855, p1, 6; "St. Anthony Items," *Minnesota Pioneer*, December 29, 1853, p2.
24. *Weekly Minnesotian*, March 17, 1855, p4, January 5, 1856, p2; Holcombe and Bingham, eds., *Compendium of History and Biography of Minneapolis*, 125.
25. Stevens, *Personal Recollections of Minnesota*, 262–63.
26. *Weekly Minnesotian*, January 5, 1856, p2.
27. "We Want an Outlet," *Weekly Minnesotian*, February 18, 1854, p2; Hayes, "Minnesota's Wandering State Fair," 13.
28. Bureau of Statistics, *Minnesota, Its Progress and Capabilities*, 9. Such projections of geographic hubs were popular at the time. William Gilpin, a prophet of Manifest Destiny and a pioneer for geopolitics, tried to establish "Centropolis" in Kansas because it was the geographic center of the nation and, therefore, would tie the nation together. Herron, "Centropolis," 25–47.
29. "Letter from the Northwest," *National Era* (Washington, DC), November 11, 1852, p183, p3.
30. "Governor's Message," *Weekly Minnesotian*, January 29, 1853, p1; Fairchild, "Sketches of the Early History of Real Estate in St. Paul," 426.
31. Session Laws of the Territory of Minnesota, Section 17, Passed by the Legislative Assembly at the Session Commencing Wednesday, January 4, 1854, 121–129. This route combined two of the previous routes. *Weekly Minnesotian*, July 29, 1854, p2; *Minnesota Pioneer*, February 16, 1854, p2.
32. *Minnesota Pioneer*, February 16, 1854, p2.

33. Kellogg, "The Rise and Fall of Old Superior," 6.
34. Oliphant, *Minnesota and the Far West*, 159; *Daily Minnesota Pioneer*, July 28, 1855, p4; Kellogg, "The Rise and Fall of Old Superior," 7.
35. "Report of the Territorial Committee of the Senate," *Daily Minnesota Pioneer*, March 23, 1855, p2; "Governor's Message," *Daily Minnesota Pioneer*, January 18, 1855, p1, 4; see also Folwell, *History of Minnesota*, 1:331.
36. *Daily Union* (Washington, DC), March 8, 1854, p2; Folwell, *History of Minnesota*, 1:328.
37. *Washington (DC) Sentinel*, July 25, 1854, p2; *Minnesota Weekly Times*, June 27, 1854, p2.
38. The founders were William P. Burrall, George L. Schuyler, Morris Ketchum, Edward Bement, R. B. Mason, and George W. Billings. At a minimum, three directors needed to be Minnesota residents, and they were Edmund Rice, Lyman Dayton, and Alexander Ramsey.
39. *Minnesota Weekly Times*, June 27, 1854, p2; Folwell, *History of Minnesota*, 1:336.
40. Folwell, *History of Minnesota*, 1:333.
41. *Alteration of the Text of House Bill No. 342*, Congressional Globe, 33rd Congress, 1st session, no. 342–serial 744, 2.
42. Folwell, *History of Minnesota*, 1:337; *Alteration of the Text of House Bill No. 342*, 33rd Congress, 1st session, *House Reports*, no. 342–serial 744, p16, 40.
43. *Daily Evening Star*, July 25, 1854, p2; *Washington (DC) Sentinel*, July 25, 1854, p2 (July 24 date on paper reflects when it was in Congress); Folwell, *History of Minnesota*, 1:329. See *Alteration of the Text of House Bill No. 342*, 33rd Congress, 1st session, *House Reports*, no. 352–serial 744, 14.
44. Folwell, *History of Minnesota*, 1:333. Folwell cites Superior, Wisconsin, Report of the City Statistician for 1892, 7–11. "Detroit, June 2," *Daily Minnesota Pioneer*, June 11, 1855, p2.
45. "House of Representatives," *Daily Dispatch* (Richmond, VA), August 5, 1854, p3.
46. "Governor's Message," *Weekly Minnesotian*, January 29, 1853, p1; "House of Representatives," *Daily Dispatch* (Richmond, VA), August 5, 1854, image 3c2.
47. *The Daily Union* (Washington, DC), February 1, 1855, p2; Folwell, *History of Minnesota*, 1:342.
48. Nichols, *Franklin Pierce*, 405; "The Administration Turned City Speculator," *New York Herald*, Morning Edition, June 30, 1855, 8 (correspondence of the *Cleveland Express*).
49. Dillon, *J. Ross Browne*, 208. Superior, Wisconsin, is built on the same location. The only remnant of the Minnesota Northwestern Railroad scheme is a neighborhood named after Billings.
50. "A Significant Fact," *Anti-Slavery Bugle*, July 11, 1857, p2, reprinted from *Chicago Press*, June 26, 1857; Lehman, *Slavery's Reach*, 65–79; Kellogg, "The Rise and Fall of Old Superior," 6. Numerous presidentially appointed administrators were slaveholders, including Rosser of Virginia, though not all of them brought slaves to Minnesota: see Lehman, *Slavery's Reach*.

51. *Minnesota Weekly Times*, September 19, 1854, p2. See Lehman, *Slavery's Reach*, 39.
52. *Minnesota Weekly Times*, August 1, 1854, p2. The closing of the land office on the day of the auction remains a mysterious event. There may have been any number of causes, from bureaucratic to political. Some evidence suggests that the delegation of Minneapolis men that traveled to Washington, DC, was successful in lobbying the General Land Office to recognize their preemption claims. The auction's cancellation may have been a result of their work.
53. *Weekly Minnesotian*, July 15, 1854, p2, July 29, 1854, p2.
54. "Repeal of the Minnesota Land Bill," *Minnesota Weekly Times*, August 15, 1854, p2.
55. National Register of Historic Places, "Railroads in Minnesota," Section E: Statement of Historic Contexts: I. Railroad Development in Minnesota, 1862–1956, 7–9.
56. "Repeal of the Minnesota Land Bill," *Minnesota Weekly Times*, August 15, 1854, p2.
57. *Weekly Minnesotian*, July 15, 1854, p2.

Notes to Chapter 6: The Steele Swindle

1. Johnston, "Minnesota Journalism in the Territorial Period," 311.
2. Flandrau, *The History of Minnesota and Tales of the Frontier*, 67; Williams, "History of the City of Saint Paul," 357, 376; Newson, *Pen Pictures of St. Paul*, 502; *Minnesota Weekly Times*, September 19, 1854, p2.
3. Holmes, *Minnesota in Three Centuries*, 2:508; Williams, "History of the City of Saint Paul," 358, 376; Flandrau, "St. Paul: The Personality of a City," 8.
4. Flandrau, "St. Paul: The Personality of a City," 8.
5. Holmes, *Minnesota in Three Centuries*, 2:508; Flandrau, *The History of Minnesota and Tales of the Frontier*, 67.
6. "A Great Metropolitan Center," *St. Paul Daily Globe*, July 27, 1891, p5–6; Williams, "History of the City of Saint Paul," 344.
7. Hudson, *A Half Century of Minnesota as Territory and State*, 24; Holmes, *Minnesota in Three Centuries*, 2:508.
8. Flandrau, "St. Paul: The Personality of a City," 8; Holmes, *Minnesota in Three Centuries*, 2:508.
9. Flandrau, *The History of Minnesota and Tales of the Frontier*, 67.
10. Schmid, *Social Saga of Two Cities*, 4.
11. *The American* (Washington, DC), September 5, 1857, p3; *Burlington (IA) Weekly Hawk-eye*, August 12, 1857, p2, reprinted from the *Chicago Democratic Press*.
12. *Daily Minnesotian*, April 3, 1857; Loehr, "Franklin Steele, Frontier Businessman," 309–18.
13. Smith laid out the addition with Cornelius Whitney, the receiver at the St. Croix Land Office. One of the first three parks in St. Paul, Mears Park was

originally known as Smith Park and was donated by George W. Farrington, Major Murphy, C. S. Whitney, and Smith: "Public Parks," *Minnesota Weekly Times*, June 13, 1854, p3.

14. The narrative of the final sale of Fort Snelling, except where noted, is based on Folwell, "Appendix (13): The Sale of Fort Snelling," *History of Minnesota*, 1:503–15; ; Folwell, "The Sale of Fort Snelling, 1857," 393–410; *Sale of Fort Snelling Reservation*; Johnson, "Fort Snelling from Its Founding to the Present Time," 427–48; Loehr, "Franklin Steele, Frontier Businessman," 309–18.
15. *National Era*, September 3, 1857, p143, p3, reprinted from *Utica Herald*; *The American* (Washington, DC), September 5, 1857, p3.
16. *National Era* (Washington, DC), September 3, 1857, p143, p3, reprinted from *Utica Herald*; *The American* (Washington, DC), September 5, 1857, p3.
17. *Burlington (VT) Free Press*, September 4, 1857, p2.
18. Folwell, *History of Minnesota*, 1:506–7. Floyd's quote comes from Folwell's speech, "The Sale of Fort Snelling, 1857," 401, which he gave nine years before he published the account as Appendix (13) in *History of Minnesota*. Floyd is quoted slightly differently in the two texts.
19. Folwell, *History of Minnesota*, 1:507; *Raftsman's Journal* (Clearfield, PA), February 3, 1858, p1.
20. Letter of Heiskell to Floyd, June 17, 1857, in the *Richmond (VA) Enquirer*, September 15, 1857, p4.
21. Letter of Heiskell to Floyd, June 17, 1857, in the *Richmond (VA) Enquirer*, September 15, 1857, p4; Kane, *The Falls of St. Anthony*, 36.
22. *Weekly Minnesotian*, May 15, 1858, p1, reprinted from *New York Times*, April 30, 1858.
23. *National Era* (Washington, DC), September 3, 1857, p142, p2.
24. *Evening Star* (Washington, DC), August 19, 1857, p2; *Hancock Jeffersonian* (Findlay, OH), August 28, 1857, p2, reprinted from the *Cleveland (OH) Herald*; *Weekly Minnesotian*, May 15, 1858, p1, reprinted from *New York Times*, April 30, 1858; Folwell, *History of Minnesota*, 1:507.
25. *National Era* (Washington, DC), September 3, 1857, p142, image 2c4–5; *Burlington (VT) Free Press*, September 4, 1857, p2.
26. *The American* (Washington, DC), August 19, 1857, p2; *National Era* (Washington, DC), September 3, 1857, p142, image 2c4–6.
27. *The American* (Washington, DC), September 5, 1857, p3; *Weekly Minnesotian*, April 4, 1857, p4.
28. *The American* (Washington, DC), September 5, 1857, p3, September 19, 1857, p3 and image 3c3–4, p3.
29. *Burlington (VT) Free Press*, September 4, 1857, p2; *The American* (Washington, DC), September 5, 1857, p3.
30. *North Iowa Times* (McGregor, IA), September 23, 1857, p1; Flandrau, *The History of Minnesota and Tales of the Frontier*, 17.
31. *Burlington (IA) Weekly Hawk-eye*, August 12, 1857, p2, reprinted from the

Chicago Democratic Press; *National Era* (Washington, DC), September 3, 1857, p142, image 2, 6.

32. *The American* (Washington, DC), September 9, 1857, p2.
33. *The American* (Washington, DC), September 5, 1857, p3; *Raftsman's Journal* (Clearfield, PA), February 3, 1858, p1.
34. *National Era*, September 3, 1857, p143, image 3, reprinted from *Utica (NY) Herald*; "The Fort Snelling Reservation," *Marshall County Republican* (Plymouth, IN), September 10, 1857, p2, reprinted from *Chicago Tribune*.
35. Folwell, *History of Minnesota*, 1:432.
36. *Council Bluffs (IA) Nonpareil*, September 5, 1857, p3, reprinted from *Chicago Press*.
37. Johnson accuses Floyd of being a part of the scheme: Johnson, "Fort Snelling from Its Foundation to the Present Time," 435.
38. *St. Paul Daily Globe*, May 19, 1890, p8.
39. Chatelain, "The Federal Land Policy and Minnesota Politics," 239.
40. Johnson, "Fort Snelling from Its Foundation to the Present Time," 435–37.

Notes to Chapter 7: The State Fair Wars

1. *New York Tribune*, September 10, 1878, p2.
2. *St. Paul Daily Globe*, September 4, 1878, p1, September 5, 1878, p1.
3. *St. Paul Daily Globe*, September 6, 1878, p1.
4. *New York Herald*, September 5, 1878, p3.
5. *New York Herald*, September 5, 1878, p3, September 6, 1878, p10.
6. *St. Paul Daily Globe*, September 6, 1878, p1.
7. *Daily Globe*, September 6, 1878, p1.
8. *St. Paul Daily Globe*, September 6, 1878, p1.
9. *The Sun* (New York), September 8, 1878, p4.
10. *New York Herald*, September 6, 1878, p10.
11. Jarchow, "Early Minnesota Agricultural Societies and Fairs," 261; Hayes, "Minnesota's Wandering State Fair," 14.
12. Jarchow, "Early Minnesota Agricultural Societies and Fairs," 256.
13. Jarchow, "Early Minnesota Agricultural Societies and Fairs," 250, 251, 256, 259; Hayes, "Minnesota's Wandering State Fair," 12–13.
14. Smalley, *A History of the Republican Party*, 313; "History of the Journal," *Minneapolis Journal*, November 26, 1903, Silver Anniversary edition, 28.
15. Smalley, *A History of the Republican Party*, 313; Atwater and Stevens, eds., *History of Minneapolis and Hennepin County*, 1:379, 380–81.
16. Smalley, *A History of the Republican Party*, 149, 153; "History of the Journal," *Minneapolis Journal*, November 26, 1903, Silver Anniversary edition, 28. Ramsey County ran along the east side of the river, including St. Anthony up to Crow Wing. Hennepin County was newly formed along the west side of the river and Minneapolis was just beginning.
17. Smalley, *A History of the Republican Party*, 314; R. J. Baldwin, in Atwater and

Stevens, eds., *History of Minneapolis and Hennepin County*, 1:381; *Stillwater Messenger*, September 6, 1859, p2.

18. Smalley, *A History of the Republican Party*, 154; "Important from Minnesota," *New-York Daily Tribune*, November 10, 1858, 6; *River Falls (WI) Journal*, November 2, 1859, 2; *Weekly Minnesotian*, November 5, 1859, 2; see also Wikipedia.org under the respective legislature number, i.e., 1st Minnesota Legislature.
19. "History of the Journal," *Minneapolis Journal*, November 26, 1903, Silver Anniversary edition, 28.
20. Atwater and Stevens, eds., *History of Minneapolis and Hennepin County*, 1:337.
21. Smalley, *A History of the Republican Party*, 148, 314; Atwater and Stevens, eds., *History of Minneapolis and Hennepin County*, 337–38.
22. Atwater and Stevens, eds., *History of Minneapolis and Hennepin County*, 385; Smalley, *A History of the Republican Party*, 315.
23. Atwater and Stevens, eds., *History of Minneapolis and Hennepin County*, 1:385; also Smalley, *A History of the Republican Party*, 315; "History of the Journal," *Minneapolis Journal*, November 26, 1903, Silver Anniversary edition, 28; Hall, *History of the Minnesota State Agricultural Society*, 132.
24. Crandall, "Minnesota State Fair and William S. King," 5.
25. Hayes, "Minnesota's Wandering State Fair," 14; Crandall, "Minnesota State Fair and William S. King," 5.
26. Hayes, "Minnesota's Wandering State Fair," 14.
27. Hall, *History of the Minnesota State Agricultural Society*, 126–28, 133.
28. Hayes, "Minnesota's Wandering State Fair," 14; Hall, *History of the Minnesota State Agricultural Society*, 129–30.
29. Hall, *History of the Minnesota State Agricultural Society*, 132.
30. Hall, *History of the Minnesota State Agricultural Society*, 133.
31. Hayes, "Minnesota's Wandering State Fair," 15.
32. Hayes, "Minnesota's Wandering State Fair," 15; *St. Paul Globe*, February 8, 1878, p1.
33. *Moorhead (MN) Advocate*, April 13, 1878, p1; Hayes, "Minnesota's Wandering State Fair," 15; Hall, *History of the Minnesota State Agricultural Society*, 136.
34. *St. Paul Daily Globe*, September 6, 1878, p1. The 1880 census would count 780,773 people.
35. *St. Paul Daily Globe*, September 6, 1878, p1.
36. "Letter From W. Fraser Rae" (occasional correspondent of the *Tribune*), "Rivalry Between St. Paul and Minneapolis, St. Paul, Minn.," *New-York Tribune*, September 10, 1878, p2.
37. *St. Paul Daily Globe*, September 2, 1878, p1; *New-York Tribune*, September 10, 1878, p2.
38. *St. Paul Daily Globe*, September 5, 1878, p1.
39. *New York Herald*, September 8, 1878, p9.
40. *St. Paul Daily Globe*, September 5, 1878, p1.
41. *Minneapolis Tribune*, February 20, 1877, p2; "A Union Fair," *Minneapolis*

Tribune, February 4, 1879, p4; "The Two Fairs," *Minneapolis Tribune*, March 19, 1879, p2.

42. "The Blindness of St. Paul," *Minneapolis Tribune*, March 24, 1879, p2, reprinted from the *Northfield (MN) Mail*.
43. "The Two Fairs," *Minneapolis Tribune,* March 19, 1879, p2.
44. *St. Paul Daily Globe*, March 15, 1879, p1.
45. Hall, *History of the Minnesota State Agricultural Society*, 137.
46. Hayes, "Minnesota's Wandering State Fair," 15; Hall, *History of the Minnesota State Agricultural Society*, 137.
47. Hayes, "Minnesota's Wandering State Fair," 15.
48. Hayes, "Minnesota's Wandering State Fair," 15.
49. Crandall, "Minnesota State Fair and William S. King," 6; Hayes, "Minnesota's Wandering State Fair," 15.
50. Johnson, *A Tale of Two Cities*, 89.

Notes to Chapter 8: Navigating the Gorge, Negotiating the Capitol

1. *St. Paul Daily Globe*, March 2, 1881, p1.
2. *St. Paul Daily Globe*, March 2, 1881, p1; Dean, "A History of the Capitol Buildings of Minnesota," 19.
3. *St. Paul Daily Globe*, March 2, 1881, p1.
4. Hartsough, "The Development of the Twin Cities (Minneapolis and St. Paul) as a Metropolitan Market," 48; Kane, "Rivalry for a River," 309.
5. Folwell, *History of Minnesota*, 3:481; "The Head of Navigation," *Minneapolis Daily Tribune*, December 31, 1875, p2; "Saint Paul Matters: The Removal Scheme," *St. Paul Daily Globe*, February 23, 1887, p2.
6. "Saint Paul Matters: The Removal Scheme," *St. Paul Daily Globe*, February 23, 1887, p2; "The Globe's Flour City Career," *St. Paul Daily Globe*, May 1, 1889, Minneapolis edition, p3.
7. Gilman, "Last Days of the Upper Mississippi Fur Trade," 123.
8. Folwell, *History of Minnesota*, 3:479–80.
9. Rogers, "History of Flour Manufacture in Minnesota," 45–47.
10. Rogers, "History of Flour Manufacture in Minnesota," 45–47.
11. Newson, *Pen Pictures of St. Paul*, 307; *Minnesota Pioneer*, January 23, 1850, p2.
12. *Weekly Minnesotian*, June 16, 1855, p3.
13. *Minnesota Pioneer*, January 23, 1850, p2, May 23, 1850, p2; Kane, "Rivalry for a River," 311.
14. *Minnesota Pioneer*, May 23, 1850, p2.
15. *Minnesota Pioneer*, July 4, 1850, p2.
16. *St. Anthony Express*, June 28, 1851; *Sauk Rapids (MN) Frontierman*, May 3, 1855, p2; Kane, "Rivalry for a River," 311.
17. *Minnesotian*, November 5, 1851, p2; *Weekly Minnesotian*, August 13, 1853, p2, June 16, 1855, p3; *Minnesota Pioneer*, April 1, 1852, p2.
18. *Weekly Minnesotian*, September 4, 1852, p2.
19. Kane, "Rivalry for a River," 310; *Minnesota Pioneer*, August 9, 1849; *Weekly*

Minnesotian, March 17, 1855, p2, March 24, 1855, p4; *Daily Minnesota Pioneer*, March 5, 1855, p2, 1855, p2; *Minnesota Weekly Times*, June 26, 1855, p3.

20. *Minnesota Weekly Times*, July 17, 1855, p1, 2; *Weekly Minnesotian*, July 21, 1855, p4; Atwater and Stevens, eds., *History of Minneapolis and Hennepin County*, 397, 779. Atwater claims the *Falls City* reached its home port many times, "the head of navigation." I couldn't confirm that. Newspapers initially reported that the *Falls City* reached Cheever's Landing; however, they retracted their announcement after hearing about the accident: see *Weekly Minnesotian*, July 14, 1855, p2.
21. Atwater and Stevens, eds., *History of Minneapolis and Hennepin County*, 1:42–43.
22. *Minnesota Pioneer*, July 28, 1853, p2. People continued attempts to ascend the gorge into the 1890s: see *St. Paul Daily Globe*, May 28, 1892, p3.
23. *Daily Minnesota Pioneer*, August 26, 1854, p2.
24. *Weekly Minnesotian*, January 10, 1857, p1. See also Josh Biber, "A Complete Guide to the Ghost Towns of Hennepin County," January 22, 2023, www.minnesotahistory.org.
25. Anfinson, "The Secret History of the Mississippi's Earliest Locks and Dams," 254–67; Kane, "Rivalry for a River," 316–17; *State Atlas* (MN), February 13, 1867.
26. Kane, "Rivalry for a River," 320.
27. Dean, "A History of the Capitol Buildings of Minnesota," 22.
28. Thompson, "A Half Century of Capitol Conflict," 240.
29. Thompson, "A Half Century of Capitol Conflict," 240.
30. Williams, "History of the City of Saint Paul," 238.
31. Henry Moss says this decision of St. Paul as the capital was made at the Stillwater convention. In the second legislative session, representatives made it official and divvied up the three foundations of their version of civilization: the university went to St. Anthony, the penitentiary went to Stillwater, and the capital went to St. Paul: Williams, *History of Ramsey County*, 182.
32. Dean, "A History of the Capitol Buildings of Minnesota," 9–10, 15; Williams, "History of the City of Saint Paul," 370–72.
33. Holmes, *Minnesota in Three Centuries*, 4:154.
34. Castle, "Reminiscences of Minnesota Politics," 560; *New National Era*, February 20, 1873, p1. The paper reports that Douglass was denied at two hotels, and that this was the second time it had happened.
35. Dean, "A History of the Capitol Buildings of Minnesota," 22.
36. *Minneapolis Tribune*, February 3, 1891, p4; *Minneapolis Daily Tribune*, February 4, 1873, p4.
37. "A Great Metropolitan Center," *St. Paul Daily Globe*, July 27, 1891, p5–6; Castle, *History of St. Paul and Vicinity*, 2:636.
38. "The 'Twin Cities,'" *Minneapolis Daily Tribune*, December 12, 1875, p2; "The State Capitol," *Minneapolis Daily Tribune*, February 13, 1875, p2.
39. *Minneapolis Daily Tribune*, October 25, 1874, p3.

40. "Let Us Embrace," *Minneapolis Tribune*, August 2, 1879, p2, reprinted from *Alexandria (MN) Post*.
41. "Saint Paul Matters: In Danger of Falling," *St. Paul Daily Globe*, February 12, 1887, p2; "They Want the Capitol," *St. Paul Daily Globe*, December 28, 1888, p2.
42. "Saint Paul Matters: In Danger of Falling," *St. Paul Daily Globe*, February 12, 1887, p2; "The State Capitol," *St. Paul Daily Globe*, February 16, 1887, p5, 6; "Saint Paul Matters: The Removal Scheme," *St. Paul Daily Globe*, February 23, 1887, p2.
43. "To Join Twin Cities," *St. Paul Daily Globe*, February 20, 1887, p4; "Must Stay in the City," *St. Paul Daily Globe*, February 22, 1887, p1.
44. "Must Stay in the City," *St. Paul Daily Globe*, February 22, 1887, p1.
45. "To Join Twin Cities," *St. Paul Daily Globe*, February 20, 1887, p4.
46. "St. Paul Matters," *St. Paul Daily Globe*, February 21, 1887, p2.
47. "St. Paul Matters," *St. Paul Daily Globe*, February 21, 1887, p2; *St. Paul Daily Globe*, February 21, 1887, p4.
48. "Must Stay in the City," *St. Paul Daily Globe*, February 22, 1887, p1.
49. "Must Stay in the City," *St. Paul Daily Globe*, February 22, 1887, p1.
50. "Must Stay in the City," *St. Paul Daily Globe*, February 22, 1887, p1.
51. "Midway Wants It," *St. Paul Daily Globe*, February 22, 1887, p8. There were fewer trees at that time, and in many places along the gorge one could see the downtown of both cities.
52. "Saint Paul Matters: The Removal Scheme," *St. Paul Daily Globe,* February 23, 1887, p2.
53. "St. Paul Matters: The Capitol Removal," *St. Paul Daily Globe*, February 25, 1887, p2.
54. "In the Midway District," *St. Paul Daily Globe*, January 27, 1889, p5.
55. "Capitol Commissioners," *St. Paul Daily Globe*, March 31, 1889, p4.
56. *Minneapolis Tribune*, February 3, 1891, p4.
57. "Discussing a Site," *St. Paul Daily Globe*, January 29, 1893, p2.
58. Dean, "A History of the Capitol Buildings of Minnesota," 27–28.

Notes to Chapter 9: The Heart of the New Metropolis

1. *St. Paul Daily Globe*, April 8, 1891, p4.
2. *St. Paul Daily Globe*, July 24, 1887, p4, October 15, 1888, p2, December 24, 1888, p2.
3. *St. Paul Daily Globe*, August 16, 1887, p8, May 30, 1889, p2.
4. *Little Falls (MN) Transcript*, April 10, 1891, p1.
5. Corrigan, *The History of St. Marks and the Midway District*, 44.
6. *Midway News*, March 1, 1890; Corrigan, *The History of St. Marks and the Midway District*, 43.
7. "Heart of the New Metropolis," *St. Paul Daily Globe,* June 15, 1890, p13.
8. *St. Paul Daily Globe*, December 25, 1889, p1.
9. "Heart of the New Metropolis," *St. Paul Daily Globe*, June 15, 1890, p13.

10. "St. Paul–Minneapolis," *Minneapolis Daily Tribune*, September 29, 1872, p2. The writer signed his initials B. F. S. and dated his letter September 22; it may have been a local posing as an outsider.
11. "Legislature," *Minneapolis Daily Tribune*, February 15, 1874, p1. Girart Hewitt, a St. Paul real estate developer, suggested the possibility of a municipal union between St. Paul and Minneapolis in the early 1870s.
12. "A Great Metropolitan Center," *St. Paul Daily Globe*, July 27, 1891, p5–6; *St. Paul Daily Globe*, April 5, 1885, p5.
13. *St. Paul Daily Globe*, November 28, 1880, p1, October 18, 1885, p11; Atwater and Stevens, eds., *History of Minneapolis and Hennepin County*, 337; Corrigan, *The History of St. Marks and the Midway District*, 41.
14. Corrigan, *The History of St. Marks and the Midway District*, 39.
15. *St. Paul Daily Globe*, February 5, 1885, p1. The legislature passed two acts: 1) As was common, they exempted the newly annexed area from the city's existing debt; 2) They prohibited saloons and the sale of liquor within four miles of Merriam Park, which was basically the entire area from the State Fair to Fort Snelling and Minneapolis to St. Paul.
16. "Saint Paul Matters: The Removal Scheme," *St. Paul Daily Globe*, February 23, 1887, p2.
17. "Let Us Embrace," *Minneapolis Tribune*, August 2, 1879, p2, reprinted from the *Alexandria (MN) Post*.
18. Cleveland, *Aesthetics*.
19. Cleveland, *Public Parks, Radial Avenues, and Boulevards*, 11.
20. *St. Paul Daily Globe*, June 21, 1885, p5; Cleveland, *Public Parks, Radial Avenues, and Boulevards*, 13, 26–27.
21. *Minneapolis Tribune*, June 17, 1886 p5.
22. "The Proposed Minnehaha Park," *Minneapolis Daily Tribune*, June 26, 1885, p3.
23. Tishler and Luckhardt, "H. W. S. Cleveland: Pioneer Landscape Architect," 283; "A Plea for Parks," *Minneapolis Tribune*, April 3, 1888, p5. Summit Lookout Park is at the top of Ramsey Street.
24. "Favors the Canal," *St. Paul Daily Globe*, September 3, 1885, p2.
25. Here and below, "Symposium of Views," *St. Paul Daily Globe*, February 19, 1888, p9; "Shall We Unite," *St. Paul Daily Globe*, December 14, 1889, p1.
26. Atwater's words are at odds with comments he made on February 16, 1888, at a joint meeting of commercial representatives from both cities. He chaired the meeting and opened by saying: "The growth of the Twin Cities has been remarkable. Thirty years ago that gentleman (pointing to H. W. Rice) predicted that St. Paul and St. Anthony would form one great municipality. But if we have accomplished a great deal as separate cities, what may we not become working for common interests? But great and strong as we are, *a great danger is looming up before us*, and we will be wise men to foresee and prevent this danger. I do not believe there is a man in either city that is not heart and soul in favor of a commercial union. What the feeling is

upon the question of one municipality, I cannot say, although I am heartily in favor of it. United we need not fear; without it we have good ground for apprehension": see Castle, *History of St. Paul and Vicinity*, 640.

27. "Saint Paul Matters: The Removal Scheme," *St. Paul Daily Globe*, February 23, 1887, p2; "Must Stay in the City," *St. Paul Daily Globe*, February 22, 1887, p1.
28. Johnson, *Another Tale of Two Cities*, 6.
29. "A City's Wrath," *St. Paul Daily Globe*, June 19, 1890, p1.
30. "A City's Wrath," *St. Paul Daily Globe*, June 19, 1890, p1.
31. "A City's Wrath," *St. Paul Daily Globe*, June 19, 1890, p1.
32. "A City's Wrath," *St. Paul Daily Globe*, June 19, 1890, p1.
33. "A City's Wrath," *St. Paul Daily Globe*, June 19, 1890, p1.
34. "A Teapot Tempest," *St. Paul Daily Globe*, June 19, 1890, p4.
35. Castle, *History of St. Paul and Vicinity*, 639.

Notes to Chapter 10: Utopian Vision Meets Contentious Reality

1. *St. Paul Daily Globe*, January 1, 1888, p19.
2. *The Story of Town and Country Club of St. Paul*, 8. The club lost the records of its early years in a fire in 1898. Subsequently, the club's early history is largely from Peet's recollections, written in 1930.
3. *St. Paul Daily Globe*, January 25, 1888.
4. "All These Toboggan Carnival Clubs Which Love the Slippery Chute by Day and Eve," *St. Paul Daily Globe*, January 25, 1888; "It's Quite English," *St. Paul Daily Globe*, January 1, 1888, p19. The Minnesota Club was on the southeast corner of Fourth and Cedar Streets in St. Paul.
5. "All These Toboggan Carnival Clubs Which Love the Slippery Chute by Day and Eve," *St. Paul Daily Globe*, January 25, 1888; "It's Quite English," *St. Paul Daily Globe*, January 1, 1888, p19; Shefchik, *From Fields to Fairways*, 2.
6. "Swell Town & Country Club," *St. Paul Daily Globe*, June 7, 1891, p1.
7. Peet, "The Beginning of Golf in Saint Paul."
8. "Swell Town and Country Club," *St. Paul Daily Globe*, June 7, 1891, p1.
9. Town & Country Club is typically not politically oriented, so the various positions of its members are not sponsored or held by the club. During this time period, however, a number of members were using the club to advance their agendas.
10. Cleveland, "Park Ways and Ornamental Parks: The Best System for St. Paul," in *Public Parks, Radial Avenues, and Boulevards*, 28. Como Avenue actually crosses the Minneapolis–St. Paul city limits in southeast Minneapolis.
11. *Minneapolis Tribune*, January 31, 1890, p3; "It's Quite English," *St. Paul Daily Globe*, January 1, 1888, p19. The other founder was W. H. Patterson. "Record of Realty," *St. Paul Daily Globe*, April 19, 1885, p5: "It is understood that they have associated with them a large number of Southern gentlemen, representing at least $2,000,000 of means, and amply able to wait and see the cities grow and meet on this common center, with the assurance of good returns for their investment."

12. *St. Paul Daily Globe*, June 21, 1885, p5.
13. *St. Paul Daily Globe*, June 21, 1885, p5.
14. *St. Paul Daily Globe*, March 24, 1885, p2, February 12, 1888, p3; Schmidt, "Pleasure and Recreation for the People," 46. McMurran and Hager were members of Town & Country. I have not found McClung associated with the club in public documents.
15. Cleveland, "Park Ways and Ornamental Parks: The Best System for St. Paul," in *Public Parks, Radial Avenues, and Boulevards*, 27.
16. *Minneapolis Morning Tribune*, April 1, 1912, p6.
17. See, for example, Minnesota Supreme Court, Case Files, General Index, and Briefs of the Supreme Court and the Court of Appeals, MNHS; Warner and Foote, *History of Ramsey County*, 243.
18. Castle, *History of St. Paul and Vicinity*, 637.
19. "Second Race," *Minneapolis Daily Tribune*, September 19, 1872, p4; "Minneapolis Trotting Park," *Minneapolis Daily Tribune*, July 13, 1870, p4.
20. *Minnesota Beginnings: Records of St. Croix County*, 45. The marriage license was issued on November 25, 1845. Ross, "Plympton's Reserve, St. Paul's Founding, and Desnoyer's New Bridge Square," 13–22. Ravoux performed the wedding to Sarah (Sally) Johnson on May 7, 1873, on his property: *Sally Desnoyer vs. Mary Jordan, et al.*, December 1, 1880, Case 2894, Minnesota Supreme Court Case Files, General Index, and Briefs of the Supreme Court and the Court of Appeals, MNHS, 7.
21. "Accident," *Saint Paul Daily Press*, October 5, 1866, p4; *Sally Desnoyer vs. Mary Jordan, et al.*, 45.
22. Adams, "Early Days at Red River Settlement," 100; Ross, "Plympton's Reserve, St. Paul's Founding, and Desnoyer's New Bridge Square," note 22.
23. The brother preceded him in death.
24. *Sally Desnoyer v. Hendrickson, et al.*, April 8, 1882, Case 14924, Second District Court, Minnesota, MNHS.
25. Young and Lightner (St. Paul) Papers, MNHS.
26. Perhaps the most successful or best-remembered utopian tale of that era was *Looking Backward, 2000–1887* by Edward Bellamy.
27. *St. Paul Globe*, March 15–April 1, 1891.
28. McAleer, *Escape Artist*; "A Coming House Warming," *St. Paul Daily Globe*, December 7, 1890, 13.
29. Robinson, *Federal City*, 11–13, 14.
30. Robinson, *Federal City*, 16, 18.
31. Robinson, *Federal City*, 17, 21, 22.
32. Robinson, *Federal City*, 22.
33. Robinson, *Federal City*, 31.
34. Robinson, *Federal City*, 33.
35. Robinson, *Federal City*, 35.
36. Robinson, *Federal City*, 35–36.
37. Castle, *History of St. Paul and Vicinity*, 641–43.

38. Castle, *History of St. Paul and Vicinity*, 641–43.
39. Corrigan, *The History of St. Marks and the Midway District*, 47–48.
40. O'Connell, *John Ireland and the American Catholic Church*, 378–79; Corrigan, *The History of St. Marks and the Midway District*, 44–45.
41. "The Site Is Changed," *St. Paul Daily Globe*, July 8, 1891, p2.
42. "The Site Is Changed," *St. Paul Daily Globe*, July 8, 1891, p2; *Minneapolis Tribune*, July 9, 1891, p3.
43. "Mr. Noyes Explains," *St. Paul Daily Globe*, July 10, 1891, p8; *St. Paul Daily Globe*, April 5, 1891, 15: Union land company to D. R. Noyes: lots 6, 7, 9, 10, and 11, block 47; lots, 9, 10, and 11, block 34; and lots 2 and 3, block 36, Desnoyer Park.
44. Corrigan, *The History of St. Marks and the Midway District*, 45.
45. *St. Paul Daily Globe*, December 25, 1889, p1; Dean, "A History of the Capitol Buildings of Minnesota," 26–30. Members were William B. Dean (Ramsey), Jay La Due (southwest corner of the state including Murray, Nobles, Pipestone, and Rock Counties), Oscar Ayers (Mower), Henry Keller (Benton, Sherburne, and Stearns Counties), and Frank Griggs McMillian (Hennepin).
46. O'Connell, *John Ireland and the American Catholic Church*, 380–81; *Saint Paul Globe*, March 21, 1905, p10.

Notes to Epilogue

1. Chapin, "A Unique Industrial Center," 20–22.
2. Hartshorne, "The Twin City District."
3. Hartshorne, "The Twin City District," 432.
4. Hartshorne, "The Twin City District," 432.
5. Hartshorne, "The Twin City District," 432.
6. Hartshorne, "The Twin City District," 432.
7. Hartshorne, "The Twin City District," 432, 436.
8. Hartshorne, "The Twin City District," 432, 438, 441.
9. Hartshorne, "The Twin City District," 438.
10. Hartshorne, "The Twin City District," 441–42.
11. Hartshorne, "The Twin City District," 442.
12. Kolderie, "Governance in the Twin Cities Region of Minnesota," 114.
13. Kolderie, "Governance in the Twin Cities Region of Minnesota," 114.
14. Kolderie, "Governance in the Twin Cities Region of Minnesota," 114.
15. Kolderie, "Governance in the Twin Cities Region of Minnesota," 114.
16. Kolderie, "Governance in the Twin Cities Region of Minnesota," 114.
17. Johnson and Harrigan, "Innovation by Increments," 212–13.
18. Johnson and Harrigan, "Innovation by Increments," 206.
19. Johnson and Harrigan, "Innovation by Increments," 212–13; Kolderie, "Governance in the Twin Cities Region of Minnesota," 125.
20. Baldinger, *Planning and Governing the Metropolis*, xiii.
21. Johnson and Harrigan, "Innovation by Increments," 212–13; Baldinger, *Planning and Governing the Metropolis*, 216; Fischer, "The Minnesota Experiment."

Note on Sources

Digital archives have improved, bringing a great number of texts to our screens along with the occasional rare find. In addition, Optical Character Recognition (OCR) gives us a fine-tooth comb to search the voluminous histories of the past.

The Minnesota Historical Society (MNHS) has an archive with an excellent searchable database for finding papers and publications. An increasing number of materials have been scanned and are available online. The *Collections of the Minnesota Historical Society* is a seventeen-volume assemblage of primary and early secondary sources. That wealth of material is augmented with decades of articles in *Minnesota History* magazine. I also benefited from materials in Hennepin History Museum and Ramsey County Historical Society and their magazines. I found most digital materials on Internet Archive (archive.org) and HathiTrust (hathitrust.org).

William W. Folwell is the preeminent historian of Minnesota, and he published *A History of Minnesota* in the 1920s. Through his work I found numerous other histories of Minneapolis, St. Paul, and Minnesota by an interesting cadre of authors. These authors were often men who were involved in politics or newspapers during the time covered in their histories, such as Henry A. Castle (*History of St. Paul and Vicinity*), Isaac Atwater (*History of Minneapolis and Hennepin County, Minnesota*), Christopher C. Andrews (*History of St. Paul*), Return I. Holcombe (*Minnesota in Three Centuries* and *Compendium of History and Biography of Minneapolis and Hennepin County*), and William H. Folsom (*Fifty Years in the Northwest*). These histories offer an intimacy with the events. Other works of this nature include *A History of the City of St. Paul* by J. Fletcher Williams, who was able to interview people who played a role in events. *Pen Pictures* by Thomas H. Newson, a newspaper editor, provides good information.

Of course I spent a good deal of time in the archives looking through papers and books. Access through digital archives enriches our research and expands the scope of material available.

Newspapers

The MNHS has newspapers online at the Minnesota Digital Newspaper Hub. As a supplement, the Library of Congress Chronicling America website has a few other Minnesota newspapers as well as a national database. Commercial services do exist; however, the public archives are excellent.

I used newspapers in a couple of ways. After reading about an event in one of the histories above, I would search the newspapers for more information. We get finer details in the newspapers that yield a more intimate story. On the pages we can see how a story sat among the other news of the day. And these databases allow us to search regional and national newspapers, which provide the bigger picture of how others viewed Minnesota issues. The newspapers can also be used to fact-check the above histories. For example, in the case of George Warner and Charles Foote's local histories, which were published as popular accounts without sources, we can verify their accounts through the newspapers.

I used newspapers for context of the Reserve sales in Part II: Chapters 4–6. Through newspapers we can follow the evolution of an issue. John Ross Browne was a well-known contemporary of Herman Melville and Mark Twain. His life is documented across several biographies, but none of them cover his time in Minnesota. He disappeared during these years. I was able to track his travels back from California and his work in Minnesota, bringing to light this part of his life.

From firsthand accounts in the newspapers we get some fairly raw stories, such as the burning of the Capitol in 1881 when the reporter/editor was on the scene. The newspapers gave the national perspective in Chapter 7 regarding President Hayes's visit to Minnesota. Reporters might have known how many people could fit in the Grandstand, and they might have monitored ticket sales, but for the most part the crowd numbers given in the newspaper accounts should be treated as estimates. Likely, because of political influence, they inflated or depressed numbers according to the publication's proclivities.

Newspapers of the nineteenth century were known for their loyalty to a political cause or a politician. They were political before they were reporters. Authors of newspaper articles could be boosters, partisan hacks, or anonymous writers. The lack of transparency could protect someone's identity and allow them to be more frank or self-promotional. The newspapers offer rich material but require a cautious read.

While searchable text in digitized newspapers is the leading edge of research today, one unfortunate fact of historic newspapers is our access to all copies. Some have disappeared entirely, of course, but some have yet to be digitized, such as Bill King's *State Atlas* and the *St. Anthony Express*, an early newspaper there. These can be found on microfilm at the Minnesota Historical Society's Gale Family Library in St. Paul.

Bibliography

Archival Collections

Minnesota Historical Society.

Bliss, John H. Reminiscences of Fort Snelling.
Fort Snelling. Papers.
Military Reserve Claim Association. Record Book, 1853–1854.
Minnesota Historical Society. Scrapbooks, 1861–1922.
Minnesota Second District Court. Files.
Minnesota Supreme Court. Case Files, General Index, and Briefs.
Ramsey, Alexander. Papers.
"Report in Relation to the Official Transactions of Willis A. Gorman."
Taliaferro, Lawrence. Papers.
US General Land Office, Stillwater Land District. Papers.
Young and Lightner (St. Paul). Legal Papers, 1842–1887.

Wisconsin Historical Society.

Wisconsin Territorial Papers, Crawford County, WI. Wisconsin Historical Records Survey.

Newspapers

The American (Washington DC)
Anti-Slavery Bugle (New Lisbon, OH)
Burlington (VT) Free Press
Chicago Tribune
Cleveland (OH) Express
Council Bluffs (IA) Nonpareil
Daily Minnesota Pioneer
Daily Union (Washington, DC)
Evening Star (Washington, DC)
Gazette (Burlington WI)
Iowa News (Dubuque, Upper Lead Mines, Wisconsin Territory)
Marshall County Republican (Plymouth, IN)
Minneapolis Daily Tribune
Minneapolis Morning Tribune
Minneapolis Star Tribune
Minneapolis Tribune
Minnesota Pioneer

Minnesota Weekly Times
Moorhead (MN) Advocate
The National Era (Washington, DC)
New National Era (Washington, DC)
New-York Daily Tribune
New York Herald
New York Tribune
Northern Pacific Farmer (Wadena, MN)
North Iowa Times (McGregor, IA)
Perrysburg (OH) Journal
Raftsman's Journal (Clearfield, PA)
River Falls (WI) Journal
St. Anthony (MN) Express
St. Charles (MN) Union
St. Paul (Daily) Globe
Sauk Rapids (MN) Frontierman
Washington (DC) Sentinel
Weekly Minnesotian

Published Works

Adams, Ann. "Early Days at Red River Settlement, and Fort Snelling: Reminiscences of Ann Adams, 1821–1829." *Collections of the Minnesota Historical Society* 6 (1894): 75–115.

Andreas, A. T. *History of Chicago: From the Earliest Period to the Present Time.* A. T. Andreas, 1884.

Andrews, C. C. *History of St. Paul, Minn.: With Illustrations and Biographical Sketches of Some of Its Prominent Men and Pioneers.* D. Mason and Co., 1890.

Anfinson, John O. "The Secret History of the Mississippi's Earliest Locks and Dams." *Minnesota History* 54, no. 6 (1995): 254–67.

Atwater, Isaac, and John H. Stevens, eds. *History of Minneapolis and Hennepin County, Minnesota.* 2 vols. Munsell Publishing Co., 1895.

Baldinger, Stanley. *Planning and Governing the Metropolis: The Twin Cities Experience.* Praeger, 1971.

Blegen, Theodore C. "The 'Fashionable Tour' on the Upper Mississippi." *Minnesota History* 20, no. 4 (1939): 377–96.

Bogue, Allan G. "The Iowa Claim Clubs: Symbol and Substance." *Mississippi Valley Historical Review* 45, no. 2 (1958): 231–53.

Bond, J. Wesley. *Minnesota and Its Resources: . . . Notes of a Trip from St. Paul to Pembina and Selkirk Settlement on the Red River of the North.* Redfield, 1853.

Bureau of Statistics. *Minnesota, Its Progress and Capabilities.* Annual report. W. R. Marshall, 1862.

Castle, Henry A. *History of St. Paul and Vicinity: A Chronicle of Progress and a Narrative Account of the Industries, Institutions, and People of the City and Its Tributary Territory.* 3 vols. Lewis Publishing Co., 1912.

Castle, Henry A. "Reminiscences of Minnesota Politics." *Collections of the Minnesota Historical Society* 15 (1915): 553–98.

Chaney, Josiah B. "Early Bridges and Changes of the Land and Water Surface in the City of St. Paul." *Collections of the Minnesota Historical Society* 12 (1908): 131–48.

Chapin, Harold F. "A Unique Industrial Center: The Midway District of St. Paul and Minneapolis." *The American City* 16, no. 1 (1917): 20–22.

Chatelain, Verne E. "The Federal Land Policy and Minnesota Politics, 1854–60." *Minnesota History* 22, no. 3 (1941): 227–48.

Cleveland, H. W. S. "The Aesthetic Development of the United Cities of St. Paul and Minneapolis: An Address Delivered in Dyer's Hall, April 20, 1888, to the Minneapolis Society of Fine Arts."

Cleveland, H. W. S. *Public Parks, Radial Avenues, and Boulevards: Outline Plan of a Park System for the City of St. Paul.* Globe Job Office, 1885.

Corrigan, Joseph A. *The History of St. Marks and the Midway District*. Church of St. Mark, 1939.

Coues, Elliott. *The Expeditions of Zebulon Montgomery Pike: To Headwaters of the Mississippi River, Through Louisiana Territory, and in New Spain, During the Years 1805–6–7.* 3 vols. Francis P. Harper, 1895.

Crandall, Bernard B. "Minnesota State Fair and William S. King." *Hennepin County History* 29, no. 2 (Fall 1969): 4–7.

Dean, William B. "A History of the Capitol Buildings of Minnesota, with Some Account of the Struggles for Their Location." *Collections of the Minnesota Historical Society* 12 (1908): 1–42.

DeCarlo, Peter. *Fort Snelling at Bdote: A Brief History.* Minnesota Historical Society Press, 2016.

Dillon, Richard H. *J. Ross Browne: Confidential Agent in Old California*. University of Oklahoma Press, 1965.

Dupre, Huntley, ed. "Territorial Daguerreotypes: E. D. Neill's Gospel of Minnesota." *Minnesota History* 30 (1949): 202–19.

"Early Days at Fort Snelling." *Collections of the Minnesota Historical Society* 1 (1902): 345–59.

Elfelt, Charles D. "Early Trade and Traders in St. Paul." 1897. *Collections of the Minnesota Historical Society* 9 (1901): 163–66.

Fairchild, Henry S. "Sketches of the Early History of Real Estate in St. Paul." *Collections of the Minnesota Historical Society* 10, no. 1 (1905): 417–43.

Fischer, John. "The Easy Chair—The Minnesota Experiment: How to Make a Big City Fit to Live In." *Harper's Magazine*, April 1, 1969.

Flandrau, Charles E. *The History of Minnesota and Tales of the Frontier*. E. W. Porter, 1900.

Flandrau, Grace. "St. Paul: The Personality of a City." *Minnesota History* 22, no. 1 (1941): 1–12.

Folsom, William H. C. *Fifty Years in the Northwest: With an Introduction and Appendix Containing Reminiscences, Incidents and Notes.* Pioneer Press Co., 1888.

Folwell, William W. *A History of Minnesota*. 4 vols. Minnesota Historical Society, 1921–30.

Folwell, William W. "The Sale of Fort Snelling, 1857." *Collections of the Minnesota Historical Society* 15 (1915): 393–410.

"Forgotten Pioneers VI: Stephen Desnoyer." *Ramsey County History Magazine* 5, no. 2 (Fall 1968): 19–20.

Forsyth, Thomas. "Fort Snelling: Col. Leavenworth's Expedition to Establish It, in 1819." *Collections of the Minnesota Historical Society* 3 (1880): 139–67.

Gilman, Rhoda R. *Henry Hastings Sibley: Divided Heart*. Minnesota Historical Society Press, 2004.

Gilman, Rhoda R. "Last Days of the Upper Mississippi Fur Trade." *Minnesota History* 42, no. 4 (1970): 122–40.

Gilman, Rhoda R. "Territorial Imperative: How Minnesota Became the 32nd State." In *Making Minnesota Territory, 1849–1858*, edited by Anne R. Kaplan and Marilyn Ziebarth. Minnesota Historical Society Press, 1999.

Goodman, Nancy, and Robert Goodman. *Joseph R. Brown: Adventurer on the Minnesota Frontier, 1820–1849*. Lone Oak Press, 1996.

Gordon, William A. *A Compilation of Registers of the Army of the United States, from 1815 to 1837*. J. C. Dunn, 1837.

Green, William D. *A Peculiar Imbalance: The Fall and Rise of Racial Equality in Early Minnesota*. Minnesota Historical Society Press, 2007.

Hall, Darwin S. *History of the Minnesota State Agricultural Society from Its Organization in 1854 to the Annual Meeting of 1910*. McGill-Warner Co., 1910.

Hall, Stephen P. *Fort Snelling: Colossus of the Wilderness*. Minnesota Historical Society Press, 1987.

Hartshorne, Richard. "The Twin City District: A Unique Form of Urban Landscape." *Geographical Review* 22, no. 3 (July 1932): 431–42.

Hartsough, Mildred Lucile. "The Development of the Twin Cities (Minneapolis and St. Paul) as a Metropolitan Market." PhD diss., University of Minnesota, 1924.

Hayes, Gordon. "Minnesota's Wandering State Fair and How It Settled in St. Paul." *Ramsey County History* 11, no. 1 (Spring 1974): 12–17.

Hennessy, William B. *Past and Present of St. Paul, Minnesota: Being a Relation of the Progressive History of the Capital City of Minnesota*. S. J. Clarke Publishing Co., 1906.

Herron, John. "Centropolis: William Gilpin, Nature, and the City of the Future." *Middle West Review* 3, no. 1 (2016): 25–47.

Holcombe, R. I. *Minnesota in Three Centuries, Volume 2: Early History—Minnesota as a Territory*. Publishing Society of Minnesota, 1908.

Holcombe, R. I., and William H. Bingham, eds. *Compendium of History and Biography of Minneapolis and Hennepin County, Minnesota*. Henry Taylor and Co., 1914.

Holmes, F. R. *Minnesota in Three Centuries, Volume 4: Minnesota as a State, 1870–1908*. Publishing Society of Minnesota, 1908.

Hudson, Horace B. *A Half Century of Minnesota as Territory and State: A Concise Account of the Principal Events in the Period of Discovery, Exploration, and Settlement, and During the Half Century of Territorial and State Government*. Minneapolis Journal, 1900.

Ireland, John. "Memoir of Rev. Lucian Galtier, the First Catholic Priest of Saint Paul." *Collections of the Minnesota Historical Society* 3 (1880): 222–30.

Jarchow, Merrill E. "Early Minnesota Agricultural Societies and Fairs." *Minnesota History* 22, no. 3 (1941): 249–69.

Johnson, C. W. *Another Tale of Two Cities: Minneapolis and St. Paul Compared.* 1890.

Johnson, C. W. *A Tale of Two Cities: Minneapolis and St. Paul Compared*, 2nd ed. Johnson, Smith and Harrison, 1885.

Johnson, Richard W. "Fort Snelling from Its Foundation to the Present Time." *Collections of the Minnesota Historical Society* 8 (1898): 427–48.

Johnson, William, and John J. Harrigan. "Innovation by Increments: The Twin Cities as a Case Study in Metropolitan Reform." *Western Political Quarterly* 31, no. 2 (1978): 206–18.

Johnston, Daniel S. B. "Minnesota Journalism in the Territorial Period." *Collections of the Minnesota Historical Society* 10, no. 1 (1905): 247–351.

Journal of the Council during the . . . Session of the Legislative Assembly of the Territory of Minnesota. M'Lean and Owens, 1849.

Kane, Lucile M. *The Falls of St. Anthony: The Waterfall that Built Minneapolis*. Minnesota Historical Society Press, 1987.

Kane, Lucile M. "Governing a Frontier City: Old St. Anthony, 1855–72." *Minnesota History* 35, no. 3 (1956): 117–25.

Kane, Lucile M. "Rivalry for a River: The Twin Cities and the Mississippi." *Minnesota History* 37, no. 8 (1961): 309–23.

Kellogg, Louise Phelps. "The Rise and Fall of Old Superior." *Wisconsin Magazine of History* 24, no. 1 (1940): 3–19.

Kolderie, Ted. "Governance in the Twin Cities Region of Minnesota." In *Regional Governance: Promise and Performance—Substate Regionalism and the Federal System, Volume II—Case Studies*, Advisory Commission on Intergovernmental Relations. Government Printing Office, 1973.

Larpenteur, August[e] L. "Recollections of the City and People of St. Paul, 1843–1898." *Collections of the Minnesota Historical Society* 9 (1901): 363–94.

Lass, William E. "The Birth of Minnesota." *Minnesota History* 55, no. 6 (1997): 267–79.

Lass, William E. "Minnesota's Separation from Wisconsin: Boundary Making on the Upper Mississippi Frontier." *Minnesota History* 50, no. 8 (1987): 309–20.

Lehman, Christopher P. *Slavery in the Upper Mississippi Valley, 1787–1865: A History of Human Bondage in Illinois, Iowa, Minnesota and Wisconsin.* McFarland and Co., 2011.

Lehman, Christopher P. *Slavery's Reach: Southern Slaveholders in the North Star State*. Minnesota Historical Society Press, 2019.

"Life and Public Services of Hon. Willis A. Gorman." *Collections of the Minnesota Historical Society* 3 (1880): 314–32.

Loehr, Rodney C. "Franklin Steele, Frontier Businessman." *Minnesota History* 27 (1946): 309–18.

McAleer, Joseph. *Escape Artist: The Nine Lives of Harry Perry Robinson*. Oxford University Press, 2020.

McNulty, Ambrose. "The Chapel of St. Paul, and the Beginnings of the Catholic Church in Minnesota." *Collections of the Minnesota Historical Society* 10, no. 1 (1905): 233–45.

Millikan, William. "The Great Treasure of the Fort Snelling Prison Camp." *Minnesota History* 62, no. 1 (2010): 4–17.

Minnesota Beginnings: Records of St. Croix County, Wisconsin Territory, 1840–1849. Washington County Historical Society, 1999.

Moss, Henry L. "Biographic Notes of Old Settlers." *Collections of the Minnesota Historical Society* 9 (1901): 143–62.

National Register of Historic Places. "Railroads in Minnesota, 1862–1956." Continuation Sheet. US Department of the Interior, National Park Service. https://www.dot.state.mn.us/culturalresources/docs/rail/sectione.pdf. Accessed November 2, 2024.

Neill, Edward D. "Fort Snelling, Minnesota, While in Command of Col. Josiah Snelling, Fifth Infantry." Reprinted from *Magazine of Western History* (1888): 171–80, 373–81.

Neill, Edward D. *The History of Minnesota: From the Earliest French Explorations to the Present Time*. 5th ed. Minnesota Historical Company, 1883.

Newson, Thomas M. *Pen Pictures of St. Paul, Minnesota, and Biographical Sketches of Old Settlers: From the Earliest Settlement of the City, Up to and Including the Year 1857*. Self-published, 1886.

Nichols, Roy F. *Franklin Pierce: Young Hickory of the Granite Hills*. University of Pennsylvania Press, 1931. Reprint, American Political Biography Press, 1993.

O'Connell, Marvin R. *John Ireland and the American Catholic Church*. Minnesota Historical Society Press, 1988.

Oliphant, Laurence. *Minnesota and the Far West*. W. Blackwood and Sons, 1855.

"Organization of Minnesota Territory." 1851. *Collections of the Minnesota Historical Society* 1 (1902): 33–46.

Orsi, Jared. *Citizen Explorer: The Life of Zebulon Pike*. Oxford University Press, 2014.

Peet, William F. "The Beginning of Golf in Saint Paul and the Early History of the Town & Country Club." October 22, 1930. Available at https://www.tcc-club.com.

"Pike's Explorations in Minnesota, 1805–6." *Collections of the Minnesota Historical Society* 1 (1902): 302–42.

Plympton, Gilbert M. *Memoir of the Life and Services of Colonel Joseph Plympton, U.S. Army, With Some Account of the Family of Plympton and the Origin of the Name*. Evening Post Steam Presses, 1881.

Ravoux, A. *Reminiscences, Memoirs and Lectures of Monsignor A. Ravoux, V. G.* Brown, Treacy and Co., 1890.

Ritchey, Charles J. "Claim Associations and Pioneer Democracy in Early Minnesota." *Minnesota History* 9, no. 2 (1928): 85–95.

Robinson, H. P. ["Optimist"]. *Federal City: Being a Reminiscence of the Time Before St. Paul and Minneapolis Were United.* Self-published, c.1891.

Rodenbough, Theophilus F., and William L. Haskin, eds. *The Army of the United States: Historical Sketches of Staff and Line with Portraits of Generals-in-Chief.* Maynard, Merrill, and Co., 1896.

Rogers, George D. "History of Flour Manufacture in Minnesota." *Collections of the Minnesota Historical Society* 10, no. 1 (1905): 35–55.

Ross, Drew M. "Plympton's Reserve, St. Paul's Founding, and Desnoyer's New Bridge Square: Decisions, Destiny, and Dreams." *Ramsey County History* 59, no. 2 (2024): 13–22.

Ross, Drew. "Reclaiming Mississippi River Boulevard." Streets.mn. January 10, 2019. https://streets.mn/2019/01/10/reclaiming-mississippi-river-boulevard.

Sardeson, Frederick W. "Description of the Minneapolis and St. Paul District." Report. 1914. https://pubs.usgs.gov/gf/201/text.pdf.

Schmid, Calvin. *Social Saga of Two Cities: An Ecological and Statistical Study of Social Trends in Minneapolis and St. Paul.* Minneapolis Council of Social Agencies (Bureau of Social Research) Monograph No. 1. 1937.

Schmidt, Andrew J. "Planning St. Paul's Como Park: Pleasure and Recreation for the People." *Minnesota History* 58, no. 1 (2002): 40–58.

Session Laws of the Territory of Minnesota. *Laws of Minnesota.* Olmstead and Brown, Territorial Printers, 1854.

Shefchik, Rick. *From Fields to Fairways: Classic Golf Clubs of Minnesota.* University of Minnesota Press, 2012.

Sibley, Henry H. "Reminiscences of the Early Days of Minnesota." *Collections of the Minnesota Historical Society* 3 (1880): 242–82.

Smalley, E. V. *A History of the Republican Party From Its Organization to the Present Time; to Which Is Added a Political History of Minnesota from a Republican Point of View and Biographical Sketches of Leading Minnesota Republicans.* Self-published, 1896.

Smith, Hampton. *Confluence: A History of Fort Snelling.* Minnesota Historical Society Press, 2021.

Snyder, C. E. "John Emerson, Owner of Dred Scott." *Annals of Iowa* 21, no. 6 (1938): 440–61.

Stevens, John H. "The Early History of Hennepin County: Address Before the Minneapolis Lyceum." Northwestern Democrat Office, 1856.

Stevens, John H. *Personal Recollections of Minnesota and Its People, and Early History of Minneapolis.* Tribune Printing, 1890.

Stevens, John H. "Recollections of James M. Goodhue." *Collections of the Minnesota Historical Society* 6 (1894): 492–501.

The Story of Town and Country Club of St. Paul, 1888–1948. Booklet, 1947.

Swierenga, Robert P. *Pioneers and Profits: Land Speculation on the Iowa Frontier*. Iowa State University Press, 1968.

Thompson, Neil B. "A Half Century of Capitol Conflict: How St. Paul Kept the Seat of Government." *Minnesota History* 43, no. 7 (1973): 238–54.

Tishler, William H., and Virginia S. Luckhardt. "H. W. S. Cleveland: Pioneer Landscape Architect to the Upper Midwest." *Minnesota History* 49, no. 7 (1985): 281–91.

Trautmann, Frederic, trans. "Johann Georg Kohl: A German Traveler in Minnesota Territory." *Minnesota History* 49, no. 4 (1984): 126–39.

US Circuit Court, Minnesota. Petition and Affidavits for Rehearing, *Geo. I. Denoyer vs. Dennis Ryan*, Exhibit "A." October 15, 1885.

Warner, George E., and Charles M. Foote. *History of Ramsey County and the City of St. Paul, Including the Explorers and Pioneers of Minnesota*. North Star Publishing Co., 1881.

White, Bruce M. "The Power of Whiteness, or The Life and Times of Joseph Rolette, Jr." *Minnesota History* 56, no. 4 (1998–99): 178–97.

White, Helen McCann. "Frontier Feud, 1819–20: How Two Officers Quarreled All the Way to the Site of Fort Snelling." *Minnesota History* 43, no. 2 (1970): 99–114.

Williams, J. Fletcher. "A History of the City of Saint Paul, and of the County of Ramsey, Minnesota." *Collections of the Minnesota Historical Society* 4 (1876).

Wills, Jocelyn. *Boosters, Hustlers, and Speculators: Entrepreneurial Culture and the Rise of Minneapolis and St. Paul, 1849–1883*. Minnesota Historical Society Press, 2005.

Wingerd, Mary Lethert. *North Country: The Making of Minnesota*. University of Minnesota Press, 2010.

Ziebarth, Marilyn, and Alan Ominsky. *Fort Snelling: Anchor Post of the Northwest*. Minnesota Historical Society, 1970.

Image Credits

Page 11 Originally published in Hampton Smith, *Confluence: A History of Fort Snelling* (MNHS Press, 2021).

Pages 30, 40, 49, 179
Maps in MNHS collections; photographs by Drew M. Ross

Pages 34, 83, 95, 114, 116, 138, 159, 160, 170
MNHS collections

Page 38 Originally produced for the US War Department's Office of the Chief of Engineers. Collected and Preserved in the National Archives. Wikimedia Commons

Page 57 George Protz, *Pocket Edition of the Original Plats of the City of St. Paul* (1883). MNHS collections. Photograph by Drew M. Ross

Page 58 Bureau of Land Management General Land Office

Page 67 Von Minden and Wippermann, Architects and Civil Engineers, St. Paul, Minnesota Territory, 1857. Photograph by Drew M. Ross

Page 80 John Ross Browne, *Harper's Weekly*, February 22, 1868. Wikimedia Commons

Page 82 Portrait by G. P. A. Healy, 1857. MNHS collections

Page 97 George W. Colton, *Colton's Atlas of the World, Illustrating Physical and Political Geography* (J. H. Colton and Company, 1856). David Rumsey Map Center, Stanford Libraries

Page 132 *Daily Globe*, September 4, 1878, p1.

Page 133 Photo by Matthew Brady, c. 1870–80. Library of Congress

Page 134 *An Illustrated Historical Atlas of the State of Minnesota* (A. T. Andreas, 1874), 28. David Rumsey Map Center, Stanford Libraries

Page 153 Edwin Whitefield, "View of St. Anthony, Minneapolis and St. Anthony's Falls (From Cheever's Tower)." Lithograph, 1857. New York Public Library

Page 156 Minneapolis plat map from 1892. University of Minnesota Digital Collections Unit scan, map 01366

Page 173 "Heart of the New Metropolis," *St. Paul Daily Globe*, June 15, 1890, 13.

Page 175 Minneapolis Park Board publication

Page 181 *St. Paul Daily Globe*, February 19, 1888, p9.

Page 198 "Midway: Between the Cities," *St. Paul Daily Globe*, October 18, 1885, 11.

Index

Page numbers in *italics* indicate illustrations.

Drew M. Ross is a writer, editor, and researcher. For his writing on local history, he won the 2024 Solon J. Buck Award from the Minnesota Historical Society for his article "White Supremacy on Parade: The Fight to Stop *The Birth of a Nation* in the Twin Cities." Previously he wrote about the life of Rocco C. Siciliano in *Walking on Sand: The Story of an Immigrant Son and the Forgotten Art of Public Service.* He began his archival experience as photograph curator at the University of Utah Special Collections, where he developed an interest in nineteenth-century photography. He enjoys many different outdoor, muscle-powered sports, from mountain biking to canoe racing, and pursues extended outdoor expeditions (river running, hiking) and Nordic ski marathons. He has been active in local politics with his district council as an advocate for parks with a special interest in developing the bike infrastructure that connects the Twin Cities. In his free time, he maintains a seventy-acre oak savanna in southern Minnesota. He lives in St. Paul, Minnesota.

Becoming the Twin Cities has been typeset in Chaparral Pro. Created by Adobe type designer Carol Twombly, Chaparral combines the legibility of slab serif designs popularized in the nineteenth century with the grace of sixteenth-century roman book lettering.

Book design by Wendy Holdman